Twyford Down

Ben Bryl.

Barbara Bryant was a Conservative Councillor representing the rural villages of Owslebury and Colden Common on Winchester City Council, when she initiated the formal opposition to the Government's choice of route for the M3 motorway around Winchester. She is married to Dudley, a chartered surveyor and has three sons. She has a deep love of the countryside which stems from her childhood, spent in the heart of Sussex. A politician with conviction, she had already fought elections on behalf of the Conservative party for nearly twenty years and was described by *The Times* as 'an unlikely challenger'. She did however remain at the forefront of the campaign, being one of the three private individuals to challenge the Government's decision in the courts and was a founder member of the Twyford Down Association. Despite the disappointment at having lost the struggle for Twyford Down she remains convinced that responsible opposition means finding practical solutions.

Graham Anderson is editor of the weekly newspaper *Construction News*. He joined the publication in 1984 and has many close friends and contacts in the construction industry. He strongly believes that successive Government ministers have allowed construction firms to take the blame for environmentally poor decisions based on bad planning and cut-price designs. He supported the completion of the M3, but believes that with more investment and vision the road could have been built in a tunnel. With better planning, the route could have avoided Twyford Down altogether.

Peter Kunzlik graduated with a first from Magdalene College, Cambridge in 1981 and was called to the Bar in 1983. He was a Fellow and Lecturer in Law at St John's College, Cambridge from 1985 to 1988 when he joined Hammond Suddards, as head of European Law, setting up their Brussels office in 1990. In the summer of 1990 he advised the Twyford Down Association on EC law and the European challenge to the UK Government's decision to proceed with the Twyford Down route. Peter Kunzlik now holds a research chair at Nottingham Law School as Browne Jacobson Professor of European Business Law.

Jonathon Porritt has been one of the most influential advocates on behalf of the environment for the last twenty years. His involvement with the campaign to save Twyford Down began during his time as Director of Friends of the Earth, but it came to prominence when he spearheaded the tactical voting campaign during the 1992 General Election. The emphasis in much of his current work is on the solutions rather than the problems, encouraging and multiplying examples of good environmental practice wherever possible. His criticism of contemporary politicians and other decision makers remains as trenchant as ever. He regards Twyford Down as a watershed in environmental campaigning.

Twyford Down

roads, campaigning and environmental law

Barbara Bryant

The Campaigner

with contributions from

Graham Anderson

Editor, *Construction News*

Peter Kunzlik

Browne Jacobson Professor of European Business Law,
The Nottingham Law School

Jonathon Porritt

Environmental Campaigner

E & FN SPON
An Imprint of Chapman & Hall

London · Glasgow · Weinheim · New York · Tokyo · Melbourne · Madras

Published by E & FN Spon, an imprint of
Chapman & Hall, 2–6 Boundary Row, London SE1 8HN, UK

Chapman & Hall, 2–6 Boundary Row, London SE1 8HN, UK

Blackie Academic & Professional, Wester Cleddens Road, Bishopbriggs, Glasgow
G64 2NZ, UK

Chapman & Hall GmbH, Pappelallee 3, 69469 Weinheim, Germany

Chapman & Hall USA, 115 Fifth Avenue, New York, NY 10003, USA

Chapman & Hall Japan, ITP-Japan, Kyowa Building, 3F, 2-2-1 Hirakawacho,
Chiyoda-ku, Tokyo 102, Japan

Chapman & Hall Australia, 102 Dodds Street, South Melbourne, Victoria 3205,
Australia

Chapman & Hall India, R. Seshadri, 32 Second Main Road, CIT East, Madras 600 035,
India

First edition 1996

Typeset in 10/12pt Palatino by Saxon Graphics, Derby
Printed in Great Britain by St Edmundsbury Press Ltd, Bury St Edmunds, Suffolk

ISBN 0 419 20270 6

A catalogue record for this book is available from the British Library

Library of Congress Catalog Card Number: 95-71098

∞ Printed on permanent acid-free text paper, manufactured in accordance with
ANSI/NISO Z39.48–1992 and ANSI/NISO Z39.48–1984 (Permanence of Paper).

Contents

Colour plates appear between pages 18 and 19.

Preface

This is the story of the campaign that failed to stop a new motorway destroying one of England's most precious landscapes at Twyford Down (Figure A and 1) outside Winchester.

Throughout, one sentiment dominated our activities. In the words of Professor Martin Biddle, President of the Twyford Down Association 'the cutting through Twyford Down is a great act of damage, possibly the greatest single act of visible destruction ever worked on the scenery of southern England. It is worth spending a great deal to avoid such an outcome because it is irreversible. Its effects will last for ever. That is the issue. All other matters are sideline.'

The campaign to save Twyford Down was of local, national and finally international significance. Locally, Twyford Down was the last undeveloped chalk downland ridge abutting Winchester, providing the magnificent landscape backcloth around England's ancient capital. St Catherine's Hill and its encircling downland ridge setting supported human habitation and civilization from earliest times (Figure 2). In the words of Biddle again, 'the proximity of downland, Water Meadow and city produced an intimate and rare backyard, perhaps unique in providing a thriving modern city with a visual perspective reaching deep into its remote past. Here, perhaps alone in modern urban England, it was possible in the course of an hour or so to walk from the twentieth century to the prehistoric past, or even to glance from one to another in the course of a moment at work or in school.'

Nationally, the UK Government disregarded its own legislation, enacted specifically to prevent loss of heritage-rich sites, and rendered impotent our conservation laws and planning regulations. The Government's obstinate and unintelligent insistence on pressing ahead with its outdated plan for the M3 motorway at Winchester has ensured it a place in environmental history for cynical landscape abuse and muddled thinking.

Internationally, the destruction of Twyford Down highlights the impotence of European legislation to protect ecologically and historically rich heritage sites in a member state when the environment becomes a defenceless pawn in grander political games.

There is an African proverb, 'when the elephants fight the grass gets trampled upon.' Twyford Down was indeed trampled in the power game played between British Prime Minister John Major and the then European Commission President Jacques Delors.

After the ten-year campaign, involving hundreds of thousands of pounds sterling, forests of waste paper, hopes and heartaches, which was, sadly, to lead to such widespread disaffection with constitutional campaigning, is it possible to say who failed Twyford Down?

Reluctantly, the only honest answer I can give is that the people and institutions who failed Twyford Down were the very same who had the power or responsibility for its protection and who aspire to care for the environment. But that is not to absolve the Major Government from responsibility. The crucifixion was carried out by the UK Government in 1992.

The cock crowed thrice many years earlier with the silence of organizations, commonly understood to be custodians of our natural heritage, at the time of discussion and route selection in the early 1980s. The time to alter decisions is before they are made and the whole disastrous fiasco could, and should, have been avoided at that juncture.

It is a sad reflection that the more hopeless the fate of Twyford Down became so the greater the involvement of certain environmental pressure groups. It is too easy to explain this away by saying that no one knew about the threat to Twyford Down until the profile reached its pinnacle in 1991. To my certain knowledge, appeals for help went unacknowledged over the years and only when it was too late to realistically hope for a change in the decision did the eco-troops start massing.

Conservationists in Britain are in danger of falling into an over-adversarial mode. Surely it is not a battle which is the objective, but the securing of environmentally sensitive solutions. The view that victory is a bourgeois concept, and that glorious defeat is better than victory must not take hold of the conservation and environment-protection groups.

And so, was it worth it? Yes, unhesitatingly yes. Winchester was worth it, Twyford Down was worth it, and our heritage is worth it. The desecration of Twyford Down was undoubtedly a tragedy. If, in its demise, Twyford Down and the landscape of England's ancient capital can become more influential than it ever was as undisturbed downland, and be the catalyst for change, so that such wanton damage is never again inflicted on the precious heritage that is the English countryside, then not only do I have no regrets but there is pride and satisfaction that our seemingly insignificant decision, taken ten years ago, and stuck to through thick and thin, was right.

Acknowledgements

This book, like the campaign for Twyford Down itself, owes its existence to the enthusiastic and generous assistance of an immense number of people; without their willingness to delve into the archives, literally and metaphorically, the book would be an even less adequate record of the monumental sum of human effort which constituted our eight-year campaign for Twyford Down.

I am indebted to *The Hampshire Chronicle* for permission to reproduce so freely from its pages. Readers of this book who are tempted to research further the whole sorry saga will find that the archives of *The Hampshire Chronicle* provide a remarkable and comprehensive record.

In particular I would like to thank Graham Anderson for his practical and objective guidance and Madeleine Metcalfe, of E & FN Spon, who took on a totally unknown quantity, both in terms of author and content – the publication of this 'anatomy' of the campaign, and its roots, is due to Madeleine and Graham.

Especially I thank Peter Kunzlik for his unselfish willingness to contribute 'The Lawyer's Assessment' and for his intellectual enthusiasm during the latter part of the campaign.

Twyford Down owes a considerable debt to Jonathon Porritt for his support and I am deeply grateful to him for providing the 'environmentalist's' overview of the fall-out from the Twyford Down débâcle.

Merrick Denton-Thompson appears throughout the book as Merrick by name, and almost always 'we' in the story will have included Merrick. It is perhaps invidious of me to refer to him as a 'key player' – he was, of course, but that understates the truth; for some eight years a large part of Merrick's life was devoted to the M3 campaign. It may therefore seem presumptuous of me to 'thank' Merrick – but nonetheless I do thank him.

To me Merrick's most outstanding contribution to the campaign was his ability to portray both the issues and the landscape itself to others. I am particularly indebted to him for his help with the book and for allowing me to reproduce, as illustrations in the book, so freely from his collection of slides which formed his 'slide presentation'.

My long-suffering family are hardly mentioned in the text, yet without their help, tolerance, intelligent interest and enthusiasm, I would have given up both the campaign and the book; without their humour and common sense I would have lost all sense of proportion, and without their support I would not have survived these years more or less intact. For a substantial chunk of their childhood James and Thomas have lived with Twyford Down and the campaign to save it; Owen, being somewhat older, had only his teenage years dominated by the campaign; all three of them, in their various ways at different ages, have contributed to the campaign, and been both a support and a levelling influence!

The debt which I (and Twyford Down) owe to Dudley, my husband, is incalculable – his intellectual, moral and emotional support has been unstinting. His level-headed involvement and tolerance (which so rarely threatened to give way) is, I am afraid, hopelessly inadequately recorded but I will be eternally grateful to him for sustaining me throughout the vicissitudes of the campaign and authorship, and for his help.

I hope the book is a fitting tribute to all those very many people who are not mentioned by name but without whose help our campaign would have been a mere shadow of itself and the passing of Twyford Down would have gone unlamented.

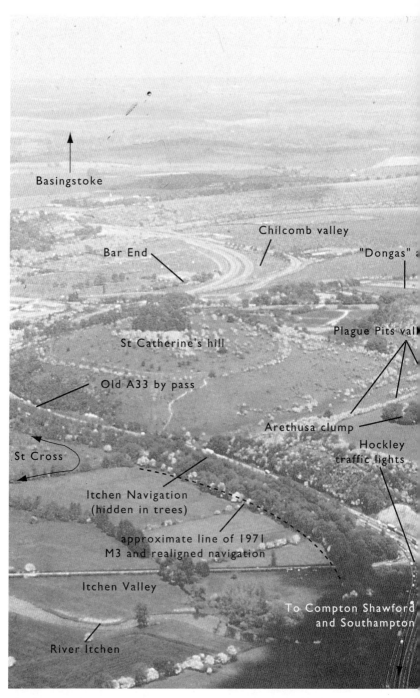

Basingstoke

Chilcomb valley

Bar End

"Dongas"

Plague Pits val

St Catherine's hill

Old A33 by pass

Arethusa clump

St Cross

Hockley
traffic lights

Itchen Navigation
(hidden in trees)

approximate line of 1971
M3 and realigned navigation

Itchen Valley

To Compton Shawford
and Southampton

River Itchen

Figure A Annotated aerial photograph of Twyford Down, St
Catherine's Hill, before the construction of the M3

orestead Escarpment

Morestead Road

To Owslebury

Roman Road

Twyford Down

ron age
llage site

Old A333 to
Twyford village

Part One

Introduction

1

Introduction to Twyford Down

Twyford Down was home to Bronze Age man. At that time man had not learnt how to drain the wet valleys and therefore he settled on the downland ridges. Originally clothed in a blanket of forest, the prehistoric landscape of southern England was interrupted by the bogs and marshes of the valleys. In what we now call Hampshire these valleys were wide, the rivers clear and slow moving, meandering through the chalk hills. The rivers sprang from the aquifers of the chalklands and flowed into the River Solent. In some places the chalk hills were so steep-sided that the forest tipped over the edge and fell in hanging woods into the valley below. The dry forest of oak, ash and beech gave way suddenly to elm and small-leafed lime trees. Alder, willow and poplar dominated the valleys below.

Locations that offered the basic requirements of survival, ready access to water, food and shelter were constantly visited by our nomadic forbears and in time, as they learned to till the land, the clearings in the great forest became permanent. The crude cultivation methods of early man were most successful on the lighter, dry soils, which meant that the chalklands of southern England attracted widespread settlement.

It seems certain that the landscape of Twyford Down and St Catherine's Hill gave Neolithic and Bronze Age man easy access to water, and its quick descent from chalk hills to valley floor offered great diversity of plant life encapsulated in a tiny area.

The steep-sided round chalk hill of St Catherine forms a pivot in the landscape at the point where the Itchen, Chilcomb and Plague Pits valleys meet. St Catherine's Hill was linked to Twyford Down and the chalk downland hinterland by a narrow 'saddle' or chalk ridge, approaching the hill from the north east.

In those far-off days, St Catherine's Hill must have been easy to defend in times of threat, and it was this juxtaposition of defence, water, fertile soils and forest remains that would have led to the consolidation of the settlement (Figure A).

An Iron Age village located on the crown of Twyford Down overlooked the compact landscape of the Itchen valley below. There was a clay cap on Twyford Down, and the village developed around a small outcrop of clay, where the soil would have been more fertile than the surrounding bare chalk soil. Although the cultivation around each of the 'houses' would have benefited from the clay, the ground would have remained wet for long after rainfall, making the village a muddy place (Figure 4).

The houses were probably round, based on a framework of short posts dug into the chalk in a circle. These posts were linked with interwoven poles made from coppiced hazel. These skeletal walls were then probably daubed with a mixture of clay and chalk bonded together with 'straw'. A central pole would have supported the roof joists and thatch cover. Beneath some of the houses, dug deep into the chalk, were the grain silos (Figure 3).

The fields around the village stretched far to the north and east, keeping to the high ground, fanning out over the ridge as Twyford Down merged with its hinterland. The fields would have been small, often less than an acre. They were located on a steeply undulating landscape and were square. The crude ploughs of that time failed to turn the soil but just broke the surface crust. The bullocks that pulled the plough were turned at ninety degrees and ploughed across the first set of furrows to till the soil for seeding. The square was the most effective shape for the fields to be cultivated at that time. Much later, when the ploughs turned the soil properly, more than just one or two bullocks were necessary, particularly on the heavier soils in the valleys and on the clays, and the square field system gave way to the long medieval strip fields, presumably to enable the teams of bullocks to be turned. In places it is still possible to identify the patterns of these long fields today.

On Twyford Down these small square fields could still be seen nearly two and a half thousand years later. All over the Down the field pattern was fossilized over centuries as cultivation shifted the soil within a family's plot, creating the curious zigzag of banks which, after construction of the motorway, are still just visible on the edge of the Hockley golf course on Twyford Down.

Through the pattern of fields ran the tracks from the village, which led to the valley for fresh water, or eastward to the extensive field system. It seems that one main track ran the full length of Twyford Down, linking the village on a flat, curved route to the huge fortification on the top of St Catherine's Hill. The entrance to the St Catherine's Hill fort is on the north side, allowing access to the fort from the ridge itself, rather than up and down the very steep sides of the Plague Pits valley. Close to the village the tracks had ditches on either side to protect the fields from animals being driven to water in the valley below. There was a dew-pond within the village itself, lined with clay. Today the site of this pond is clearly visible – the Arethusa Clump of trees on the western face of Twyford Down has grown up in the old pond (Figure A).

It is – was – a remarkable place, a place of international significance. And we have built a motorway right through the middle of it. Why should such a place be treated with less care than, say, St Paul's Cathedral?

THE HISTORIC TRANSPORTATION CORRIDOR AT WINCHESTER

Immediately to the east of the heart of the ancient city lie the Winchester Water Meadows, through which flows the River Itchen, and which are abutted on the side farthest from the city by St Catherine's Hill, which forms the western edge of the South Downs (Figure A).

A north–south transportation corridor has been recorded in the valley since Bishop Godfrey de Lucy made the Itchen navigable in the late twelfth century, by building a canal, the Itchen Navigation.

In the late nineteenth century the Didcot, Newbury and Southampton railway line was constructed to the east of the Itchen Navigation. In the early twentieth century the 'old Twyford Road' was built on the eastern side of the railway line, which was closed in the 1960s.

In the 1930s, after some debate, a dual carriageway bypass to Winchester was constructed to the east of the 'old Twyford

Road' – but abutting on the footings of St Catherine's Hill and necessitating trimming back the westerly face of St Catherine's Hill.

Though construction of the bypass was completed before the outbreak of war in 1939, it was not opened to the public until after 1945, although it was used by the military before that.

By the 1960s, discussions had started about how to improve the London to Southampton trunk road. In the late 1960s a stretch of dual carriageway, on the A33, was opened from Compton, just south of Winchester, bypassing the rapidly expanding settlement of Chandlers Ford, and extending to Bassett on the northern outskirts of Southampton.

SUMMARY OF PROPOSALS PRIOR TO 1983

In 1970, the Government published its plan to continue the M3 motorway from a point to the south of Basingstoke, at Popham, passing just east of Winchester to Compton where it would link with the new Chandlers Ford bypass.

In the 1970s (and for years to follow) there was a strong view in Winchester that the logical line for the proposed M3 motorway would be to pass to the west of Winchester, meeting the planned M27 motorway on the north-west outskirts of Southampton. Such a route would have passed through arable countryside, avoiding the settlements of Compton, Shawford and Otterbourne and the proximity to Winchester. Many of the older residents in and around Winchester believe that the influential owners of the land to the west of Winchester were instrumental in persuading the Government to adopt a route for a motorway which followed the line of the A33 bypasses of Winchester and Chandlers Ford.

Those that did not support that westerly route argued for the expansion of the existing transport corridor along the line of the bypass. As a historical transport route, the area had already been disrupted, so any environmental or archaeological damage would be minimized.

In 1971 Inspector Burrows held a Public Inquiry into the 'line order' for the Popham to Compton section of the M3, proposed at that time to be six lanes at Winchester, leaving the old A33 bypass intact for local traffic. The plan was to build the new motorway to the west of the old A33 bypass, intruding into the Water Meadows between St Catherine's Hill and Winchester, and necessitating the physical relocation of the Itchen Navigation westwards into the Water Meadows (Figure A).

The 'line order' Inquiry discussed only the route of the motorway. A subsequent Inquiry would be held into any compulsory purchase requirements. The route of the motorway proposed at that time included a controversial section passing through countryside just to the north of Winchester. In 1973 the Government approved this route for the motorway from Popham to Compton.

In Winchester opposition was growing to the damaging proposals which would have resulted in ten lanes of highway between the foot of St Catherine's Hill and Winchester. The construction of the new motorway, and relocation of the old Navigation, would, in addition, have caused major physical disruption to the Water Meadows themselves.

In 1976 a Public Inquiry was held by Major-General Edge into the compulsory purchase orders to enable acquisition of the necessary land in the vicinity of Winchester and St Catherine's Hill, much of which was owned by Winchester College.

Local residents in Winchester, landowners and others had formed the Winchester M3 Joint Action Group. This powerful alliance dominated the Public Inquiry and forced Inspector Edge to allow discussion not only of matters relating to land acquisition but also to debate again the route and need for a motorway. The Inquiry was the scene of much passionate and articulate opposition to the Government's plan and went on for a full year, closing in 1977 on the anniversary of its opening.

The Winchester M3 Joint Action Group argued in favour of abandoning the construction of a six-lane motorway, with its associated disruption to the Water Meadows, and proposed improving the existing A33 bypass by widening and straightening and by the construction of a flyover to remove the bottleneck at the junction of the A333 (today the B3335) Portsmouth traffic with the A33 Southampton traffic.

The colourful scenes at the Inquiry, and the strength and ferocity of the local opposition, were to result in Inspector Edge recommending reconsideration of the Government's plan for the M3 at Winchester. However, Edge did not recommend any change to the proposed route north of Winchester.

In 1980, the newly elected Conservative Government announced that it accepted Inspector Edge's recommendations for a 'fresh study of the proposals for the most sensitive section of the proposed Winchester Bypass improvement in the vicinity of the Water Meadows.' On 16 September 1981, Kenneth Clarke (at that time Parliamentary Under-Secretary of State for Transport) announced the details of this 'fresh study'. He said that engineering consultants, Mott Hay and Anderson, had been appointed to prepare it. The press announcement continued:

> The consultants have been informed that the scheme will need to deal satisfactorily with the substantial and growing volume of traffic using the existing road.
>
> Any new construction should so far as possible enable traffic to continue to use the present A33 Winchester Bypass during construction in order to avoid the serious problems that would be caused by the diversion of traffic through Winchester.
>
> The new scheme will need to have the highest possible measure of acceptance by the local authorities, other interested parties, and most important of all, by the general public. The present traffic problems and the accident record are bad so that the scheme will need to be completed as quickly as possible.
>
> We have particularly asked the consultants to pay full regard to environmental factors in the very sensitive areas with which the scheme is concerned – in particular at St Catherine's Hill, the Itchen Navigation, the water meadows and the Compton/Shawford area. They will want to consider the comments of the Inspector who conducted the 1976/77 public inquiry. The study will also include an examination of the standards to be adopted for the future improvement of the Compton to Bassett section of A33 (Chandlers Ford bypass)...

On 15 February 1983 Mr Turnbull, on behalf of the consulting engineers Mott Hay and Anderson submitted his firm's appraisal study and recommendations to the Transport

Department. The report recommended completing the M3 motorway via a cutting east of St Catherine's Hill through Twyford Down.

Part Two

The Campaigner's Story

2

The campaign to save Twyford Down begins

The campaign to save Twyford Down from destruction by the M3 motorway was begun one day in March 1985. A chance lunchtime meeting between my husband, Dudley, and one of his colleagues at Hampshire County Council, Merrick Denton-Thompson, who was the County Council's landscape architect, was to lead to the start of our eight-year crusade against the Government's plan to destroy Twyford Down.

Twyford Down, Plague Pits Valley, and St Catherine's Hill, formed a magnificent undeveloped landscape backcloth, situated less than a mile from Winchester Cathedral (Figure 2). Back in the spring of 1985 the historic name of Twyford Down was little known, except to local people in Winchester and to archaeologists. Farmed for thousands of years, Twyford Down, and its hinterland of the South Downs, remained undeveloped and largely undisturbed, despite the intensive farming methods of the mid-twentieth century.

By 1985 the new section of the M3 motorway from Basingstoke had been built only as far as Bar End on the edge of Winchester, in the valley floor below Twyford Down, and its escarpment, the Morestead Ridge.

The Government's original intention had been to complete the M3 on a route to the west of both Twyford Down, and St Catherine's Hill, which was close to the River Itchen, and would have left the old A33 bypass as a local road, creating ten lanes of traffic between St Catherine's Hill and Winchester. The residential area of St Cross, with its magnificent Norman abbey, and Winchester College, the famous public school founded in the fourteenth century, would have been dominated by such a motorway, and their unique surroundings destroyed forever.

Not surprisingly there had been a massive outcry against this plan in the 1970s. The citizens of Winchester and the 'establishment' of Winchester College, and its old boys, had united in the campaign. What became known as the '1976 J(oint)A(ction)G(roup)' which brought together all the local residents was remarkably successful. Spending tens of thousands of pounds, mobilizing hundreds of supporters (many of whom held positions of influence) the 'JAG' campaign culminated in an explosive Public Inquiry and was successful; in 1979 the Government abandoned the plan to add six lanes of new motorway in addition to the then existing bypass in the valley around Winchester.

In 1981 Kenneth Clarke, at that time responsible for roads, announced that the Government had appointed a firm of consulting engineers, Mott Hay and Anderson (MHA), to look at alternative ways to complete the missing link in the London to Southampton M3 motorway. The Government's brief to the consultants stated that 'the new route should respect the special environment around Winchester and should have the support of the local authorities, and the general public.'

Two years later, in June 1983, the Government publicly announced that it was accepting the recommendations of the consultants, Mott Hay and Anderson, that the best way to complete the M3 was on a route to the east of St Catherine's Hill in a deep cutting through Twyford Down. The statutory process leading to a full Public Inquiry was initiated a year later in 1984.

Personally I'd had some direct (albeit slight) involvement in the Mott Hay and Anderson consultations. Early in 1978 my husband, Dudley, and I had moved down to Winchester from London. For a time we lived in Twyford where I took on the part-time post of clerk to Twyford Parish Council; this fitted in with my increasing family commitments, not the least of which were our twin boys who were born in 1980. The boundaries of Twyford Parish included part of the existing A33 Winchester bypass, and Twyford Down, so the Parish Council had the status of a 'statutory objector' in the planning process, and an obvious, even if rather low-key, involvement in the consultations.

Intuitively I had considered that the plan (which was to become known as the Cutting route) to thread the M3 just east of St Catherine's Hill was an unnecessarily dramatic over-reaction by the Government to the dilemma of how to complete the M3

motorway as it passed Winchester. The plan necessitated the
motorway rising up from the valley floor at Chilcomb, across the
Morestead ridge and then into a cutting through the undisturbed downland before dropping down through the face of
Twyford Down back into the valley at the Hockley traffic lights,
notorious for lengthy traffic queues at busy times. In 1982
Twyford Parish Council had voted to support the proposal to
route the M3 through Twyford Down, though as an employee I
had no say in its decision. Personally I remained dubious about
the whole plan, but the MHA representatives were very persuasive. Obviously the motorway needed to be completed; perhaps
the solution of merely enlarging the existing A33 was too sim-
plistic and not practical. I supposed that my concerns about the
damage to the unspoilt downland were misjudged.

The old Roman Road from Winchester to Silchester passes
through the hilltop village of Owslebury, the ancient route
marked by yew trees. The sides of the lane are worn down by
years of use and the ancient hedgerows and trees form a canopy
over the road. The old road is joined by the more modern road
to Winchester just west of the hamlet of Morestead and follows
the Roman Road over the top of the Morestead Ridge, dropping
down past St Catherine's Hill into the outskirts of Winchester at
Bar End (Figure A). In the early 1980s my daily journey between
our new home at Owslebury and Winchester followed this
ancient highway. As I drove out of Winchester, homeward
bound, up the sharp hill on the escarpment and along the
downland ridge I would glance back down at the newly constructed part of the M3, tucked low in the valley and wonder
again at the wisdom of dragging the concrete, the vehicles and
the urbanization up the hill to spoil the undisturbed, rolling
chalk downs. No one, apart from Dudley, seemed to share my
growing misgivings. All the authorites, local and national,
apparently agreed with the plan.

In 1983 I had been elected as the Conservative councillor for
Owslebury on the Winchester City Council, at a local by-elec-
tion following the death of the previous councillor. Although we
had been active in Conservative politics in London, I'd had no
desire for local political involvement in Winchester – imagining
in any case that the local Conservative Association must be
crammed to bursting with the politically astute as well as the
great and good. However, it is often surprisingly difficult to find

people willing to stand as candidates for local councils and Dudley encouraged me to stand for election. We fought the campaign, which fell during the 1983 General Election, hard, and vastly increased the Conservative vote. I soon found myself attending meetings of the City Council at Winchester Guildhall. Once elected it had taken me a while to find my way around the system, but it was evident that Winchester Council was solidly supportive of the Government's latest plan for the M3. At the time of the formal publication of the proposals in June 1984 Winchester Council had confirmed its continuing support for the Cutting route. Winchester Council had been a member of the local councils' joint working party during the earlier consultation phase and had thus been party to the decision by Mott Hay and Anderson, Hampshire County Council, and ultimately the Transport Department to propose routing the M3 east of St Catherine's Hill, through Twyford Down.

In 1984 there was no debate within Winchester Council about the merits of the M3 Cutting route. I had been getting to know my colleagues on the Council, some of whom had been very active during the 1976 campaign opposing the Water Meadows route. I received the very firm impression that these people believed the new route east of St Catherine's Hill was the ideal solution, and one which they had fought hard to achieve. It was clear, too, that the paid officers of the Council shared this belief. Indeed, the Planning Officer of Winchester Council in his evidence to the 1985 Public Inquiry described the plan as 'bold' and an 'imaginative solution', and the result of a 'close working relationship' with the consultants, Mott Hay and Anderson.

The chance meeting in the spring of 1985 between Merrick and Dudley, which was to have such far-reaching repercussions, took place over lunch in the staff restaurant of Hampshire County Council. The restaurant is housed on the top floor of Ashburton Court, a 1960s office block, perched above the heart of Winchester with magnificent views across Winchester, the Cathedral and St Catherine's Hill and distant views of the South Downs, stretching as far as Butser Hill near Petersfield on a clear day. Over lunch their conversation turned to the distant scenery and what the planned motorway would do to the landscape. Until that moment neither had been aware that they shared misgivings about the planned route through Twyford Down.

Figure 1 **Aerial photograph of Twyford Down, St Catherine's Hill.** The landscape of Twyford Down, St Catherine's Hill and the St Cross Water Meadows before construction of the M3.

Figure 2 The lost landscape of Twyford Down. A view from the south of Twyford Down with St Catherine's Hill on the left, before construction of the M3.

Figure 3 Reconstructed round houses as they may have been in an Iron Age village.

Figure 4   The Iron Age Village. Sketch showing the Iron Age village as it might have looked in 500 BC.

Figure 5   The Dongas. Medieval trackways or drovers' roads, some 20ft deep, eroded by feet over hundreds of years.

Figure 7   The famous photomontage of the Cutting route through Twyford Down, produced in 1984. 1985 Public Enquiry: M3 Bar End to Compton. © Crown copyright.

Figure 11   The Tunnel Route. The likely visual impact of the tunnel route.

Strengthened by the discovery that they were not alone in deploring the plan, Merrick and Dudley decided that we should all three meet to discuss our concerns. The next day we sat down together and spent a long evening talking through the subject. It was to be the first of literally hundreds of such meetings over the years of our campaign.

A landscape architect by profession, Merrick had been the landscape adviser to Hampshire County Council for some years. His criticism of the Twyford Down route had been long-standing. In 1983 he had written, under the pen name of 'Capability', an article in the magazine, *Landscape Design*, describing the proposed Cutting route as 'being in disastrous conflict with the topography' and that the 'excessive amounts of surplus chalk created by the chasm (the cutting out of Twyford Down) will apparently be used to regrade the western side of the Itchen Valley,' completely remodelling the landscape with the new road running high up on the new levels. Merrick described the proposed Cutting route as an 'arrogant' solution.

Merrick was dismayed that the County Council, which rightly enjoyed an excellent reputation for its imaginative and effective conservation and countryside policies, was supporting, perhaps unwittingly, a solution to the problem of completing the M3 which in his professional judgement was so damaging in landscape terms. As an individual who understood and cared deeply about the countryside, its landscape and the environment, Merrick was personally grieved at the prospect of the destruction of Twyford Down.

Dudley, a chartered surveyor, was a senior officer in Hampshire County Council's Estates Department. Before coming to Hampshire he had worked in London and been involved for many years in public inquiry and compulsory purchase work in London's East End. His objections to the route were that the damage to the landscape was needless; and that the 'switchback' nature of the planned route, which would bounce the road across the hilltop ridges, was obviously out of context with the grain of the existing landform. He always argued that the route was designed as an engineering *tour de force* having little regard to scale, or human context, reminiscent of the 1960s high-rise blocks designed by men who proudly belonged to the school of 'brutal architecture'.

I came at the problem without Merrick's technical understanding of the landscape, but with a strong sense of injustice:
we believed that the pros and cons of the route through
Twyford Down had not been debated, and we were beginning
to suspect that the impact and scale of the engineering works
and the remodelling of the landscape had not been understood
by the public or even by the decision-makers.

That first evening our discussions revolved around the
Twyford Down route itself, the opportunities that existed to
precipitate a proper debate about the choice of the route, and
whether any of the three of us could, and should, take positive
action to do so.

Merrick explained some of the technical characteristics of the
route. Despite the fact that I had been involved in a small way in
the consultation process that had led to the selection of the
route, and that both Dudley and I had visited the public exhibitions mounted by Mott Hay and Anderson and the Transport
Department in 1983 and in 1984, we had only a very superficial
understanding about the engineering or design details. For
instance, we knew that the motorway was to go into a cutting
roughly where it crossed the Morestead Road, but I had not
realised that in order to do so the motorway would have to be
elevated on a man-made embankment some 30 ft above the
existing ground level, to take it up from the valley floor at
Chilcomb onto the Morestead ridge; or that at the other end of
the cutting there would be a man-made embankment, using the
chalk spoil from the cutting, right across the Water Meadows
and would then rise steeply, along the western side of the valley,
to take the motorway over the London to Southampton railway
line near Shawford. The whole landscape would be changed.

As Merrick explained the scale and detail of the engineering
works, and the consequential remodelling of the landscape, I
began to understand why he had called the Twyford Down
route an 'arrogant' solution. My earlier, inexpert reservations
were reinforced by what Merrick told us that evening, and I
became increasingly convinced that the route would be a dreadful mistake. I was sure, too, that many other people were
unaware of the magnitude of the works.

It soon became clear to all three of us that immense damage
would be inflicted on the landscape by the suggested route
through Twyford Down; equally, we all recognized that the

missing link in the motorway must be completed. The M3, the main route from London to Southampton had been built as far as the outskirts of Winchester. The motorway continued just south of Winchester, linking into the new M27. The existing Winchester bypass was totally inadequate and completion of the motorway was clearly essential.

The option of simply expanding the existing A33 bypass had been discussed by the newly appointed consultants, Mott Hay and Anderson, with some of the consultees (including Twyford Parish Council) in 1981, but that option had been abandoned, along with a number of other suggested routes, in favour of the route east of St Catherine's Hill in a cutting through Twyford Down.

In the spring of 1985 we knew little of the process that had led MHA to opt for the Cutting route through Twyford Down. The MHA recommendation in favour of the Cutting route had been sent to the Government in February 1983, accompanied by a substantial appraisal study document. From this document, the Mott Hay Anderson Technical Appraisal, it appeared that the decision to opt for the Cutting route had been based on the consulting engineers' assessment that the Cutting route would be environmentally superior and attract greater public support than the other alternative possibility (which the consultants had worked up in some detail) of expanding the A33 bypass.

The consultants had identified a number of advantages of a route on the line of the old A33 bypass, but had apparently abandoned it in substantial measure on the grounds that, in order to accommodate a full three-lane motorway, with acceptable geometry, such a route would necessitate a large cut up the western face of St Catherine's Hill, almost to the outer ramparts of the ancient hill fort, which would attract opposition. Merrick, with his professional knowledge, believed that the amount of the cut into the face of St Catherine's Hill could be reduced dramatically. He promised to study the MHA technical drawings of their route on the old bypass, and redesign the route to minimize the damage to St Catherine's Hill.

Even then, though, we realized that much of Winchester, and its institutions, had enthusiastically embraced the concept of the area between St Catherine's Hill and Winchester becoming free from traffic for the first time in fifty years. The people of Winchester, and particuarly the St Cross area and Winchester

College, saw the banishment of traffic to the 'east of St Catherine's Hill' and the re-unification of Winchester and St Catherine's Hill as a very real amenity gain. Merrick's design adjustments to the route on the old bypass might overcome the damage to St Catherine's Hill, but they could not offer the removal of traffic from the area between St Catherine's Hill and the Water Meadows.

So, we asked, how could we avoid the damage to the unspoilt downland, complete the motorway, and still offer the 'gain' of the removal of the old bypass? After a while the obvious answer came to us – a tunnel under Twyford Down. If the tunnel followed the horizontal alignment of the Transport Department's own Cutting route would it even be necessary to alter any of the formal paperwork (the statutory procedures) already published for the Cutting route? A tunnel would be more expensive, but it was already obvious that the Cutting would be a vast engineering undertaking. Would the tunnel be that much more difficult? After all, there were many road tunnels across Europe.

As the evening wore on the conviction grew on each of us, not only that these counter arguments should be publicly aired but that for us to allow the decision on the Cutting route to be approved by default, so to speak, was unthinkable. The purpose of the forthcoming Public Inquiry was to hear 'objections and representations' – it was entirely the appropriate time for us to submit our objections and comments, and to suggest alternative routes.

Late that night we decided to formally object: that the basis of the objection would be the damage which the Cutting route would inflict upon Winchester's landscape setting, and that this damage was needless since two alternative routes for completing the M3 existed. After some discussion we agreed that the objection should be entered in my name, as an elected councillor, and because of the fact that both Merrick and Dudley were employed by Hampshire County Council, which supported the Cutting route.

As soon as we had made the decision we began the preparatory work. It was already March, and we had little time with the Inquiry due to start in May. The most obvious tasks were to assemble the factual evidence supporting our case and to work on the concepts of our two chosen alternatives so that they became credible, and to involve other people in our project who would add weight to our cause and in particular plug the gaps in our expertise or knowledge.

Neither Merrick nor I knew anything about the construction of tunnels. It was pointed out to us, however, that if we proposed a tunnel as an alternative route at the Public Inquiry the Transport Department team would be obliged to 'work up' our concept in sufficient detail for the Inquiry to have a realistic discussion on the merits of such an alternative. It seemed to Merrick and me that we need not spend any of our very limited resources, time, energy and of course money, on developing the tunnel proposal. It was only later I realized that this was a serious misjudgement and that the tunnel was to be permanently hampered by the lack of expert advice at the earliest stage in its conception. Generally, objectors' alternatives will be as good as the guidance given to those burdened with developing them for the Inquiry. In the case of the Twyford Down tunnel this was doubly so, since the concept itself was novel, and involved engineering techniques seldom used on road projects in the UK, though of course commonplace on mainland Europe, particularly in Austria and Switzerland.

The historic and archaeological importance of Twyford Down, St Catherine's Hill, and the area of the old Roman Road at the Morestead Ridge, on the northern end of the proposed Cutting, was a further area in which both Merrick and I knew our knowledge and expertise was deficient.

It was a simple matter to augment our existing knowledge of the history of the area, and the 'feel' of the place, especially the area around the Roman Road, where the deep hollow-ways, worn as much as 20 ft deep by medieval man and his stock passing to and from the commercial hub of Winchester, had a special quietness. Over the years I had often walked our labrador dog there, and loved the area for its short downland turf and the way the butterflies seemed to sit and sun themselves on the sheltered sides of the tracks (Figure 5).

But we knew that if our objection was to be taken seriously at the Inquiry the archaeological case would have to be made by a professional (and if possible an eminent) archaeologist.

Professor Martin Biddle was just such an eminent archaeologist with strong Winchester ties, who had been Director of the Winchester Research Unit since 1968. He was a well respected figure in Winchester and had been closely involved with the archaeology excavations on the northern section of the M3 built as far as the outskirts of Winchester. Neither Merrick nor I had ever met Martin, nor were we aware whether he was among those who welcomed the Twyford Down route and would consider that by objecting at the forthcoming Public Inquiry we would be rocking the boat in an irresponsible way. It was therefore with some trepidation that I telephoned Martin. I was vastly relieved to find, first, that he understood what I was saying and, second, that he agreed with our objections to the Cutting route. After a little thought, and having read the MHA appraisal study, Professor Biddle agreed to give the archaeological evidence to support our objection at the Inquiry.

Our 'team' was instantly greatly enhanced. The intellectual and moral support which Martin and Birthe, his wife, gave us during the remaining eight years of the campaign proved invaluable. Martin's ability to get straight to the nub of an issue and to articulate that succinctly was a remarkable asset to the campaign. At both Public Inquiries his incisive mind and professionalism gave great force to our opposition to the Cutting route. Some years later, as president of the Twyford Down Association he was to write to the Government, 'The Cutting through Twyford Down is a great act of damage, possibly the greatest single act of visible destruction ever worked on the scenery of southern England. It is worth spending a great deal to avoid such an outcome because it is irreversible. Its effects will last for ever. That is the issue. All other matters are sidelines.'

We had about two months between our original decision to take up the cause on behalf of Twyford Down, and the opening of the Inquiry. Starting from scratch there was a daunting amount (and variety) of work to be done. Both Merrick and I made contact with a wide range of people in the relevant professions, conservation groups, and local organizations, while Dudley undertook much of the background research and paper work.

Merrick contacted the branch of the Nature Conservancy Council (now English Nature) responsible for Hampshire and learned that the Nature Conservancy Council was distinctly unhappy with the plans for the Twyford Down route, and the impact on the species-rich Water Meadows (a Site of Special

Scientific Interest, SSSI for short) where so much of the excavated chalk from the Cutting would be deposited. The Nature Conservancy Council (NCC) did in fact formally object at the Inquiry, despite a letter, dated 20 June 1985 from the Estates Bursar at Winchester College expressing the hope that NCC would not support an alternative route on the line of the old bypass, saying, 'The College will take very strong exception to this as it seems to take us right back to stage one, and is bound to stir up a hornets' nest... The College, being the major landowner involved, fully realises it cannot take an isolationist view and if we are to have a bypass would prefer it to be where it does the least damage, i.e. the preferred route (Twyford Down Cutting). I hope you will be able to reassure me that you will not be supporting this alternative (to route the motorway on the bypass).' In the event, NCC stuck to its guns, objected at the 1985 Inquiry and supported either of our alternatives, the tunnel or the bypass route, both of which it maintained minimized the damage to the ecology of the area.

In the run up to the Inquiry we were concerned that there seemed to be so litttle public discussion about the forthcoming Inquiry, and a sense that the whole thing was merely a matter of form. Having made the decision to oppose the Cutting route, with the objective of achieving a less damaging means to complete the missing link in the M3, we were anxious to involve as many people and the public at large as possible. The obvious way to do this was by getting the issues aired in the press and elsewhere. We started with a letter to the Winchester weekly local paper, *The Hampshire Chronicle*. A pillar of Winchester life for more than two hundred years, the *Chronicle* is well read and renowned for its old-fashioned reliability.

Come the Friday morning there the letter was – appropriately set alongside the formal public notice of the Public Inquiry. I wondered what sort of response it would attract. In fact, I was surprised by the many local people who commented that they shared those views but believed they must be mistaken, or that the route had to be built because there was no alternative.

The letters column in *The Hampshire Chronicle* one week later carried three letters supporting our objection. All three letters suggested a tunnel. One of the letters, from a resident of the village of Compton, Peter Savage, exhorted readers to 'Act now at the public inquiry, show interest, support those involved, write to political leaders, or, when it's too late, face the issue of why you didn't do something when you had the chance.' Earlier in his letter Savage wrote, 'A cheap solution is not right for the people here today, nor for those of tomorrow; the damage will outlast the planners and consultants of today. Tunnel through Twyford and Compton Down, go under the railway – minimise the damage, even add to the environment. And why not? If we always opt for the cheap and easy then we set our values for today and tomorrow, *and tomorrow is not afforded the luxury of a vote!*' I cannot recall ever meeting Mr Savage, but how I wish those in a position to help had done as he asked, and how sad it is that those organizations responsible for the heritage that was Twyford Down did not heed his words and act in 1985, when the destruction could perhaps have been avoided.

The campaign which Merrick and I mounted was deliberately rational and measured because we wanted to avoid a repetition of the highly emotional 1970s campaign, and because we were determined not to discredit a sound cause with inaccuracies.

During our preparations for the Inquiry Dudley (a chartered surveyor) and I spent many hours sifting through and studying the plans, documents and paperwork made available to the public six weeks before the Inquiry. These documents are known as Deposit Documents and constitute the DoT's written case for its preferred route, along with engineering drawings and such other material, for instance regional and national development policies, which are relevant to the route in question. In the Public Library one afternoon Dudley turned up the DoT drawing (known as Section T–T) showing the Twyford Down Cutting, in cross-section, at its deepest and widest point, more or less on the face of Twyford Down (Figure 6). In one sense a simple line drawing, its impact was staggering. We both gasped at the enormity of the chasm, with cars and vans, drawn to scale, dwarfed at the bottom of the Cutting. Up to then I certainly had not even begun to guess at the sheer scale of the engineering and construction that the Cutting involved.

Sharing our discovery with Merrick a couple of days later I could hardly believe it when he told me that while working on the landscape cross-sections in preparing our case for the Inquiry, he had discovered that this critical landscape cross-section drawing was incorrect; it showed the Cutting too narrow, by about the equivalent of one lane in each direction. In

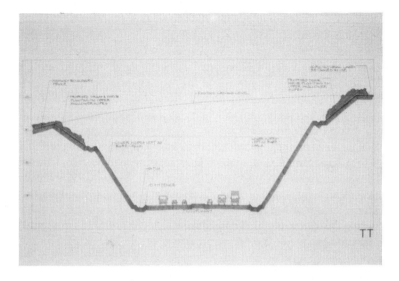

Figure 6 Cross-sectional drawing, known as Section T–T. The original cross-section produced by the DoT's consultants, showing the Cutting in Twyford Down near Hockley.

fact no allowance had been made for the rock-fall ditches, which were part of the design to allow for the chalk face of the Cutting to crumble. When the opportunity arose during the Inquiry I challenged the Department of Transport team with this alleged error; after checking the drawings themselves they admitted that Section T–T had indeed been incorrectly drawn and it was subsequently amended.

The Department of Transport produced a photomontage (a picture of a particular view of a route made by superimposing the dimensions of a road onto a photograph of the existing landscape or view) showing the Cutting at this angle; it was to prove a spectacular tool throughout our campaign and was repeatedly used by the press and on television (Figure 7).

The deeper we delved into the subject, as we read all the documents relating to the forthcoming Inquiry, particularly the evidence to be presented by the DoT itself, the choice of route began to seem less and less logical. We began to ask when was the Cutting route chosen, by whom was it suggested? We asked those questions in the spring of 1985, but there were no clear answers. In the course of the 1985 Inquiry more information was revealed, but this served only to increase the opacity which surrounded these fairly simple questions which were basic to the whole problem – the Government had asked that a route be selected which respected the environment and, most important, was acceptable to the public and to local organizations. And yet a route had been chosen which, by 1985, we believed failed miserably on both counts.

There is apparently no record of any body, corporate or individual, claiming the Twyford Down route as their own idea. That is not so suprising with hindsight, but curiously, even in 1983 when publicly proposed as the ultimate solution to the dilemma of the M3 and Winchester, no one claimed it as their own idea. Certainly the consultants, Mott Hay and Anderson, and the Department of Transport, and others, argued its merits robustly, but who actually first suggested it?

There may be clues in a report from the County Surveyor of Hampshire County Council (HCC) to the Council's Planning and Transportation Committee. In this short report, dated 1 March 1982, entitled 'M3/A33', the County Surveyor writes:

> Members will be aware that the Secretary of State approved Orders for the construction of the M3 between Popham (Basingstoke) and Bar End (Winchester) but appointed Consultants to undertake a 'fresh look' at the length of A33 south of Bar End to Chilworth (Southampton). Progress on the approved section (i.e. between Basingstoke and Winchester) however has been delayed in consequence of a challenge in the High Court regarding the validity of the Orders. Inter alia the plaintiffs included Winchester College.

[The report continues:]

> Recently I was advised that the College have withdrawn from the High Court action and that the other plaintiffs were likely to follow suit on the understanding, but not conditioned upon the following:

> > I) That the study being carried out by the Consultants (MHA) would be extended to examine not merely the section south of Bar End, but also the opportunities of a new route to the east of St Catherine's Hill.

II) That the works carried out by the Secretary of State between Popham and Bar End would not be prejudicial to such an opportunity...

[The report closed:]

The County Chief Executive has been involved in the discussions of this matter and he and I recommend that the Secretary of State for Transport be advised that the County Council welcome withdrawal of the High Court action and support the proposal that a route east of St Catherine's Hill should be studied as one of the options for the improvement of the A33 between Winchester and Southampton.

The Mott Hay Anderson Appraisal presented to Government in 1983 reported that 'A further economic factor in favour of Route D (the Cutting route) is the avoidance of possible loss of benefits should the promotion of a road in the Itchen Valley (the alternative of incorporating the motorway into the then existing A33 bypass) lead to further long delays at a Public Inquiry. Contributiors have suggested that this would be the case now that the technical feasibility of a route east of St Catherine's Hill has been demonstrated' (Appraisal Document 1.10.4.8.11).

However the Cutting route came to be promoted, it appears to have been grasped as the way out of the seemingly never-ending dilemma. Both Hampshire County Council and Winchester City Council opted for the Cutting route, as did the Winchester Preservation Trust and the M3JAG, stating 'the Group's view is that a scheme [has] now been devised by which the motorway would be hidden from sight and sound in the most sensitive area near the city, and indeed the DoT [has] gone further and made it possible to restore the valley to the condition pertaining before the construction of the Winchester bypass' (David Pare, Winchester M3JAG to the 1985 Public Inquiry).

However it had been chosen, in the spring of 1985 our researches served only to convince us that the Cutting route was a mistake – indeed that it would ruin Winchester's landscape backcloth, destroying part of two Scheduled Ancient Monuments, part of a Site of Special Scientific Interest and severing the westerly extremity of the South Downs from the rest of the Area of Outstanding Natural Beauty.

The more we researched the background papers, and the more detail that emerged, the more convinced we became that the Cutting route would inflict irreparable and visually prominent damage on the area around St Catherine's Hill, and on the Itchen Valley and the Water Meadows at Twyford. The scale of the earthworks (or chalk works) would be gigantic, necessitated solely by having to find somewhere to spread the excavated chalk. The Cutting would be 1000 metres long, and 30 m (104 ft) deep and 120 m (400 ft) wide at the point where the motorway emerged from the face of Twyford Down, before going over the valley at Hockley. At that time it was estimated that 1.3 million cu. metres of chalk spoil would have to be excavated from the Cutting (in fact by 1994 the figure had been adjusted to some 2.1 million cu.metres). Much of this vast quantity of disturbed chalk would be deposited in the valley at the northern and southern entrances to the Cutting to enable the route to climb into the Cutting. It seemed increasingly obvious to us that it was the need to dispose of the chalk that caused the Transport Department to make up the level of the motorway across the valley and that this explained the commitment to putting the motorway over, rather than under, the railway line.

The sides of the Cutting were to be left as 'bare raked chalk' – that is, white. The public exhibitions had included a model depicting the route when completed. Looking down at the model displayed at the exhibition I found it impossible to understand the impact of the route on the landscape, and indeed to relate what I saw on the table to the existing land-scape of Twyford Down around which I had walked so often. That may of course have been my untrained eye, but it was, after all, an exhibition for the *public* and presumably the purpose of the model was to explain the scheme to those unable to inter-pret technical drawings. The fact is that the model gave an excellent two-dimensional image of the proposed motorway and side road links. Its vertical scale, however, was so minuscule that the huge Cutting in Twyford Down was little more than a groove, the huge rolling landscape looked virtually flat. Trained eyes, too, criticized the model. It is notoriously difficult to create an effective model unless an enhanced vertical scale is adopted. For the 1987 Inquiry the Countryside Commission, the organiza-tion with responsiblity for the countryside and landscape, produced at considerable expense an attempted improvement. Whereas the DoT model could have been part of a model rail exhibition, the Countryside Commission model was diagrammatic, showing the contours in different colours but was still hopelessly difficult to interpret – someone rather unkindly referred to it as the Neopolitian ice cream.

Not only was the Transport Department's model difficult to interpret, but it had shown the sides of the Cutting as green, grassed over. Having seen the model at the public exhibition in 1983 I was surprised to discover during our researches that the cutting sides were planned as bare chalk. The model was duly amended and when it appeared at the 1985 Public Inquiry it showed white sides to the Cutting, but by then many had been misled; others would have only discovered the true situation by attending the Public Inquiry!

Later, during the 1985 Inquiry, the Transport Department team was challenged by objectors about the model, and the changes to the sides of the Cutting depicted. The DoT conceded that the model had been amended to take account of the evolving design of the proposals. Dudley Leaker, the Inspector holding the Inquiry, later reported, 'The original model, albeit amended, was on display at the Inquiry, and the DoT maintained that when viewed from a low level it gave a fair indication of the impact of the scheme.' I suppose it might have if you were the size of an ant.

So far as public support for the Cutting route is concerned the public consultation exercise which preceded the Government's adoption of the route has been the subject of much criticism over the years since 1985. Members of the general public, elected councillors and a leading expert on public opinion assessment have all identified serious shortcomings in the process.

Apart from the public exhibitions, at which the model previously described appeared, full-colour publicity brochures were distributed widely in the Winchester area. The first of these brochures was produced in February 1983 when the Government announced 'an opportunity for the public to comment on the consultants' report (MHA recommendation in favour of the Cutting route) before deciding whether to proceed to the next stage.' The February 1983 brochure gave no indication of the vertical alignment of the Cutting route which would be necessary to construct the horizontal alignment across the rolling landscape; the brochure failed to give details of the damage to the historic sites affected, omitting any reference to the Roman Road and hollow-ways scheduled ancient monument at the northern end of the Cutting, and depicted the second Scheduled Ancient Monument (the Twyford Down Iron Age settlement site) by an asterisk, which the motorway appeared to avoid.

Importantly, the brochure offered only one solution to the long-standing problem of how to complete the M3 – namely, the recommended preferred route through the Down. The brochure showed no alternative routes for completing the missing link in the M3. Surprisingly, the incongruity of a public consultation document with only a single option seems to have passed almost unnoticed at the time.

This defective brochure was widely distributed in and around Winchester, and three exhibitions were held. According to the DoT 1600 people visited the exhibitions, and 270 written responses were received by the DoT, of which 155 expressed general support (for the scheme). The population of Winchester exceeds 30 000, that of the villages along the route about another 5000 – hardly a ringing endorsement of the proposals.

In the summer of 1984 a further publicity brochure was published, accompanying the Government's decision to proceed with the Cutting route. Although both Scheduled Ancient Monuments appeared in that second version these were still shown only as asterisks, with absolutely no indication of the actual boundaries of the sites, or of the impact that the proposed route would have upon these archaeological remains, and again incorrectly showing the motorway skirting the sites, in one of which the 400 ft Cutting in the motorway was to be centred. The 1984 brochure also failed to give any indication of the vertical alignment of the route, and of the magnitude of the earthworks, though the areas to receive the excavated soil were shown as 'remodelled'.

The role played by the Landscape Advisory Committee (LAC) in the process that led to the selection of the Twyford Down route had troubled Merrick for some years. This advisory committee to the Department of Transport has subsequently been disbanded, by Mr MacGregor, Transport Secretary, in 1994, but at the time of the route selection process for the M3 at Winchester the Landscape Advisory Committee provided the Transport Department with independent landscape advice as part of the Department's route selection processes. The Transport Department maintained only a very small Landscape Section within its own staff.

Despite the fact that the Landscape Advisory Committee's report, following the Committee's visit to the site in 1983, endorsed the Transport Department's plan to route the motorway through Twyford Down, and that the Department's case was to rely upon this 'independent' endorsement as an objective professional assessment which justified the choice of the Twyford Down route, the LAC report (its recommendations in effect) was not made available to the public until objectors brought the matter to a head during the course of the Inquiry in June 1985. Merrick, however, had been present during the site visit of the LAC to the proposed route, and thus we had some information about the process by which the Transport Department's Twyford Down Cutting route had come to be endorsed by this professional adviser. He had long been concerned that the Landscape Advisory Committee seemed to have taken a somewhat superficial approach to the complex issues. That may be the case, or it may be that the LAC, like the local authorities and others, were very conscious of the long-standing deadlock at Winchester and, having been persuaded that the only option was to go through Twyford Down, the Committee took what it regarded as a 'responsible' or reasonable decision simply 'to go along with the route'.

Sadly the history of the early consultations, by the consultants and Transport Department, resulting in the Twyford Down route seems to be littered with organizations who subjugated the specific interests and responsibilities of their own particular discipline in the interests of what was thought to be 'the common good'. But the decision-making process is built upon consultation of the interested parties so that a balance can be struck between those competing interests. Shakespeare's 'to thine own self be true, and...thou canst not then be false to any man' may have referred to individuals, but the same holds true for organizations. However well intentioned, I think that the decision-making process at Winchester was distorted by muddled thinking on the part of various organizations, such as the Landscape Advisory Committee, and Countryside Commission.

Time was to show the calamitous effect that the silence of the national environmental agencies and others had on the outcome at Twyford Down. If they had argued for their own constituencies at the earliest stages of route selection, the tragedy would undoubtedly have been averted.

Shortly before the Inquiry was due to open Merrick and I realized that we needed to raise the public profile of our objection – without quite realizing what was happening, the decision to object to the Twyford Down Cutting route was developing into a campaign. We were concerned that there was a sense of public apathy and tiredness in the lead-up to the Inquiry and there was a feeling that the decision about where to put the M3 was a foregone conclusion.

We realized that the level of awareness in Winchester was such that 'visual aids' would be needed to stimulate a real understanding of the reasons for our objection. One evening we all three sat down to work out what we could do to explain the impact of the Cutting on the landscape. Merrick suggested marking the sides of the Cutting, as it would emerge from the

Figure 8 The black polythene seen from across the valley. Picture of the black strips marking out the Cutting, taken from across the Itchen Valley – May 1985.

Figure 9 Marking out the route on Twyford Down. Campaigners laying the black polythene on the line of the Cutting – May 1985.

shoulder of Twyford Down, with black polythene sheeting – the agricultural kind used by farmers between rows of potatoes. At that time it was a novel and imaginative way of identifying a route, athough since then various ingenious ways of marking routes have been used – vehicles parked bumper to bumper, whiteboards held skywards for the press photographers in helicopters at the Devil's Punchbowl, Hindhead, and the voting 'X' on Twyford Down itself during the 1992 General Election campaign. But for us and Twyford Down the simple black polythene worked in 1985 (Figure 8).

It was a good idea, but proved a major undertaking: obtaining the landowner's permission, and agreeing to compensate him for the damage to the crop in the field at the time, buying and transporting the polythene, and laying a quarter of a mile of it, six feet wide, on the steep slope of the Down on a windy day! (Figure 9) Four-wheel-drive vehicles, surveyors and a team of beefy volunteers laid out the polythene; local BBCTV were persuaded to film it and our first television coverage went out on the early evening local news the day before the 1985 Inquiry opened on 19 June 1985.

3

The 1985 Public Inquiry

The Public Inquiry opened on 19 June 1985 in Eastleigh Town Hall, a red-brick Edwardian building set in a small public park in the railway town of Eastleigh. The Inspector, Dudley Leaker, was an architect by profession, with qualifications in landscape architecture. His career had included work in Africa and he was the author of a number of books on the Third World.

The 1985 M3 Public Inquiry was to last for 27 days to 8 August 1985 (Inquiries traditionally do not sit on Mondays). It considered the eight-mile section of M3 from Bar End (Winchester) to Bassett (Southampton). Throughout, the whole affair was kept fairly low key and informal – which was in part a reflection of Inspector Leaker's own approach and a dramatic reversal of the scenes at the earlier 1976 Public Inquiry which suffered such noisy disruption.

The Transport Department's recommended route on the southern section of the proposed link would merely improve to motorway standard the existing sub-standard dual carriageway that ran from Compton past Eastleigh to Southampton. There were many objections from local residents to that section of the proposal, mostly relating to the impact on residential property adjoining the road. There was no suggestion to consider alternative routes to that provided by the existing road.

The objection we mounted was confined to the relatively short section around Winchester where the Transport Department planned to put the motorway in a cutting through Twyford Down. We proposed instead either a tunnel under Twyford Down, or expanding the (then) existing A33 Winchester bypass to full three-lane motorway with hard shoulders and central reservation.

Before the Inquiry we discussed extending our case to include objection to the proposed embankment taking the motorway over the London to Southampton railway line (the Hockley to Compton section), but decided on balance that the issues were much more complex, required much more research and would stretch our very limited resources too far, diminishing the strength of our present case.

The high-level crossing of the Water Meadows, built on the chalk excavated from the Cutting, and the motorway crossing over the top of the London to Southampton railway line at Shawford remained the 'Cinderella' in the campaigns that followed, because the potential damage was more difficult to identify visually, and the area lacked the statutory designations which protected Twyford Down. Latterly the high-level crossing of the valley and over-rail link has come to be regarded as equally, if not more, damaging than the Cutting itself, and has had a huge impact on the landscape around the villages of Shawford, Compton and Twyford.

Our turn to present our case to the Inspector came some four weeks into the Inquiry. The 'Twyford Down' team consisted of Merrick, who had worked enormously hard producing the technical drawings for the bypass alternative in addition to the rest of his evidence, with Professor Martin Biddle, the archaeologist, and Morag Ellis, the pupil barrister whom Merrick had persuaded to represent us. Behind the scenes, of course, our families were offering every kind of support. We were a small but happy band of pilgrims.

In his report of the proceedings Inspector Leaker was to write 'It could be said that the main opposition to the DoT's proposals in the St Catherine's Hill area was grouped around Mrs Bryant and her supporters.'

The objection we mounted was prefixed by the statement that we did not dispute the need to complete the 'missing link' to the M3, but that this should be done by a solution that would respect the magnificent landscape backcloth to Winchester, and referred to the fact that the City of Winchester was the ancient capital of England, renowned for its surrounding landscape of which the twin hills of St Catherine and Twyford Down were the major feature.

The essence of the case I sought to present was summed up in my formal statement to the Inquiry, thus: 'My purpose in objecting is to prevent the undoubted scenic intrusion of the cutting, and to preserve this unique part of our heritage – something to be preserved for future generations whose transport requirements will differ from our own and who will see in a different perspective the desecration of a landscape steeped in the history of our City, undisturbed, and remarkable for its flora and fauna and yet so close to developed centres of population.'

While giving my evidence I tried to convey the special nature of Twyford Down, and particularly the hollow-ways area, known locally as the Dongas. This area was a Site of Special Scientific Interest and a Scheduled Ancient Monument protected for its rich downland habitat. At one point Inspector Leaker interjected to ask whether I felt there was 'a genius loci of the place.' Those were the words Inspector Leaker used, but they fairly articulated what I had been attempting to describe. Leaker's Inquiry Report carried his version of that exchange, 'She referred to the genius loci of this place. It had an intrinsic value and special feeling which was always mystical and quite unique.'

Merrick gave his evidence on behalf of both the South West Chapter of the Landscape Institute and me. His objection focused on the effects of the Transport Department's Cutting route, which would go through the East Hampshire Area of Outstanding Natural Beauty (AONB), destroy a significant part of the St Catherine's Hill Site of Special Scientific Interest (SSSI) and by severance jeopardize the survival of the remnant of the SSSI left on the east of the Cutting. This would reduce the biological viability of the site as a whole, and would cause immense disruption to the landscape, creating a visual intrusion which could never be reinstated.

Merrick drew attention to one particular matter which concerned him as a professional with responsibility for conservation. He said, 'The current proposal by the DoT would affect the SSSI, AONB and historic features which include two Scheduled Ancient Monuments. Encroachment on just one of these should take place only in exceptional circumstances but, given a viable alternative route, damaging all three at once was totally unacceptable in planning as well as conservation terms. Opportunities to experience the open downland landscape and the transition to a historically and biologically important landscape are regrettably very few. Their further erosion should not be accepted.'

The point that the Transport Department (i.e. the Government, or Crown) was proposing a development by any private developer which would have been totally unacceptable was one made frequently by us all; the inequity in the system of Crown developments, and the conflict between the interests and responsibilities of various Government Departments recurs throughout the saga.

Merrick presented his alternative route for completing the M3 on the route of the old A33 bypass. He showed how this route could be contained within the disturbed communication corridor, which had been created over several centuries by the Itchen Navigation canal, the old Twyford Road, the former Didcot to Newbury railway line, and the bypass, and this could leave undisturbed the canal's tow-path, the Navigation canal and the land between the Itchen Navigation canal and Winchester (Figure 10).

Although Merrick was appearing as 'my' witness his position as the Hampshire County Council Landscape Architect did not

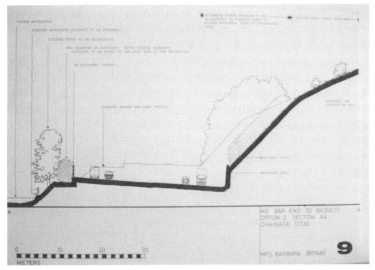

Figure 10 A motorway on the old bypass, west of St Catherine's Hill. How it would have been possible to build the M3 by adaptation of the existing bypass. The drawing shows the cut made in 1935 to build the bypass, the disused railway line, the old road to Twyford, the tow-path and Itchen Navigation.

pass unnoticed, of course. The Transport Department counsel, earning his keep, spent a while attempting to devalue Merrick's professional provenance in an effort to lessen the importance of Merrick's evidence. The exchange became slightly tawdry, and typically confrontational owing to the Transport Department's inevitable desire to undermine any and every possible alternative route so that the Published Route (which had been recommended to ministers and so forth) would not be discredited at the Inquiry.

The Hampshire Chronicle carried a large article under the headline 'Ignore County Opinion, Says Architect'. Hampshire County Council was strongly supportive of the Transport Department's Cutting route and, as Hampshire's Landscape Architect, Merrick put rather more than his head above the parapet.

The Oxford archaeologist, Professor Martin Biddle, presented a comprehensive assessment of the archaeological impact of the Twyford Down Cutting route. He explained that the area of Twyford Down affected by the Cutting was an extensive prehistoric landscape. The Iron Age and Roman–British settlement on Twyford Down was associated with the field systems, and 'the whole preserved an archive of information on social, economic and historical aspects concerning settlements in the Itchen Valley over at least half a millennium.' Martin Biddle drew the Inspector's attention to the fact that, although the principal document produced in connection with route selection, the 1983 Mott Hay Anderson Appraisal Report, made reference to the archaeological sites of the settlement and fields, and the remains of the Roman Road in the Dongas area, the Report failed to make any mention of the two Scheduled Ancient Monuments in the important comparison of Route A3 (bypass) with Route D (Cutting), where the relationships of these two routes to the Area of Outstanding Natural Beauty and Site of Special Scientific Interest were, however, taken into account.

Biddle sketched the history of the north–south communication corridor to the west of St Catherine's Hill over the last 300 years, which included the construction of the Itchen Navigation in 1710, and the Didcot–Newbury–Southampton Railway in 1883 (of which the brick-built Hockley Viaduct remains), and commented that there was no disguising the fact that this corridor was essentially derelict land, and that the reinstatement of it would be an artificial solution and would be no recompense for the extensive destruction of previously untouched land east of St Catherine's Hill. He concluded that the Cutting route would be unacceptable on those, and other grounds, but doubly so because it was unnecessary.

During our preparations for the Inquiry we were frequently reminded of the difficulty of communicating the very special character of the landscape under threat. Merrick suggested we submit a video as evidence to the Inquiry. We could see no reason why such an audiovisual aid should not be accepted as evidence, and as always once Merrick was fired up with an idea he set about making it happen. Portsmouth College of Art undertook to produce a video for us at a nominal cost. I believe it was the first time a video had been used in evidence at a Highways Inquiry. Ms Ellis had to spar a little with the DoT Counsel to persuade Inspector Leaker that the video was permissible evidence, and then for a few minutes the magic of the undisturbed downland, the butterflies and the tiny plants, microscopic but critical in the biological chain, and the magnificent countryside and Water Meadows penetrated the vapid atmosphere of the Inquiry.

The Dongas hollow-ways, worn down by generations of medieval man heading for the bustling commercial centre of Winchester, providing undisturbed chalk downland turf and shelter for colonies of Chalk Hill Blue and, more rarely, Brown Argos butterflies, were explained. Martin Biddle was filmed on the crest of the Down, giving a vivid perspective of the undisturbed rolling downland, and man's habitation of it.

Our suggestion to complete the motorway by a tunnel under Twyford Down was an entirely new concept. Government guidelines require the Transport Department to 'work up' any alternatives put forward by objectors at Inquiries. Not knowing the first thing about tunnels, and without engineering expertise at my elbow, I was quite unable to instruct the consultants so as to ensure that the optimum tunnel scheme was produced. Much later I learned that it is necessary to appoint one's own experts to properly direct the DoT's engineers to make certain that an objector's concept is most sensitively produced. But experts cost money and we were on a tiny budget. In the absence of any better guidelines I suggested to the DoT team of engineers that the tunnel should be on about the same line as the Cutting route.

The DoT did a fair job of that – the tunnel portals appeared just about at the base of the Cutting – half way up and pretty well full frontal on Twyford Down. When our turn came for discussion Inspector Leaker, and the world, was told that the tunnel portals would be almost as damaging as the Cutting. The rest of the Down would have been undisturbed, admittedly, but to have the tunnel stuck up in the air with full bore portals was obviously not the intention and a mistake that would long remain with us.

Only much later, after we had appointed our own professional tunnel engineers, did I realize how far adrift my 1985 tunnel, called J3 for the purposes of the Public Inquiry, had been. In 1987 Burslem Engineering Associates Limited (BEAL), specialist tunnel consultants, were to write, 'The alignment of the proposed tunnels as shown...appears to virtually transpose the tunnels on the open cut route. The motorway layout at each end has been designed to accommodate the cutting through Twyford Down. The route has not therefore been evolved with tunnelling principally in mind. A fresh look...may well provide a more economical route for the tunnelled scheme.'

It was clearly damaging to submit such a camel of a proposal at the Public Inquiry. Inspector Leaker was later to come to this conclusion in his official report of the 1985 Public Inquiry, 'I believe there were also people who would welcome this solution, but doubted its practicality.'

The condemnatory criticisms made of the 1985 (J3) tunnel were to resurface time and again, and to be repeated by Government Ministers and others long after I had withdrawn the proposal and it had been superseded by the M3JAG tunnel and low-level crossing of the valley (called JAG3) proposed at the 1987 reopened session of the Inquiry.

At the 1985 Inquiry the two principal local authorities, Hampshire County Council (HCC) and Winchester City Council (WCC) were both supporters of the Transport Department's scheme. Both councils had likewise supported the earlier, 1970s plan to route the M3 alongside the existing bypass, in the valley. Both HCC and WCC counter-objected to our alternative bypass route (P1) but chose to remain 'neutral' on the tunnel.

The Council for the Protection of Rural England, Winchester College, the Hospital of St Cross (not a hospital in the modern sense, but The Trustees of the Hospital of St Cross and Alms

House of Noble Poverty, the oldest charitiable institution in the UK, founded in 1136, situated on the western edge of the Winchester Water Meadows), the Joint Action Group, The Winchester Preservation Trust, and The Royal Fine Arts Commission were among those joining the local councils in supporting the Transport Department's Cutting route. Also recorded as supporters of the route were the Automobile Association, the British Road Federation, the Royal Automobile Association and the Confederation of British Industry.

Opposition to the Transport Department's Cutting route came from local individuals (though some of those, whose letters criticizing the Cutting were published in the local paper sadly did not write direct to the Public Inquiry – their authors no doubt believed their opposition was publicly recorded; unfortunately the Inspector can only take account of material formally submitted to him at the Inquiry) and from the Winchester Ratepayers Association and, nationally, by way of a letter in *The Times* (and to the Inspector at the Inquiry), from Dr Miriam Rothschild, CBE, FRS. Dr Rothschild's letter deplored the desecration of Twyford Down by the proposed new route.

There was a little flurry at the Inquiry the day the letter appeared in *The Times*. Such cogent and influential support was a great fillip to our cause. Interestingly, Dr Rothschild's uncle had been chairman of The Roads Beautifying Committee in the 1930s. This quaintly named group had viewed the route of the Winchester bypass, recommending that it be kept 'west of St Catherine's Hill.'

I had contacted Dr Rothschild before the Inquiry opened. By return of post Dr Rothschild replied, saying she had fought two major road inquiries, she dreaded them, but would be pleased to help. Over the succeeding years Dr Rothschild helped and worked behind the scenes for Twyford Down.

Miriam Rothschild is a remarkable, and formidable, personality with a great intellect. She is a distinguished zoologist, writer and lecturer. A daughter of the Hon. Charles Rothschild, who founded the Society for Promotion of Nature Reserves (SPNR) and represented Great Britain at the first international conference on conservation in Berne in 1913, she grew up at the centre of the new conservation movement and served on the first National Trust's Committee for conservation, and the Executive of the SPNR for 30 years and has remained in the forefront of

environmental activities, both at home and abroad. It is not possible to quantify the impact of her influence and contacts upon
the campaign for Twyford Down; at a personal level she was a
marvellous support, always ready to talk and share problems.
She knew the ups and down, and strains of what we were
attempting, and always had a reassuring word, or would try
'just one more' contact. As well as her letter to *The Times*, she
wrote directly to the Public Inquiry, that July in 1985, and to the
environment minister, William Waldegrave, and to the roads
minister of the time, Lynda Chalker. Many years later in 1992
she accompanied Sir William Wilkinson, Chairman of English
Nature to 10 Downing Street with Friends of the Earth to lodge
a protest at the route chosen across Twyford Down.

Miriam Rothschild never opposed the principle of completing the M3 motorway, but it appeared to her inexplicable that
the old A33 Winchester bypass had not been modified and
adapted to serve the purpose. Adaptation of the existing road
seemed an obvious solution and she was amazed that it had not
been more fully investigated in view of the inevitable desecration of this most beautiful landscape if the road was driven
across the top of Twyford Down.

Discussing Twyford Down and the M3 nearly ten years later,
Miriam Rothschild identifies the key elements which led to the
conservation disaster at Twyford Down as, first, the inexplicable
choice of route, presumably due to the lack of understanding of
the environment by the Transport Department and their engineers, and, second, the signal failure on the part of the conservation bodies to be sufficiently forcible in their objection to the
proposed route. This, she says, emphasized the perennial lack of
cooperation and understanding between the different ministries
involved.

She says she found it extremely depressing to witness still
more destruction of what is left of our unspoilt countryside: 'It is
extraordinary that if a famous picture comes on the market and
is about to be sold, a large sum of money is immediately made
available to retain it in this country. Yet, a picture merely
changes walls, and other people, say in America, can enjoy it.
Yet at Twyford Down the same authority (the Government)
destroys forever thousands of years of irreplaceable beauty and
the enjoyment of countless generations.' Not surprisingly, back
in July 1985 Miriam Rothschild's initial foray into the debate

about the M3 motorway and the future of Twyford Down made a considerable impact on the Public Inquiry.

Neither the Countryside Commission nor English Heritage (then Historic Buildings and Monuments Commission) appeared at, or contributed to, the 1985 Inquiry. In the case of English Heritage this failure to appear, or contribute, occurred despite a letter from the Programming Officer (the administrator of the Inquiry), on 8 June 1985, asking that a representative from HBMC should attend the Inquiry to answer questions on the nature and extent of the Ancient Monuments. Inspector Leaker received no reply from English Heritage.

The absence of the Countryside Commission, and indeed its lack of opposition to the Cutting route was to be discussed at the reopened Inquiry in 1987, but the full explanation was revealed only recently. While writing this book I came across revealing notes in the Countyside Commission files relating to the M3 motorway at Winchester, and I have discussed this with David Coleman, the present Regional Officer at the Countryside Commission.

David Coleman's understanding is that, some time in the summer of 1981, Patrick Leonard, the then Director (South) of the Countyside Commission was taken to Winchester by a senior member of the regional DoT office. Patrick Leonard 'stood in various places, such as the Water Meadows', and was briefed on the possibility of upgrading the existing A33 bypass, but was told that this would involve the removal of a substantial new slice up to the upper ramparts of the western (Winchester-facing) face of St Catherine's Hill. Leonard was apparently told of the difficulties the DoT anticipated arising from this potential, very visible scar, and asked whether, if the DoT went for a route east of St Catherine's Hill, the Countryside Commission would stand back from the debate.

This expedition seems to have been a not unnatural attempt to informally ascertain the likelihood of a route east of St Catherine's Hill incurring objection from the Countryside Commission. Apparently Patrick Leonard gave a verbal undertaking that, since it appeared that either of the alternatives to completing the M3 – a route west of St Catherine's Hill (on the bypass) or a route east (through Twyford Down) – would cause immense damage, the Countryside Commission would keep its own counsel on the matter, and not object to any Transport

Department proposal for a route east of St Catherine's Hill. Accordingly, the Countryside Commission did not appear at the 1985 Public Inquiry nor submit comments or representations.

Later internal Countyside Commission memos in the 1980s reveal considerable discussion as to whether the Countryside Commission still remained bound by Leonard's unwritten undertaking, particularly when Merrick Denton-Thompson's lobbying indicated that an alternative route existed, which would respect the landscape designations. This internal debate was finally resolved in 1986 and resulted in the appearance of the Commission at the reopened Public Inquiry in 1987. Sadly though, the Commission arrived six years too late to easily influence the outcome.

Unchecked by two of the major environmental watchdogs, the Transport Department and its consultants had been producing a scheme on the assumption that the Twyford Down Cutting route was tacitly acceptable to the Countryside Commission, the custodian of the East Hampshire Area of Outstanding Natural Beauty (of which Twyford Down formed the final ridge), and English Heritage, the guardian of two affected Scheduled Ancient Monuments.

The objections which we mounted at the 1985 Inquiry made a substantial impact. Inspector Leaker's report of the Inquiry was to say, of my J3 tunnel (which had been cobbled together from my vague instructions to the DoT engineers), 'but this proposal also deals in intangible values and the preservation of our heritage. So it is with some reluctance that I have to conclude that this alternative...is one I *cannot* recommend for acceptance in spite of its superiority in respecting sensitive areas of environmental and historic importance' (Leaker 10.21.4).

The part played (or perhaps more accurately the part which was not played) by the Countryside Commission and English Heritage was the subject of considerable discussion and examination over the coming years and may have prompted the DoT to recognize this shortcoming, which would probably have resulted in judicial review of any decision taken on the 1985 Inquiry evidence alone and thus may have led to the decision by Government to re-open the Inquiry in 1987. Nevertheless, the absence and silence of these organizations caused the public at large and others to seriously underestimate the damage to the landscape and to the protected sites. It also left the Transport

Department and minister sufficiently insulated from the real issues to allow the damaging scheme to proceed. The level of support, tacit or articulated, from such a wide range of reputable organizations for the DoT's route through Twyford Down and over the railway line made opposition from individuals seem insignificant.

During the Public Inquiry in the summer of 1985, objectors nagged away at the DoT and its witnesses. A number of short-comings in the general process of road planning, and the Twyford Down case, came to light.

It became clear that John Kelsey, the landscape consultant employed by the consulting engineers, Mott Hay and Anderson, had been appointed only on 9 May 1983 – after the initial round of public consultation, and certainly after the local councils had made decisions to support the Cutting route. Kelsey confirmed 'a preferred route [had already] been chosen at the time of my [firm's] appointment.' Kelsey subsequently stated that he had not the opportunity (or presumably remit) to consider alterna-tive routes. Indeed his firm was appointed following route selec-tion and thus his job as landscape consultant was simply cosmetic: to make the best out of the chosen route.

In our preparatory work for the Inquiry we had come across the evidence given to the Public Inquiry in the 1970s by the Transport Department's chief landscape adviser, Mr Porter. Porter had stated that any route *east* of St Catherine's Hill should be rejected on landscape grounds.

In the spring of 1985, I was unclear about the exact role and function of landscape archictects within the Transport Department and to what extent those landscape architects would have been involved in route selection. During the 1985 Public Inquiry I raised this with Roger Kent, a Transport Department landscape architect working on the M3. Responding to one of my questions Kent said, 'From the strategic point of view, I personally feel the route should be west of St Catherine's Hill. The routes investigated to the west could be improved.'

In other words, routes on the bypass could, and should have been further investigated, as evidenced by Merrick's work in producing our alternative bypass option.

The failure to explore in greater depth the possibility of inserting the M3 on the old A33 bypass has been an issue which has bothered a number of people over the years – even Prime

Minister Thatcher was apparently to ask, 'Why can't it (M3) go on the bypass?' when being lobbied some years later. Discussing the route selection process, and the MHA appraisal of the options, David Coleman of the Countryside Commission later asked 'Why did Merrick's bypass route – which avoided the damaging cut into the face of St Catherine's Hill – which was proposed at the 1985 Inquiry, or the Countryside Commission's alternative proposed in 1987, not emerge earlier, when the Transport Department and its consulting engineers were study- ing the alternative options in 1982?' Often, of course, the most obvious discoveries are the last to be made, but it does seem strange that in the course of such a very thorough trawl through a wide range of options, originally 14, finally whittled down to the two finalists, A3 (bypass) and D (Cutting), that those carry- ing out the planning and selection procedure did not go that one step further and consider the comparatively simple, and really very obvious, adjustment which would avoid the scar on the face of St Catherine's Hill, given as the official reason for rejecting Merrick's bypass route.

During the 1985 Inquiry, however, we established that the Government's chosen route for the M3, the creation of the engi- neering consultants, had been chosen for its alleged environ- mental benefits, against the (personal) judgement of the DoT's landscape officer, and only about 12 years after the most senior Departmental landscape architect had rejected consideration of a route on that alignment.

The Public Inquiry in 1985 served as a forum at which we met others who were to become key players in the campaign in the years to come. Prior to the Inquiry we had been largely isolated from other people opposed to different aspects of the DoT route. Our decision not to extend our objection to the section crossing the valley and over the railway had been taken because we did not feel competent to deal with those issues effectively, certainly not within the short time-scale available to us. We did not know that objection was to be made to the over-rail crossing by Richard Parker, a consulting engineer, newly resident in Twyford, who was experienced in Highway Inquiry work. On the opening day of the 1985 Inquiry Richard Parker made an immediate impact upon the proceedings when he challenged the DoT on a whole range of technical matters, with the DoT team failing to respond adequately to his requests for informa- tion (including the report of the Landscape Advisory

Committee). Our objection to the Cutting, the source of the vast quantities of chalk spoil, and Parker's objection to the high-level crossing of the valley, the receptacle for the chalk, ran in parallel during the 1985 Inquiry. Later, Parker was to become a leading member of the campaign where his technical expertise was the backbone for much of our activity. His family, too, were always there to help, encourage and sustain us through the eight years ahead.

Richard Parker conducted his own case, probing the Transport Department witnesses on their evidence. He eventually ground out of them that the gradients on the proposed motorway and its slip-roads (one of which was to have a 7 per cent gradient) were such that in normal circumstances crawler lanes would be provided for heavy vehicles – but that was not possible at M3, because it would have meant widening the cutting still further. Additionally, the stopping sight distance would be below standard, due to the gradient and curve, requiring formal dispensation from the DoT's own standards for motorway design. So, the Cutting route would be sub-standard, too.

After Richard Parker had completed his cross-examination of the Transport Department's Project Manager, Ian Caws, representing the Transport Department, re-examined his own witness, saying at one point 'the Minister would take account of information arising from the Public Inquiry.' I gained the understanding that statements made at an Inquiry by Departmental witnesses formed part of 'policy'.

Years later, in 1993, after the final decision had been made to build the Cutting, our new MP, Gerry Malone, arranged for a small group of us to meet with the then Roads Minister, Kenneth Carlisle. There was discussion about the finish on the motorway, black top (bitumen) or concrete. Despite indications at the Public Inquiries that black top would be used, the civil servants present when we met with the Roads Minister quite clearly stated that this was not the case, unless such an undertaking had been repeated in the Minister's Decision Letter. Since verbatim recordings of Inquiries rarely if ever form part of the official record of the Inquiry (and did not at M3) this raises a question as to whether undertakings given to objectors during cross-examination should be formally recorded or whether the whole process might not be more effectively executed by some sort of exchange of letters.

The Public Inquiry closed on the evening of Thursday, 8 August 1985. It had sat for 28 days, had received over 150 written submissions, heard more than 70 witnesses and marked the start of the eight-year debate on the future of Twyford Down. In closing the Inquiry, Inspector Leaker had thanked all those who appeared for presenting their case in a positive reasonable and civilized manner. Reporting the close of the Inquiry the local *Hampshire Chronicle* described how the Inquiry had been 'always relaxed and informal,' but that the 'tunnel scheme dominated the Inquiry and support for this proposal grew as the Inquiry progressed.' How Inspector Leaker was to react would not be made public until April 1987.

Within days of the 1985 Inquiry formally closing, I was disturbed to be told about an irregularity in the process, possibly to the disadvantage of our alternative suggestion that the M3 could be completed by adaptation of the old A33 bypass.

Towards the end of the 1985 Inquiry a programme of site visits had been arranged by the programming officer. At the end of a Public Inquiry site visits are arranged to view, on the ground, the Department of Transport route, and objectors' alternatives. A schedule is agreed and published and both the DoT and objectors are entitled to attend. The Guidance Notes for Inspectors make it clear that although the Inspector is free to make as many independent, unaccompanied visits as he likes, formal site visits after the close of the Inquiry may only be undertaken by prior arrangement, notified to all parties, and that no discussion on the merits of a proposal may be undertaken since the Inquiry is formally closed, and any 'discussion' could be 'evidence' which may only be given on the floor of the Inquiry.

A programme of site visits around Winchester had thus been organized, and on Tuesday, 13 August I attended the Bar End to Hockley section visits (Figure 12). Robin McCall, our solicitor friend and grand old man of Winchester, Alan Weeks of the local Ratepayers Association, and I walked the route, accompanied by Inspector Leaker, the Department of Transport Project Manager, Peter Davies, and a number of other members of the DoT 'team' at the Inquiry, including John Kelsey, the landscape architect to the Department of Transport's team.

The route of the Cutting had been marked out beforehand by the DoT team with post markers. Inspector Leaker, who was a relaxed and amiable man, chatted informally with everyone until we reached the shoulder of Twyford Down, about where the Iron Age Village site used to be; he walked away from the group, standing alone in the afternoon sunshine and looking down to the valley below towards Shawford. That part of

Figure 12 Inspector Leaker's site visit on the Dongas with the old road in the background. Left to right: Alan Weeks, (Winchester Ratepayers), the author, Peter Davies, Dudley Leaker, and Robin McCall, CBE, Freeman of the City of Winchester. (*Reproduced by kind permission of The Hampshire Chronicle*)

Twyford Down was private arable land (belonging to Winchester College but farmed by a tenant farmer) and it is very unlikely that Inspector Leaker would have made a private visit to that vantage point before the formal site visit. He was, however, standing more or less in the middle of the proposed Cutting at its widest and deepest point, looking down on the valley far below which contained a wide strip of ancient Water Meadows, the River Itchen with its 'gin-clear' waters, the old bypass tucked down in the landscape and the main railway on the far side of the valley. Perhaps he was visualizing the impact of the huge engineering operation that would be involved in excavating the vast quantities of chalk from beneath him and building up the embankments to carry the new motorway across the valley and over the top of the railway line.

At the end of the afternoon I bade formal farewell to Inspector Leaker, since the remaining site visits were to be made to various points on the southern, Compton to Bassett section, with which I was not concerned.

On the following Friday, 16 August, I received a telephone call from a fellow objector, John Pilkington. What Pilkington told me came as a bolt from the blue, and was disturbing. Apparently an unscheduled site visit had been made to St Catherine's Hill the previous afternoon, and the subject under discussion was our alternative bypass route, known as 'P1', and it was said that inaccurate remarks had been made about this 'P1' alternative. Only Inspector Leaker and representatives of the DoT team and of the County Council had been informed of the visit. I had no way of knowing at whose instigation that extra visit was arranged.

I telephoned the Department of Transport regional office at Dorking, which confirmed that the visit had occurred, and agreed that no attempt had been made to contact me, or any other objector. Whatever the proprieties were or were not of this additional, unannounced site visit, officials gave no indication that there was anything amiss in the DoT team involving the County Council or the Inspector, in this way, or in the unscheduled site visit.

However, others were disturbed. Whatever the real reason for the extra visit its secretive nature aroused suspicion that those in favour of the Cutting route were trying to give themselves an unfair advantage by exerting additional pressure on the Inspector and discrediting our bypass alternative.

The Inquiry was formally closed. I telephoned the Inquiry Programming Officer who told me that since the Inquiry was closed there was no means of communicating with the Inspector. It appeared that the only recourse was via the Council on Tribunals, an organization set up in 1958 to oversee administrative procedures involving statutory inquiries, such as a trunk road Public Inquiry.

With hindsight, that is a fair summary of what I eventually managed to find out. It required considerable research, and a round of increasingly frenetic telephone calls to establish that there was nothing I could do by then, apart from register my concerns. So I wrote formally to the Council on Tribunals, who replied, on 22 August 1985, saying:

> The role of the Council on Tribunals in planning matters is to advise the Government on procedures at public inquiries generally. They cannot become involved in the merits of a case. If they do take up a point of procedure it

has to be after the completion of the Inquiry – that is after the decision has been made; otherwise it might be thought that the Council were trying to influence the decision...

The 'decision' was not made until nearly five years later, on 27 February 1990, by which time the significance of this injustice had been overshadowed by so much else. Why the additional site visit was arranged, or at whose request, and what difference it may have made to events remains impossible to judge. What is clear is that the additional visit contravened the Government's guidelines on the conduct of Public Inquiries.

Some eighteen months later another flaw in the process, also directly relating to our bypass alternative, came to light with the publication in 1987 of Inspector Leaker's report of the 1985 Inquiry, when the Secretaries of State announced their decision to reopen the Inquiry – a decision taken, they said, to hear evidence from English Heritage and the Countryside Commission, the two environmental watchdogs who had not been involved in the 1985 part of the Inquiry.

This injustice would have been avoided if a recommendation of the Franks Committee (The Report of the Committee on Administrative Tribunals and Enquiries 1957) had been implemented. Although accepted by the Government in the Report on the Review of Highway Inquiry Procedures in 1978 the recommendation that 'all parties (at an Inquiry) should have an opportunity to propose corrections of fact in the first part of the Inspector's Report before it is tendered to the Minister' had (and has) not been implemented. Obviously the first part of an Inspector's Report (i.e. Report of the Proceedings, the second part being Findings of Fact and Conclusions) would have to be made available to all parties at the Inquiry to enable implementation of this. Had we been able to see a draft report of the proceedings we would have been able to correct the following crucial error.

At the 1985 Public Inquiry Hampshire County Council (HCC) had formally counter-objected to our bypass alternative, called 'P1'. As is customary the HCC proof of evidence was made available prior to its actual presentation to the Inquiry. The written proof stated 'the cut which P1 would necessitate into the western face of St Catherine's Hill would be between 14 and 19 m high.'

While giving his evidence the HCC planning officer volunteered a modification to the proof. He withdrew reference to alleged damage to the western face of St Catherine's Hill caused by the construction of P1. Much attention had been focused by those objecting to our alternative 'P1' on the alleged necessity for a 'cut' up to the upper ramparts on the western face of St Catherine's Hill, which would have been visible from Winchester. Withdrawal of that part of the HCC proof acknowledged that 'P1' did not involve such damage. Subsequently confirming the withdrawal of this part of the Hampshire County Council's evidence the planning officer wrote on 12 August 1986, 'The County Council witness volunteered a modification while presenting his evidence, withdrawing para 10 as a result of the drawing prepared in support of scheme P1. Such was the timing of the presentation of the revised drawings that para 10 could not be deleted from the typed text. However, the Inspector acknowledged the withdrawal of that paragraph' (letter from HCC Planning Officer 12.8.86).

Surprisingly, Inspector Leaker's report repeats the statement relating to the 'cut' in to the face of St Catherine's Hill in the original, written proof and does not record the fundamental amendment made by the planning officer: 'the effect of this would be to raise the cut at its highest point right to the foot of the Iron Age Earthworks (upper ramparts)' (Leaker 6.22.33). Quite how Inspector Leaker failed to incorporate the radical amendment into his report must remain a matter for speculation, but the effect was clear cut – a possible alternative to the Cutting route was being ruled out on the basis of incorrect information.

With hindsight I do wonder quite why we did not explore the potential of the Government's failure to implement the undertaking to give objectors an opportunity to correct factual errors in the Inspector's report of the proceedings, and challenge the Department of Transport on this critical safety net. But I think it was because we were amateurs in the Highways Inquiries game (as most objectors were in those days – the advent of Alarm UK and the vastly increased profile of the damage caused by the roads programme has remedied somewhat the problems of inexperience faced by so many objectors). We were not sent a copy of the Inspector's report in advance of publication, so we did not know that there were any matters of fact requiring correction until the Inspector's report was eventually published, along with the Ministers' decision in April 1987. By that time, the issue was overtaken by the reopening of the Inquiry.

It is interesting to speculate what the possible outcome, and effect on the whole saga, might have been if we had attempted to take out an injunction preventing a Ministerial decision until after Inspector Leaker's Report of the Proceedings had been made public. As it was the uncorrected evidence went unchallenged: an error which resulted in consistent repetition by opponents of 'P1' that a route on the bypass had to involve substantial damage to the face of St Catherine's Hill. This misinformation was to be repeated again in the Hampshire County Council report to its Planning Committee in May 1987 when the HCC was considering its position in the run-up to the reopened Inquiry (HCC Planning and Transportation Committee 18.5.87). It is not possible to evaluate the impact on the M3 debate of this continued misconception about damage to St Catherine's Hill.

Public Inquiry Inspectors are sent to purdah from the moment they formally declare an Inquiry closed. Previously there to serve the interest of public debate, the Inspector is no longer contactable by the public. The report he produces is kept secret, and when completed is delivered direct to the developer of the scheme, the Department of Transport, which proposed the scheme in the first place. Ministers will say they are unable to discuss any aspect of the scheme on the grounds that it is all *sub judice*. Although the Public Inquiry system in the UK is highly adversarial it is not a court of law – hardly even quasi-judicial. In effect, at the moment the Inquiry closes, but long before it is completed (in the sense that the Report completes the Public Inquiry) it ceases to be part of the public process and becomes a secret part of Government's policy making. Once delivered to the Department of Transport it may be considered at their leisure, and in private.

When they are so minded, the Secretaries of State announce a decision. Then, and not before, does any body, public, private or corporate, have sight of the report of the proceedings, and leaking the contents of the report can even invite the attentions of the security services.

This contrasts with arrangements for development control Inquiries, where the Inspector's report is made available to all parties, developer and others, upon completion and before the DoE make a decision. The difference of course is that in the case of Highways Inquiries the Government, DoT and DoE are applicant (developer) and decision-maker. While there will be many situations involving two (or more) arms of Government, it would seem the more important in such circumstances that justice is not only done, but seen to be done, and a complete revision of these aspects of Highway Inquiries is long overdue. It is hard to square political commitment to open government with such secretive procedures being allowed to persist.

4

September 1985 to April 1987 – The Road to Damascus

During the 1985 Inquiry with the attendant local publicity many supporters of our objection had emerged, giving us increased confidence. For the first time there was open public discussion of the merits of the Department of Transport Cutting scheme. Whatever else we had done we had exploded the myth that the Cutting route would be good for the environment. A new and crucial stage had been reached in the history of the M3 around Winchester, already more than a decade old.

At the end of 1985 we relaxed a little. We believed our objection had been well presented at the Public Inquiry, though I am afraid that I for one considerably underestimated the shortcomings in the proposal we had made for the tunnel under Twyford Down. We believed that there was a chance Inspector Leaker would support my objection, and recommend that the DoT route be dropped. Dudley, with his years of experience in local government, was the most doubtful, fearing that the political and bureaucratic convenience of pushing ahead with the Cutting route would be too powerful to overcome.

In the aftermath of the Inquiry we all reverted to normality, catching up on day-to-day life.

Following the close of the Inquiry in August 1985, the Twyford Down debate was in suspense while Inspector Leaker prepared his report, although the issue was never far from our minds. The subject of M3 and Twyford Down was a frequent topic of conversation for all of us, socially, at work, and for me particularly as a councillor on Winchester City Council; additional information and reactions kept coming our way so, although very little seemed to be happening, we were building up our contacts, and I felt local people were becoming increasingly unhappy as awareness grew of the enormous impact which the Cutting route would make upon the landscape.

Ten months after the first Public Inquiry, information was leaked to Merrick that Inspector Leaker's report had been delivered to the Department of Transport in the summer of 1986. Because of the Transport Department's curious protocol of secrecy there was no official confirmation that civil servants or ministers had received the document, but Merrick's information proved to be correct.

In an effort to establish whether the Report had been submitted to the Transport Department I wrote to the Department of the Environment asking if they could confirm that the Report had been completed, and asking also if they could confirm whether the document had been sent to any of the participants at the Inquiry, including the DoT. I asked for a copy of the Report, offering to pay any necessary charges.

The reply, dated 21 July 1986, which I received from the Department of the Environment and Department of Transport 'Common Services' office at Bristol was revealing. '(Your letter) has been *forwarded to the Section now responsible for this Inquiry.*'

On 25 July 1986, an official from the *Departments of the Environment and Transport South East Regional Office*, at Federated House, Dorking, wrote to me, 'I can confirm that the Inspector ...has recently submitted his Report to the Secretaries of State for the Environment and for Transport. As you will appreciate, a large number of detailed and complex issues were raised at the Inquiry and these will need to be carefully considered by the Secretaries of State in reaching their decisions. This will take some time, but the Secretaries of State have indicated that they hope to announce their joint decisions by the end of the year. The Inspector's report will not be published until the decisions are announced but, as an objector, you are entitled under the Highways (Inquiries Procedure) Rules 1976 to receive a copy. This will be sent to you with the Secretaries of States' decision letter.' In other words, responsibility for the project had now passed to its promoter, the Department of Transport, before the findings of the Inspector's Report were known. So, we would not have an opportunity to correct any errors of fact.

The exchange of letters illustrates why there is such public concern about the Highway Inquiry process. The whole procedure had moved from a Public Inquiry to a series of confidential internal procedures and decisions were being taken by the very department which promoted the scheme. Objectors (and presumably all parties at the Inquiry apart from the Transport Department, the promoting authority) are denied the right to see the Inspector's final report until crucial decisions have been taken. Quite clearly, no minister having once confirmed the advice of his department can easily change the decision without loss of face and humiliation unless forced to do so by litigation by objectors, who seldom possess the financial or other resources to do so.

The joint structure of the the Environment and Transport departments in this process is little more than a transparent device to lend some credibility to the scheme. This point was taken up by a leading article in *The Times* in November 1990 (Figure 13). It was to be 18 months after the close of the 1985 Inquiry before the Secretaries of State, or their officials, finally bit the bullet and announced the next stage in the affair. Admittedly our campaigning and lobbying activies over the latter half of that period may have thrown a spanner in the works and slowed down the process, but long periods of apparent inactivity are quite common while the Transport Department digests an Inspector's report. Delay in the decision-making process, often blamed on objectors to schemes, arises more commonly from cumbersome and leisurely bureaucratic processes and the execution of such processes.

From the information leaked to Merrick it seemed clear that Inspector Leaker was recommending the Cutting route as the best choice. It appeared that we had underestimated the importance the Inspector would attach to the objections raised by Hampshire County Council, Winchester College and others to the bypass alternative and apparently the Inspector had been convinced of the superiority of the Cutting route – or at least the inferiority of any alternative route on offer, and in particular the politics of putting a route on the old bypass, west of St Catherine's Hill, and the cost, delay and uncertainty of the particular tunnel route we had proposed.

The leaking of the Leaker Report therefore focused our minds rather sharply: if something was not done, quickly, the Cutting route would be approved and Twyford Down would be lost for ever. Spurred on by this news, Merrick and I began to

THE TIMES SATURDAY NOVEMBER 3 1990

1 Pennington Street, London E1 9XN Telephone 071-782 5000

TWYFORD DOWN BUT NOT OUT

In a tranquil corner of Hampshire the limits of national sovereignty are being tested by lovers of the English countryside. Led by Barbara Bryant, they have just lost a High Court action to protect Twyford Down, the magnificent hill outside Winchester through which the transport department would like to blast a motorway cutting. The campaigners have two weeks in which to appeal against the judgment, so risking still greater legal costs than those they have incurred already. Mrs Bryant has even sought help from Brussels against the Conservative government she supports.

More than two years have passed since a European Community directive, which requires governments to make an environmental impact assessment before embarking on big engineering projects, came into force in Britain. Mr Justice McCullough ruled that the decision on Twyford Down had already been made before 1988, and that the law could not be applied retrospectively. Yet controversy has continued ever since 1985 over whether a tunnel rather than a cutting should be built, at an extra cost now estimated at £90 million.

The case highlights several weaknesses in the British decision-making process. If, as both the transport and the environment departments claim, the essential decision on Twyford Down was taken at an early stage, in what sense are ministers taking them? By the time officials pass upward a road scheme for approval, there is little room for manoeuvre for politicians who may wish to take account of environmental objections omitted from the original analysis. No minister likes to be seen to climb down on an official decision. Even if he is so minded, an environment secretary is unlikely to gain extra money from the Treasury to force his transport counterpart to change his mind on a road plan. Ministers are thus stuck with bad decisions and the law can usually be wheeled out on their side.

That some members of the government know that Mrs Bryant is right about Twyford Down has been demonstrated by the eloquent silence of the environment secretary, Chris Patten, whenever the transport secretary, Cecil Parkinson, proclaims government unanimity on this road. More than silence is now required from Mr Patten if the government is to be saved from severe and well-deserved embarrassment. In his recent white paper, Mr Patten hinted that all departments considering large projects should in future incorporate a quantified "green" factor into their cost/benefit analysis. That way lies the future.

Consideration of environmental externalities in all planning decisions should now be axiomatic. Transport externalities are, after all, used to justify new roads in the first place. If convenience to car users is judged an economic "return" on an investment, why should the same not apply to the convenience of local people, to the pleasures of pedestrians and to the benefits for society of natural beauty?

To be sure, balancing an irreplaceable landscape against the £90 million of a tunnel under Twyford Down is not easy. But then justifying the motorway itself required just such cost/benefit juggling. Congestion between Winchester and Southampton will be eased by the road. Amenities in Winchester and its environs will be damaged by the cutting. If the prime minister cannot bang together the heads of the Treasury and the two departments involved, the least she can do is shelve the whole project until prosperity returns.

Figure 13 'Twyford Down but Not Out'. A leading article in *The Times*, November 1990. *(Reproduced by kind permission of Times Newspapers.)*

lobby environmental organizations, cajoling our friends and acquaintances in an effort to persuade organizations and individuals to object publicly to the Cutting route, and to marshal public opinion to force the Department of Transport to rethink its proposal.

In order to give a detailed and credible picture of the damaging route, we needed visual aids – only the most experienced professional was otherwise able to fully comprehend the complexities of the scheme and landscape. Merrick devised a form of presentation, using two slide projectors side by side, with twin screens, to create a panoramic view, enabling direct before and after comparisons, and carrying a great deal of information in an economical way. The slide presentation became highly polished; it was an invaluable tool for our campaign and was shown to audiences of all sizes from small local groups to major meetings at Winchester Guildhall and other venues.

In 1986 we focused the campaign on local contacts, assuming that if the two local councils, Winchester City Council and Hampshire County Council could be persuaded to change their policies and use their powers and influence to protect this historic landscape then there would be a fighting chance of success.

Merrick gave scores of presentations in 1986. Depending on the organization receiving the presentation, either Merrick made the presentation on his own, or both he and I would go along. The campaign was demanding on our time, our energies and on our families, but nonetheless very rewarding. Almost without exception as we explained the details of the Cutting route, and the impact it would have on the landscape, scales fell from the eyes of those watching.

Despite the consultations which had taken place in 1983 and 1984 it was remarkable how few people were aware of the real impact of the scheme, and the fact that acceptable and some less expensive alternatives did exist. The depth and width of the Cutting, its bare chalk sides, the gradients on the road itself, the height of the embankments built from the displaced chalk were barely understood. Nor was the extent of the damage to the valley and water meadows or the impact of the high-level embankment, constructed with the chalk excavated out of the Cutting, which was to carry the motorway across the valley and over the main London to Southampton railway line.

We recognized only too well that to bring about a change in attitude to the DoT Cutting route we had to get under the skin of the local establishment to make them aware and to produce a reaction.

Winchester is different. Once the ancient capital of England, a major commercial centre in medieval times, it is now a small town. Its reputation and status is far greater than the town today would otherwise warrant – like Oscar Wilde's woman, everyone likes it because it has a past. In the 1939-45 world war it escaped bombing despite the proximity to Southampton, which was flattened because, it is said, Hitler wanted to be crowned King of England at Winchester!

The City with its population of some 33,000 is comparatively affluent, and well-connected. Winchester Cathedral and Winchester College, historic and magnificent institutions, enjoy a network of influence throughout the British establishment and have done so for many centuries. The Mayoralty of Winchester is the oldest in England, and the City and surrounding shire countryside drips titles. The 'county-set' is a major influence, as Winchester's MPs have found sometimes to their misfortune. The local newspaper, *The Hampshire Chronicle* has been published since 1772, pre-dating even *The Times*, and changing only gradually over the centuries.

Things change slowly in Winchester; residents put down deep roots. Despite the national, even global, lives of many residents it remains distinctly parochial. David Cowan, a border Scot and chief executive of Winchester Council said to me once, 'Whenever I don't understand Winchester, I go home and read Trollope's *Barchester Chronicles*, and then it all becomes clear to me!'

The task of bringing about a change in attitude of those who could influence the Government thus involved not only mobilizing the local population, but also touching key points of influence, such as Winchester Preservation Trust, Winchester College, the local branch of Council for the Protection of Rural England, the Cathedral, the ancient institution of the Hospital of St Cross, and a network of social contacts, unseen but powerful.

I sought first to try to bring about a change in the Winchester City Council and its support for the Cutting route. As an elected Conservative councillor I tackled the task with that magic tag 'elected member'. Ken Livingstone, the left-wing Labour MP and former leader of the Greater London Council (perhaps not convinced of the power of the ballot box) may have said, 'If Voting Changed Anything They'd Abolish It,' but the fact is that if people have voted for someone, electing them to office, it bestows a unique authority in the constitution, and provides at the very least a handle to open doors.

Winchester Council's policy of support for the Transport Department proposal to complete the M3 with the Cutting route had developed and consolidated over many years and was by then firmly entrenched. In its evidence to the 1985 Public Inquiry Winchester Council said, 'the Council [have] enjoyed close working relations with Mott Hay and Anderson [the consultants] in the preparation of their Report of February 1983 [the Mott Hay Anderson Appraisal] and [have] accepted that the choice of route past Winchester depended chiefly on environmental considerations.'

In his own evidence to that Inquiry, Winchester Council's Director of Planning referred to a 'most worthwhile and reward-ing partnership with the Consultants – Mott Hay Anderson have been represented at meetings of the Review of Planning in the Winchester Area Steering Committee and officers of all the local authorities involved have attended meetings of the "Technical Committee" established by Mott Hay and Anderson and the Department (DoT).'

In 1986 officials of the Winchester Council were continuing the implemention of the policy, developed since 1981, of sup-port for the Cutting route; and could do no other until such time as the policy was altered. Thus, my approach was directed to my fellow elected members, who had the power to change the policy if they chose.

The campaign to 'convert' the Winchester Council between the autumn of 1986 and September 1987 provides a study of the complexities of securing change in local government policies and attitudes, and explains how such change was ultimately brought about at Winchester. Merrick told me that it was scarcely possible – that would almost certainly have been the case if the discus-sions within Winchester Council had taken place in isolation, rather than as part of a much wider public campaign which was gaining momentum. This wider campaign was creating a climate in which previously held views about the wisdom of the Cutting route were being increasingly questioned. As it was, the various arenas of both local and national activity fed off each other, par-ticularly of course in Winchester itself where so many people are involved in more than one organization.

As a first step it seemed important to me that I should explain to my Council colleagues why I believed the Cutting route was a mistake, indeed a disaster, and how we proposed the missing

M3 link could be completed. Merrick and I began giving the slide presentation to small groups of Winchester councillors. Many demands are made on local government politicians, most of whom give freely of their time and energies to the communities they serve. I developed a pattern of offering the presentation to small groups of councillors about an hour before a Committee meeting which would be convenient for their diary. All that I asked was that they turn up a bit early.

Merrick and I merely explained the case, colourfully and convincingly – the platter was laid before the councillors, but it was left to them whether and what they picked from it. Some of the councillors were horrified by what they saw. Some were less convinced, and some stepped back because they feared the muddle and uncertainty which would be created by an admission that the Department of Transport had got it wrong.

It soon became clear that, while they knew the general route of the motorway, most councillors were unaware of the environmental impact of the scheme, and were less than happy that neither English Heritage nor the Countryside Commission had appeared at the 1985 Inquiry. It seemed that some might even wish to oppose the Cutting route, though any precipitous move to propose a change of policy would be premature and could consolidate Winchester Council's policy of supporting the Cutting.

A substantial number of my colleagues had always regarded the high-level crossing of the valley (taking the road over the railway) with a great deal of criticism, or even hostility, though sadly that does not appear to have been communicated formally to the Department of Transport. As mentioned earlier, the high-level crossing of the valley is the Cinderella of the story, but the grass-roots instincts of local politicians were fundamentally right. These local instincts about the high-level crossing and the very damaging embankment crossing of the Water Meadows and the London to Southampton railway line were unfortunately never converted into proper campaigns; throughout attention remained focused on the damage to Twyford Down, overshadowing the devasting effects that the Department of Transport route would have elsewhere.

One of the most important presentations we gave was in the Wykeham Room of the Guildhall to a small group of councillors, including Councillor Patricia Edwards, chairman of the Winchester Council Planning Committee, and thus responsible for steering Winchester Council's policy on M3. Edwards is a diminutive blonde, of Irish descent, with a sharp, disciplined mind who always does her homework. She was well respected, by foe and friend, as an able, experienced and sincere politician, and highly competent chairman of her committee. She fought her corner hard, and rarely lost.

She had held the chair for the past three years, and had taken the committee through the 1985 Public Inquiry representing Winchester Council's support for the Department of Transport's Cutting route. Edwards watched our presentation carefully, asked just a couple of questions and left, only saying thank you and good night. Merrick was alarmed at her silence and feared the worst.

Edwards says now, 'There's no doubt that the close working relationship between Mott Hay and Anderson and Winchester Council was new in the early 1980s – that opportunity for the Council to work with the DoT's people was very novel, and one of the changes which had resulted from the 1976 Public Inquiry. The novelty of this probably blunted our critical faculties during the consultations. I'd had doubts about the DoT route for some time, the Cutting and, more important, the whaleback crossing of the railway line (the high-level crossing). But it seemed the only answer and better than going through the Water Meadows. The enormity of the cutting was never evident to us until we saw Merrick's presentation. I was horrified when I found out the sides of the cutting were to be bare chalk.' The reason for Edwards's silence while we showed our presentation is obvious.

By the autumn of 1986, with still no sign of the Inspector's Report, I was 100 per cent confident that a majority of councillors would support a plea to Government to have the Inquiry reopened, principally on the grounds that two of the Government's own conservation 'watchdogs' had not been represented at the Inquiry. This would be a major breakthrough, which would receive all party support and which could provide the foundations for the first step towards a change in Winchester Council's policy of support for the Cutting route.

I was only too well aware of the potential damage to the campaign that would have resulted from any unsuccessful votes at

Winchester Council. I had never forgotten the politicians' axiom taught me years earlier – if you can't count, you shouldn't be in politics! At each stage it was only when I was absolutely confident of sufficient support that I was prepared to push the campaign to change Winchester Council's policy a step further.

By the autumn of 1986 I was confident that the time was right to ask my colleagues to fire the first shot across the Transport Department's bows by formally expressing the Council's concerns surrounding the 1985 Public Inquiry into the Twyford Down Cutting route. I discussed the procedural problems and logistics of how to get this matter on to the Winchester Council's agenda. A formal motion made directly to Council, in my name, was the only option in the time available and would allow my colleagues, the elected members, to debate the absence of English Heritage and Countryside Commission from the Inquiry as a matter of principle, without the need for officers' reports. Officers' reports have to go through a six-week committee cycle which would have been time-consuming and inevitably would have raised the wider issue of the Council's existing support for the Department of Transport route.

Elected members have the right to make policy, but since the officers have to implement the policy, and have an obligation to ensure that at the very least the policy complies with the law, councillors are well advised to discuss policy initiatives with senior officers. I arranged to meet with the principal officers involved to discuss the terms of my proposed motion. The meeting was constructive and helpful, although one of the staff present somewhat petulantly complained that I was creating a lot of work 'simply on a whim'.

But, however arrogant the remark may have been, the exchange picks out an element in the decision-making process which is frequently overlooked or whose impact is underestimated – namely, that officials regard change as troublesome! Just like any of us, local government officers and Department of Transport officials are reluctant to unpick a piece of work only to have to do it again, particularly if change involves rethinking a professional principle. The way to overcome this obstacle is to convince the bureaucracy that it will be less troublesome to change than not to change.

After the meeting with the senior officers I went away to finalize the text of the motion. Dudley and I spent a lunch-hour refining the wording, and at 2 o'clock I delivered the notice of motion to the Chief Executive. It read:

That this Council:

1) Calls upon the Secretaries of State for the Environment and Transport to publish without further delay and before any ministerial decision is made the Inspector's Report on the recent M3 Bar End to Bassett Public Inquiry

2) Requests the Secretaries of State to call for such further information as they may consider necessary and ensure that any ministerial decisions flowing from the Public Inquiry are made only after full consideration of all relevant information.

The Chief Executive scanned the words carefully – was his mind working overtime on what sort of, or where, an amendment could be inserted during the debate which could suddenly transform the motion into one of objection to the route? I expect it was, certainly in his shoes I would have been wondering whether the apparently bland motion was all I really had in mind. But it was, because I had no intention of being precipitous – after five years the Council needed time to adjust.

David Croker agreed to second the motion. He had been a Winchester councillor since 1979, and an active member of the Winchester Joint Action Group in the 1970s. At the 1985 Inquiry Croker had restricted his evidence to the impact upon the villages of Compton and Shawford, the area which he represented. He had been one of the first group of four councillors to watch Merrick's slide presentation, and along with the other three, had been immediately convinced of the need to reopen the Public Inquiry, because, as he put it, 'there had been corruption of the process.' From that moment on he had been a great support to me at the Winchester Council.

Despite my confidence that I had done my homework, nevertheless I was nervous before the meeting. There were after all 54 councillors who were members of the Council, across all political interests and all of whom would be attending. But, remarkably, the motion was carried unanimously, and the following day the City Secretary wrote to the DoT officially conveying the message 'I should be obliged if you would let me know whether...the Secretaries of State are satisfied that they have obtained all relevant information on which to take a decision.' No Government Department could afford to ignore such a shot across the bows from a Statutory Objector. We had got to first base!

In order for Winchester Council to go the next step and alter its policy away from support of the Department of Transport route, the Planning Committee would have to discuss the matter, briefed by officers' reports, and then recommend a revised policy for adoption by full Council. To allow for the fairly long run-in time for preparation of the necessary reports and still have any hope of the Council changing its policy in time to make any difference to the fate of Twyford Down it was important to get the process moving at Winchester Council.

In 1986 the Conservative Group (of which I was a member) controlled the Council, and held the chair of all committees. A change in council policy was unthinkable unless the controlling group sanctioned such a change.

The Conservative Group of Winchester Council met on 30 October 1986 a few days after the motion had been agreed by Council. The minutes of that Group meeting record that 'Bryant, Edwards, the chairman of the Planning, and the Group Chairman should present a joint statement (to Group) and recommendation to be debated as soon as possible.' A joint statement signed by the chairman of the Planning Committee and the chairman of the ruling political Group would be a considerable power-base and could be expected to carry the day.

The Conservative Group met again on 13 November, and agreed that 'in principle this Group supports efforts to achieve a tunnel for the completion of the M3...'. Among the other political parties on Winchester Council, Liberal Democrats, and Labour, there was a majority moving towards support for a tunnel and objection to the damaging Department of Transport route.

This political debate was taking place against a background of increasingly public discussion of the reservations about the Department of Transport Cutting route, which were apparently (and belatedly) being expressed by English Heritage and the Countryside Commission.

On 12 December 1986 the Winchester Council received a reply from the Department of Transport, 'The Inspector's Report will, in accordance with normal and well-established practice, be published when the Secretaries of State...announce their decisions about the scheme and not before...' and then, after a paragraph, 'But if new information comes to light after the close of the Inquiry which is germane to the decisions to be reached, the Highways (Inquiries Procedure) Rules 1976 contain the provision whereby the inquiry can be reopened...'.

That sounds fairly dry now, but coming in a letter from the Department of Transport at that time it was explosive. Local BBC Television certainly thought so, and Bruce Parker, BBC South's experienced presenter, did the piece. It was recorded late in the afternoon and on that occasion apparently they 'literally ran down the corridors with the tape' to get it on air, accompanied by a studio interview with Bill Rogers, a former Secretary of State for Transport. Bill Rogers said if he were Secretary of State he would look very carefully at the need to reopen the Inquiry: 'these are very reputable organizations indeed. They've come forward with some new evidence...maybe it's necessary to reopen the Inquiry.' There was a wave of speculation that the Inquiry would be reopened.

By the end of 1986 a statutory authority, namely Winchester Council, was asking awkward questions of government departments. A substantial power base had been secured within the elected members, but as yet there was no formal mechanism to give the Council the opportunity to reappraise its policy. In due course the Government's decision to reopen the Public Inquiry would provide that opportunity. The irony, of course, is that none of the 'evidence' justifying the reopening of the Inquiry was 'new'. The fact that even those most closely involved had not appreciated the exact nature of the project under discussion must raise serious questions.

5

June 1986 to April 1987 – National organizations reappraise the damage and impact of the Cutting route

In the summer of 1986, when Inspector Leaker's Report had first been 'leaked', the possibility of a challenge in the High Court (technically 'judicial review') to any possible decision by Government to go ahead with the Cutting had been discussed between Merrick and me. At that time we were still only two individuals, supported by family and friends, campaigning as a unit.

The difficulties and uncertainties which we believed would be associated with a High Court challenge, and the probable costs to us as simply two families deterred us. The compromise of pressing for a reopening of the Inquiry to hear the missing evidence from the Countryside Commission and English Heritage seemed at once both more responsible and constructive, less awe-inspiring.

We did not know it at the time, but apparently at least one arm of Government, the Environment Department, was, by the summer of 1986, itself promulgating the possibility of reopening the Inquiry.

It seems probable that we had underestimated the legal potential of the absence of the two conservation watchdogs, the Countryside Commission and English Heritage. What would have happened if instead of pushing for the Public Inquiry to be reopened we had let Government make a decision – presumably in favour of the Department of Transport Cutting route – and then had challenged that decision in the courts? We have since been advised that we would have stood a good chance of persuading the courts to overthrow such a decision because of the absence of evidence from the country's two principal environmental watchdogs. Instead we put rather too much faith in the Public Inquiry process, assuming that if all the facts were properly presented to an Inquiry Inspector the Cutting would be thrown out.

Merrick was hearing rumours out of the Transport Department, and other information came our way from a number of contacts in and around Government. We seized upon these snippets of information but unfortunately I think they merely served to focus our minds on one or two specific issues, rather than the whole canvas of the decision-making process. The services of a well-informed lobbyist at that time would have done a great deal to clear the opacity of the process with which we were surrounded, and might have enabled us to focus the energies of our vastly increasing power base of local and national support to better effect.

In the autumn of 1986 the concept of the tunnel solution remained just that: an attractive idea but lacking technical support. The Transport Department had poured technical scorn on my embryonic J3 tunnel at the 1985 Inquiry and, according to the leaked reports in the press, Inspector Leaker's report of the Inquiry had agreed with the Department.

Outside the immediate confines of central Winchester the general view was that the bypass was the obvious place for the motorway, but among the Winchester establishment, there remained strong opposition to any suggestion of a route on the bypass, or 'west of St Catherine's Hill'.

This opposition arose from a real fear that 'on the bypass' would end up being 'through the Water Meadows' rather than on the old A33 bypass, and also from ignorance about the impact of the Cutting route through Twyford Down and the 'whaleback' crossing of the railway line, which combined to lead to a rose-tinted spectacles notion that idealized the east of St Catherine's Hill route to one of being the 'perfect solution': out of sight – and out of mind.

For us there was an increasingly obvious dilemma: the alternative incorporating the bypass was the cheapest and, in ecological terms, a quite harmless and practical option. On the other hand I felt that the tunnel would be a superb solution, both protecting the environment and offering an 'amenity' gain: in other words not only would Twyford Down be saved, but Winchester would have the added benefit of traffic-free access to St Catherine's Hill and the South Downs beyond. Admittedly the tunnel would be very expensive, but both of these alternatives kept the motorway low in the landscape and would take the motorway under the railway line – avoiding the 'whaleback' high-level crossing over the valley.

Merrick, the professional landscape architect, while arguing the glories of the tunnel, remained absolutely convinced that the bypass was the right place for the motorway. He was heard to remark, 'The tunnel cost is about £80 m – that's a whole year's funding for this country's conservation bodies.' He also found the Cutting route indefensible when compared to widening the existing bypass, which would not damage the scheduled sites, would have avoided the Itchen Navigation and the Water Meadows in that area, would have been absorbed into the existing landscape, and was estimated, at that time, to cost some £7 m less than the Cutting route.

For my part, my opposition to the DoT route had grown out of an instinctive love of the countryside, rather than any technical background, and a distrust of a decision, made without public debate, to raise the existing road out of the valley floor and high up the scarp face of Twyford Down.

As I listened to the influential locals reacting to our slide presentations I think I came to recognize a reality – a route on the bypass, however obvious, logical and economical, was not politically practical. Talk of a bypass route was like a red rag to a whole herd of bulls and to pursue that option would simply harden attitudes in favour of the Cutting route. This strong reaction against any suggestion of a route along the line of the old A33 Winchester bypass (despite being the choice of the earlier generation of objectors), was articulated clearly to me by Dr Chris Gillham, then chairman of the Winchester Preservation Trust's Planning Committee, after I had made the slide presentation to the Trust.

Gillham wrote on behalf of the Trust, thanking me for the presentation, but identifying three main reasons for rejecting our suggested route on the bypass: 'Firstly, if the traffic projections are nearly right (and *regardless of overall national figures, motorways generate their own traffic*), there would be the strong threat remaining of a Dual 4 demand in fifteen or twenty years time. It would be very much more difficult to propose a widening of the Cutting [interestingly Gillham's understanding of road planning and economics led him to foreshadow the secret 4 Lane Study in 1989/90 but he completely underestimated the DoT's willingness to put that in the Cutting] than further incursion into the Itchen Valley. Certainly assurances could be sought that no widening would be contemplated but very few of those who have been the strongest objectors to the M3 could any longer trust any assurances from the DoT, however strongly phrased.'

Gillham continued, 'I believe that a return to a valley route now would be politically impossible to bring about. Too many people have seen advantages to Winchester which they won't easily let go. The Preservation Trust also has to make a presumption in favour of Winchester's [urban] interests. The cost to the City of even the valley scheme [our bypass route known as P1] you propose and more so in what is risked in say 20 years time, means that Winchester Preservation Trust would be failing seriously in its duty to Winchester if it did not oppose a bypass route.'

And then, 'The Trust had wearied from all the previous struggles and whilst we asked for a tunnel at the last Inquiry we never really seriously believed it was politically possible at that time. Now there is a glimmer of hope. We thank you for stirring our blood again, but can we all wholeheartedly go for a tunnel? We should get together again soon.'

The views expressed by Gillham succinctly sum up the attitude of the influential voices of the City at that time. Indeed, Professor Martin Biddle held the view that an upgrading of the bypass would be the acceptable solution; as an archaeologist and a pragmatist, he believed that the retention of the motorway in the valley floor in the already disturbed communications corridor of the former railway, old Twyford Road, and the A33 bypass was the correct place for it. Nonetheless he recognized the political reality and was to put his whole weight behind the campaign for a tunnel at the 1987 Inquiry. He had no quarrel with a route on the bypass, but recognized the need for everybody to pull together and present a united front in an effort to defeat the Cutting route.

There is a widely held belief that the option of going on the bypass was strongly favoured by some members of the

Government in 1986 and by staff in the Department of the Environment.

John Browne (MP for Winchester 1979–1992) had a private meeting with the Prime Minister, Margaret Thatcher, early in October 1986. According to the report in the *Hampshire Chronicle* (24 October 1986), Mr Browne had forty minutes with the Prime Minister, who asked for a summary of the points, which she promised to present to Mr Moore (Secretary of State for Transport) personally. Rumour had it that the Prime Minister looked at the plans, and asked why the motorway wasn't going on the bypass.

Be that as it may, as time went on the complexities and heat of the debate about M3 grew and the Department of Transport dithered. Our campaign had disturbed a hornet's nest.

The principal opposition to any route on the bypass identified and shared by the Winchester Preservation Trust was focused around Winchester College and St Cross. Any decision favouring a bypass route would have incurred the wrath of those two groups at least.

Earlier in the year, Maldwin Drummond, a Commissioner at the Countryside Commission wrote personally to the Secretary of State for Transport, Nicholas Ridley. Mr Drummond wrote explaining that the Countryside Commission had not given evidence to the 1985 Public Inquiry... 'the Nature Conservancy Council [later known as English Nature] and HBMC [which became English Heritage] support Mrs Bryant's alternatives, and personally I have no doubt the Commission would have joined them...but I believe it is important – even at this late stage – for you to be aware of the reason for the Countryside Commission's silence and to urge the [bypass] alternative.' There had been discussion as to whether the Commission itself should write to Ridley, but it was felt that a personal letter from a Commissioner to the Secretary of State was more appropriate since the matter could be kept at a personal, rather than a 'corporate' level.

Merrick was giving presentations to MPs, members of the House of Lords, and leading lights in the conservation movements. I was contacting friends from the past now in Government, local residents were lobbying in high places and Winchester's MP was actively involved in the debate.

It has been said that the additional workload for civil servants created by a single parliamentary question delayed the Transport Department's decision by a week – what then was the impact of forty minutes of the Prime Minister's time, let alone all the other fronts on which we were then attacking?

In Winchester itself local groups and societies were looking again at the DoT scheme, and in some cases reconsidering their own policy and attitudes.

The Winchester Preservation Trust, with around 5000 members, a former British ambassador to the United States as its president, and a reputation for 'running' Winchester, is a well organized group. After a good deal of consideration it decided to support the tunnel, and to change its policy to one of opposition to the Cutting route. Giving evidence to the reopened Inquiry in 1987 on behalf of the Preservation Trust, Dr Chris Gillham, explained, 'At the 1985 Inquiries the Trust underestimated the adverse environmental effects of the PR [Cutting] route...and unless a tunnel solution is accepted, which is clearly practicable, this section of the M3 should not be completed...'.

The Winchester branch of the Council for the Protection of Rural England (CPRE) had supported the Cutting route at the 1985 Public Inquiry, saying, 'We reaffirm that we believe the proposed new route to be as good as can be achieved in all the circumstances. Clearly if money were no object a full tunnel might be favoured by some people, but since we understand the cost could add something approaching £100 m to the bill, with the burden of lighting, ventilating and maintenance for all time, we do not consider such a solution can be contemplated.'

The CPRE is a national charity, highly respected in Government and the environment movement. The branch committees commonly comprise people who have involvement with (and loyalties to) other interests in the area – in 1986, for example, the Winchester branch membership included Wing Commander John Nunn, Vice-Chairman of the Winchester Council Planning Committee, and Robin Chute, the Estates Bursar at Winchester College. In small communities this is inevitable and not necessarily wrong. However, in the case of Twyford Down the CPRE local branch apparently received no initial guidance from HQ on the pros and cons of the Cutting route and its impact on a nationally protected landscape.

One of our nightmares at the time was of a 'Yes, Minister' type scenario in the Transport Department's headquarters in Marsham Street:

> *Minister to Sir Humphrey* What on earth are we doing trying to destroy Twyford Down? I keep getting awkward questions from all sorts of people.
>
> *Sir Humphrey* It's not quite like that, Minister. The County Council and the local landowner, Winchester College, support it.
>
> *Minister* But I'm told it's an environmental disaster.
>
> *Sir Humphrey* Oh, no. We chose it on environmental grounds, and the Council for the Protection of Rural England supports our scheme. [Minister gives up and returns to his mountain of paper.]

Perhaps it didn't happen like that. But the method by which national groups decided policy on Twyford Down, and the implications of such decisions, were a matter of considerable concern.

When the Inquiry was eventually reopened in 1987, the CPRE had joined many others on the Road to Damascus. Giving evidence, CPRE now stated, 'At the 1985 stage of these Inquiries CPRE opposed a route following the line of the bypass; a tunnel was regarded as risky...whilst the PR (Cutting) aligned away from the city and valley was too *uncritically accepted and supported*...A decision in favour of a...tunnel under the Downs, an under-line crossing of the railway and low-level crossing of the valley should be taken without delay.'

At national level the Countryside Commission was reassessing its policy on the M3. The Countryside Commission was debating internally whether it was bound by its earlier unwritten undertaking not to oppose a route to the east of St Catherine's Hill, made in 1981. After internal discussusions, and presumably in the light of the very considerable interest being shown by at least some of the Commissioners, a decision was taken to put the Commission's whole weight behind objection to the DoT route.

But in Parliament ministers were having to reply to questions from MPs who represented constituencies to the south of Winchester, pressing for an early decision. Sir David Price, the veteran MP for Eastleigh, was particularly critical of the delays:

'It seems to me that every route round Winchester has objectors. But at some point the Minister has got to bite the bullet and come up with a line for the route, and get on with it!' In February 1987, Sir David Price wrote to me: 'As you know I am not taking part in your arguments as to how the M3 should go round Winchester. As one who is not a Wykehamist, I would not presume to take part. All I am trying for is that the Secretary of State should get a move on. I have described the Ministry of Transport as a tortoise amongst Government departments. I wish he would come out of hibernation!'

The Transport Department received Inspector Leaker's report of the 1985 Public Inquiry some time in the late spring or early summer of 1986. The Environment Department appears to have been canvassing the possibility of reopening the Inquiry by July, at which time parts of the Inspector's Report had been leaked to the press. The Transport Department, or Secretaries of State, took at least nine months to announce a decision, which when it came was hardly courageous. Many months, or years, passed while the Department of Transport digested Inspectors' Reports before coming to decisions, despite ministers' and others' continual reiteration of the urgent need for the completion of the motorway at the earliest opportunity.

Objectors are frequently accused of delaying the implementation of road schemes. Undoubtedly this is sometimes the case. It may be that merely exercising their legal rights, such as appearing at a Public Inquiry, prolongs the process, but on other occasions delay is the sole objective and time-wasting tactics are employed. Parliamentarians regularly filibuster and 'talk out' Private Members' Bills. However, responsibility for many of the delays associated with road planning and implementation rests solely with the Department of Transport whose leisurely approach to these matters creates undue pressure for instant decisions by others.

On 10 April 1987 the uncertainty and speculation was ended. The formal announcement from Government read 'because of the environmental sensitivity of the route between Compton and Bar End Inquiries (that is the CPO and Line Order Inquiries) should be reopened...and should hear evidence from the Countryside Commission and English Heritage and any new evidence on the relative merits of the PR and objectors' alternatives not previously submitted...'.

The Minister's decision to reopen the Inquiry did not come as a great surprise to Merrick, Dudley or me. Quite apart from the rumours and leaked information there had been plenty of straws in the wind. None the less the formal announcement came as a relief.

With the announcement came the official publication of Inspector Leaker's report of the proceedings of the 1985 Inquiry, together with his 'Findings of Fact' and 'Recommendations'. Inspector Leaker recorded the support for the tunnel alternative and, explaining his reasons for rejecting the tunnel proposal, which I had presented to the Inquiry, as an acceptable alternative, said, 'In terms of conventional economics this alternative would be a poor investment...because of its high extra cost it presumably could only be carried out at the expense or deferment of worthwhile projects elsewhere in the country. But this proposal also deals in intangible values and the preservation of our heritage [and] so it is with some reluctance that I have to conclude that I cannot recommend [this alternative] in spite of its superiority in respecting sensitive areas of environmental and historic importance.'

Today, nearly ten years later, Dudley Leaker says he believes he took the right decision in recommending that the Cutting route should go ahead, given the circumstances and the evidence presented to him. He says: 'I am afraid that I find it difficult to cast my mind back to those worrying days and their serious issues but I am still of the opinion that my recommendations at that time were right and based on the evidence submitted.'

But if Leaker believes he took the best decision, he also sides with those who say the system itself is flawed. A widely experienced Public Inquiry Inspector, he agrees wholeheartedly that Highway Inquiry procedures are too lengthy, too adversarial and too expensive. He says more attention needs to be given to consultation, with better technical help for those involved, especially major objectors. He adds that a tunnel would have been the best environmental solution to the Twyford Down problem. But he says the real issue was that there was no truly acceptable route given the line of the M3 already constructed north of Winchester. The options had already been greatly restricted.

'I believe that given the "springing point" for the continuation of the road southwards (from Bar End) (Figure A) there was no totally acceptable route possible and the basic mistake was made much earlier and farther back northwards (that is, just south of Basingstoke) when less environmentally damaging lines could have been considered *in toto.*'

Saying this, Dudley Leaker backs up what many local people in Winchester have long argued – that the Government's approval of the M3 route from Basingstoke to Bar End pre-empted consideration of an alternative which could (and many would say should) have avoided the ultra-sensitive area around Winchester, its ancient downland setting and the water meadows.

In the early 1970s there had been public discussion of a route for the M3 to the west of Winchester, on a more or less direct line south from the junction of the M3 and A30 near Basingstoke to the M27 on the north-western edges of Southampton. In March 1971 the *Hampshire Chronicle* published a map showing alternative suggested routes to be put to the forthcoming Public Inquiry, which included two variations on this 'west of Winchester' route. Even in 1995 Winchester folklore still lays the blame for the failure of this apparently logical route to gain credibility at the door of landowners to the west of Winchester.

Whatever the reason, it is disturbing and saddening to see that the abject failure of UK Governments to propose and implement a cohesive, strategic road-building policy led to the destruction of an important part of England's heritage, but that this absence of a strategic and properly planned policy also resulted in the expensive charade of the 1985 and 1987 Public Inquiries.

However, back in the spring of 1987 we had only the written words of Inspector Dudley Leaker's report of the 1985 Inquiry to rely on. We believed that his report recognized the potential benefits of a tunnel and, heartened by these findings, we believed, somewhat naïvely, that free to present all the evidence of the environmental damage to the reopened Inquiry we would achieve a different route for the M3. By that time we had a substantial group of local and national organizations and individuals supporting our objections. It seemed likely that the reopened Inquiry and the opportunity it presented would act as a catalyst for everyone to come together and unite against the Transport Department. Coupled with our immediate euphoria was a slightly sickening awareness that the really hard work was about to start. I daresay our families viewed the news with mixed feelings, too. On the other hand, for the first time in two years we were surrounded and supported by a wide range of exceedingly competent and influential groups.

6

April 1987 to August 1987 – Prelude to the reopening of the Public Inquiry

With the Government announcement of the decision to reopen the Public Inquiry, the debate on how to complete the M3 at Winchester came even more sharply into focus, if that were possible. The announcement brought to an end a lot of the uncertainty and provided the trigger for the various groups and organizations to embark on a detailed reappraisal of their support for the Cutting route.

In Winchester activity reached new heights. The councils of the two parishes directly affected by the route, Twyford, and Compton and Shawford, held public meetings, and all the local interest groups discussed what and how they could contribute to the debate. General election fever was rife, too, and the campaigners considered putting up a candidate to fight the Winchester constituency. There was no serious expectation that such a candidate would win, but the M3 debate would certainly make headlines. However, it was decided that, with the reopened Inquiry now announced, the public reaction would be rather negative and this idea was abandoned – for the moment.

Despite the high profile debate on the route of the M3, and the press publicity that had been achieved highlighting some of the damage that the DoT route would inflict upon Winchester's landscape, we wanted to produce a leaflet describing the objections to the DoT route and explaining the alternatives. We hoped to be able to deliver the leaflet to all households in the area, communicating directly the main arguments of our case. Merrick, having managed to persuade one of our local benefactors to pay for the printing of the leaflet, set about producing the

artwork. The leaflet, called 'M3 and The National Heritage'
explained the bones of our objection to the Department of
Transport's Cutting route.

Later, when summing up for the DoT at the end of the
reopened Inquiry in 1988, David Altaras, counsel for the
Department of Transport, spent a considerable amount of time
criticizing the leaflet 'M3 and The National Heritage', which he
claimed was inaccurate because we had not spelt out that the
Department of Transport Cutting route meant that the old
bypass road would be abandoned (Figure 14 – the sketch map
reproduced on the leaflet). That Altaras thought this a justified
use of his time may be commendation enough, but referring to
the DoT's proposal to return the old A33 bypass 'to countryside'
and the drawing in our leaflet he said, 'Lawyers have a word for
it, *suppressio veri, suggestio falsi* – if you suppress the truth you
suggest a falsehood' (PI Doc. R256 P34 Para A). We felt bitter as
the Department of Transport leaflets had carried far greater
inaccuracies. Altaras clearly did leave an impression as his
words were quoted fully in the Inspector's Report of the Inquiry.

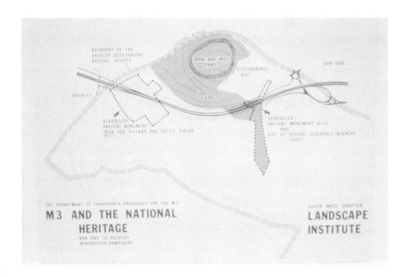

Figure 14 M3 and the National Heritage. Drawing, made by Merrick
Denton-Thompson in 1987, showing the relationship of the Twyford
Down route to the Scheduled Ancient Monuments, Site of Special
Scientific Interest and an Area of Outstanding Natural Beauty.

Closing addresses are heard uninterrupted. Listening to Altaras in the silence of the Inquiry I had some difficulty in remaining silent. Single-handed, so to speak, Merrick, Dudley and I had produced the 'M3 and The National Heritage' leaflet. The vast resources of the Department of Transport and its consultants had produced a formal public consultation document on behalf of HM Government upon which the whole of the public consultation and decision-making process had relied and which (i) omitted entirely any reference to one statutory conservation designation (the Roman Road Scheduled Ancient Monument) and (ii) had shown the Iron Age village site, adjacent to Twyford Down as a star – just avoided by the DoT route. If our plan suggested a falsehood it could be said that the DoT consultation document amounted to misrepresentation.

In the summer of 1987 we had distributed 'M3 and The National Heritage' throughout Winchester, and some of the surrounding villages. We were well pleased with increasing awareness of the issues, and the growing debate. In addition to the leaflet, and public meetings, Dudley had obtained permission for a large visual display to be placed in an empty shop window in the heart of Winchester. Situated just beside the Cathedral the display looked professional, and was a talking point among locals and visitors.

During the months that we had been campaigning in earnest it had become increasingly obvious that the Transport Department's claims that their proposed route enjoyed widespread public support were unfounded. In every stratum of 'the public' (local councils, conservation and amenity groups, private individuals) we had encountered countless examples of misunderstandings of the scheme, and of opposition to the route. In spring 1987 a very clear picture presented itself to us of reservations, or even downright opposition to the route, which simply did not stack up alongside the Transport Department's claims of widespread public support for their scheme. We realized of course that this mass of anecdotal evidence would be easily dismissed by the Transport Department as unrepresentative and unscientific.

With the announcement of the reopening of the Inquiry we were spurred to consider how an independent survey of public opinion might be obtained, which would provide tangible proof of the anecdotal evidence we believed existed. We decided that a priority in our campaign should be to try to secure a full and proper research report to test whether the terms of the Government's original brief for the scheme had been met; these terms had been set out in Mr Clarke's ministerial statement saying, 'the scheme...will need to have the highest possible measure of acceptance by the local authorities, other interested parties, and most important of all, by the general public.' (16 September 1981)

We were fortunate perhaps that John Hanvey, chairman of the Harris Research Centre, and a leading member of the Association of Market Survey Organisations, was one of Dudley's oldest friends. Their friendship went back to the days when both were councillors on Islington Council in north London. For fifty years Islington had been Labour-controlled, but the Conservatives had swept the board in 1968 at the height of Prime Minister Harold Wilson's unpopularity – not just taking control, but ousting all but a dozen or so of the former Labour councillors from the council, and unexpectedly sweeping into office a score of bright young professionals (among them a sprinkling of future national politicans) with varying degrees of commitment to local politics. Hanvey had steadily climbed his own particular tree in market research, and the combination of his political acumen and professional skills led to his role as market research adviser to the Conservative Party and Prime Minister Margaret Thatcher, for whom he had the highest regard.

Dudley discussed with John Hanvey the problems we had identified with the assessment of public opinion. Despite the undoubted pressure that John Hanvey was under in the lead-up to the announcement of a general election (we got to anticipate general elections when John refused invitations on the grounds that his diary had to be kept clear!) he came down to Winchester one Saturday in April 1987. John had no particular 'green' credentials and no interest in the location of the final section of the M3. But he became as concerned as we were about the process by which the route had been selected and the implications for the Conservative Party.

It soon became clear that a privately commissioned full research exercise in the form of a public opinion poll would cost in the region of £10 000, and that since such funds were not available to us (in those days) another way to obtain a scientific assessment of public opinion would have to be found.

That Saturday night John left with a full brief, and a ready willingess to come back to us with some sort of solution which might enable the vital questions to be properly answered. We felt that this opinion poll was crucial if we were to succeed at the reopened Public Inquiry. One of the reasons which the Department of Transport used to justify the Cutting route was the level of public support it alleged the Cutting route enjoyed. We had to be able to show that such support did not exist. The methodology underpinning the opinion poll had to be as professional as possible if it was to carry sufficient weight.

The actual thinking and the system finally adopted was submitted to the reopened Inquiry in 1987 and John Hanvey's reasoning, the solution which we evolved and its conduct are best taken from his evidence, which was given to the 1987 Public Inquiry:

> Whilst it is a traditional and valid form of consultation to invite interested parties to submit their views to an Inquiry, these views tend to be representative only of the people or organisations who make them and presuppose a level of knowledge, interest and articulence which is not necessarily representative of the wider population in the area concerned. I considered therefore that it was necessary to supplement it by carrying out a systematic survey of the relevant population.
>
> The objects of the survey were broadly –
>
> (i) to establish awareness on a number of criteria –
>
>   (a) awareness of the proposals in general
>   (b) awareness of the former Public Inquiry and any associated consultation
>   (c) awareness of the current state of the proposals.
>
> (ii) to establish preferences towards –
>
>   (a) the routes available
>   (b) their interaction with sites of historical association or national beauty or existing man-made features.
>
> (iii) to establish attitudes to the extent and nature of information made available and to consultation.

The universe for the survey

Given the specific interest in the Bar End to Compton motorway link, the appropriate population to be consulted was judged to be all wards of Winchester City plus the Parishes of Badgers Farm, Chilcomb, Compton, Olivers Battery and Twyford. This covered an area about 2 miles equidistant east and west of the Preferred Route, over a length of some 5 miles and covered the entirety of the Parishes involved. The total area of survey covered some 17 square miles overall.

Sampling frame

Outside the Inner Metropoliatan Areas the level of electoral registration is highly efficient and the electoral registers covering the Universe were collated as a sampling frame and stratified geographically using the reference letters of each section of the electoral register.

Sampling process

From this stratification of the electoral registers a clustered systematic probability sample was drawn. The total electorate was 29 640 and every 296th name was selected as a cluster 'starter', yielding 100 clusters. A further seven names were selected at intervals of ten on each side of the starter, producing, theoretically, a total sample of 1500. In the event one register was only sufficiently large to yield twelve (rather than 15) names so the final sample was 1497.

Survey administration

The 40 or so volunteers available to help administer the survey had neither the training nor skills to undertake in-person interviews. It was therefore decided to develop a system which did not rely on these particular skills for valid results. A self-completion questionnaire instrument was developed which was delivered by volunteers (who had been briefed) between 15 and 20 June 1987. Completed questionnaires were collected between 17 June and early July 1987 and a few which had been sent by post to the Landscape Institute's headquarters in London were forwarded to the local Branch for inclusion in the survey. Up to three attempts were made to collect the questionnaires.

Survey documentation

Each respondent was sent:

(a) a letter explaining the purpose of the survey and giving assurances of individual confidentiality

(b) a questionnaire

(c) a separate signature slip stating that the named individual had indeed participated in the study

(d) a return envelope.

The Opinion Research Report was in time submitted to the reopened Inquiry as part of the evidence of the Landscape Institute. John Hanvey's conclusions recorded that Mott Hay and Anderson's public participation exercise was already five to six years old. He stated that he was satisfied that the survey carried out on behalf of the South West Chapter of the Landscape Institute was conducted in a professional manner and to the same standards as a survey conducted by a commercial organization. John also stated that he was satisfied that the reponses to the survey were a realistic representation of the views of the public in the area of survey.

And so what were the results of the survey? They were by any standards dramatic, so much so that they provoked a remarkably strenuous and lengthy response from the Department of Transport's counsel when summing up at the close of the 1987 Inquiry. But that is to go forward too far in time – in the late summer of 1987 we awaited the results of the survey with a good deal of anticipation. In all, 864 fully completed replies were received, which in John's professional opinion was significantly higher than could have been expected for this type of research.

The results were staggering – of the 94 per cent who claimed to be aware of the proposals to extend the M3 only 4 per cent thought they had ever been invited to submit suggestions or comment to the consultants. Only 58 per cent claimed to know the route proposed. The survey showed only 9 per cent support for the route, with 91 per cent of opinion divided roughly equally between support for the bypass and the tunnel. We felt vindicated by the survey results, which accorded so much with the anecdotal evidence.

With the change of heart of the Winchester Preservation Trust, CPRE and the many meetings of various local organizations all discussing the motorway proposals, the old Winchester Joint Action Group (JAG) met again. JAG was first formed in the mid-1970s and had proved a powerful coalition, which had fought and defeated the Department of Transport's proposal to complete the M3 through the water meadows between St Catherine's Hill and Winchester itself in 1976.

In the early 1980s JAG had been a key player in discussions with the consultants, Mott Hay and Anderson, during the early consultations about how to complete the motorway following the withdrawal of the Department's earlier proposal. Meetings between JAG and the consultants are recorded in December 1981, and October 1982, along with some seven letters received by the consultants from JAG. It seems that JAG had gradually faded and responsibility for speaking on its behalf rested entirely with the one-time Chairman, David Pare. JAG is recorded as one of the organizations that supported the Department of Transport's Cutting route at the 1985 Public Inquiry.

In the late spring of 1987 a rejuvenated JAG elected David Croker as its new chairman and decided to invite the various amenity groups, parishes, objectors and prominent individuals to meet together, and to include Merrick and me; I think it was the first time that either of us felt we were being treated as 'insiders' by Wintonians.

Among the people who came to the first proper meeting of the re-assembled Joint Action Group were veterans of the 1970s' campaign; some of these people Merrick and I were meeting for the first time, although we had met others in their various capacities in Winchester's local community. In addition to repeating much of the by now well-publicized criticisms of the Cutting route Merrick and I were able to tell JAG new information about the costs and practicality of a tunnel.

During the previous autumn Merrick and I had been very busy campaigning to increase support for our opposition to the Cutting route. Almost all our spare time at evenings and weekends was taken up with meetings, presentations to local groups or individuals, and lobbying. Meanwhile, Dudley had tried to find a means to answer, and better, the Department of

Transport's technical criticisms of the tunnel as a realistic and achievable alternative way of completing the M3. After some dogged research and discussions and meetings with a number of civil engineering contractors he made contact with the contracting company, Fairclough.

In November 1986 Dudley received a letter from the local divisional director of Fairclough's Southern Division, giving a budget assessment of the Department of Transport drawing of the 1985 J3 tunnel which revealed a dramatic reduction in the DoT's own estimate of around £80 m. The letter also identified a major disadvantage of the J3 tunnel, namely that the western portals would have to be widened to accommodate the slip roads at Hockley (as per the DoT Cutting scheme). The letter went on to say, 'Whilst, as a company, there have to be some reservations, politically, regarding our involvement, it is equally in our interest to see progress towards a resolution of the problem and hopefully another construction contract coming on the market in the near future.' Indeed, discussions with various major contractors at that time revealed a very pronounced caution against offending the DoT, a potential client. This caution was to surface again in 1991 at the time of the private finance tunnel investigation.

Although Fairclough was apparently interested in the possibility of working with us, in the event it did not prove practical, but as a result of this contact with Fairclough Dudley was put in touch with Geoffrey Thornton of Burslem Engineering Associates Ltd. A bluff Yorkshireman in his mid-fifties, Thornton had specialized in tunnel and shaft engineering for over twenty years, eighteen of those years at the sharp end of the business as a contractor with a great deal of his life spent underground. Since 1984 he had been a partner and director of BEAL, a consulting firm specializing in tunnels and underground projects. By lucky coincidence, Geoff Thornton was already involved with a feasibility study for the DoT twin road tunnels to be driven through chalk for the proposed A27 Brighton bypass. Clearly, there was much in common between tunnelling through the chalk of the South Downs at Brighton and at Twyford Down (the western edge of the South Downs).

In order to fund a tunnel feasibility study and our Inquiry costs Merrick and I had managed to achieve some financial help from local benefactors. The fund raising was coming along well – many small but very welcome contributions, and suddenly one superb gift of £5000.

From discussions with BEAL and from their initial report, we were able to tell the meeting of JAG in the spring of 1987 that it was practical and technically possible to build a much improved version of my 1985 tunnel, and that this evidence should be put to the Inquiry, due to reopen in June.

As we anticipated, the JAG Group membership included many groups and individuals vehemently opposed to any route on the bypass, and the meeting decided that a tunnel was the only acceptable method of completing the M3 around Winchester. Subsequently the umbrella group, Winchester M3 Joint Action Group, was formed, comprising two parish councils, most of the amenity groups and residents associations in Winchester, along with a number of individuals and support from the main political parties.

The initial euphoria that had come with the announcement that the Inquiry was to reopen was now replaced by growing concerns at the inadequacies and possible abuses of the planning system which were being revealed, and the chaos that resulted.

On thorough reading of Inspector Leaker's Report, I and other campaigners considered the opportunity to readdress the impact on the landscape and environment of the Cutting route might be severely inhibited by the continued appointment of Inspector Leaker, who had confirmed the Department of Transport's Cutting route through Twyford Down, and on an embankment over the railway line.

Dudley checked out the Government's own guidelines on what the Highway Inquiry Procedure Rules had to say about reopened Highway Inquiries, and found the following:

> If the re-opened Inquiry is to deal with a matter on which the Inspector, who held the original Inquiry, has already expressed an opinion, a different Inspector will probably be appointed to hold it (Notes for Guidance of Independent Inquiry Inspectors. Highways Act Oct 1981 para 108).

Letters were soon on their way to ministers at the Department of the Environment seeking a change in the appointed Inspector. We were concerned that the reappointment of Inspector Leaker, who had reached conclusions and made recommendations following the 1985 Public Inquiry might prejudice the objectors' case at the reopened Inquiry. Certainly it was not easy to see how Leaker's reappointment complied with the expressed wishes of the Secretaries of State, in announcing the decision to reopen the Inquiry 'that the decision process is not only fair to all the objecting interests, but is clearly seen to be so.'

'M3 Motorway Extension, Winchester Proposed Reopening of Public Inquiry' was how we titled a letter to the *Daily Telegraph* reciting our concerns about the continued appointment of Inspector Leaker – the *Telegraph* changed the title to 'Fair Play at Winchester'.

Winchester Council, a statutory objector, also wrote. But the Council's solicitor addressed the Council's letter more appropriately to the person responsible for the appointment of Inspectors – the Lord Chancellor's Department, seeking an 'explanation as to why Mr Leaker had been appointed as the Inspector when he has already made recommendations on the subject at issue.' Mr Hanratty, from the Lord Chancellor's Department, replied, stating that 'Mr Leaker has an advantage that no other person can have in that he will have heard all the evidence at the Inquiries.' The letter from Mr Hanratty (22 June 1987) masterfully manages not to address the question posed by the Winchester City Council as to whether the appointment of Mr Leaker in the circumstances of his having already made recommendations on the subject, was or was not in accordance with the official 'Guidance Notes for Road Inquiries.'

On 26 June Winchester Council was informed by the DoT that the Inquiry 'due to reopen on 30 June will need to be adjourned because of an injury to Mr Leaker. Apparently he broke a leg while hill walking, and is undergoing an operation.'

Poor Mr Leaker. But incredulity was by now starting to set in. Had the Transport Department and Environment Department really spent the better part of a year deciding to reopen the Inquiry without thinking through the propriety of (or even whether they could get away with) reappointing the same Inspector?

Max Cross, the Supervisor of the Independent Panel of Inspectors, stepped into the breach to attend the June 30 reopening.

On 1 July Mr Cross wrote to Mr Leaker, confirming that he had opened the Inquiry and adjourned it to 23 July, having advised those present of 'your regrettable accident' and referring at one point in the letter to the fact that 'further views were briefly expressed which were opposed to your appointment for this reopened inquiry.' On 6 July the DoT Inquiry Progamming Officer, Eric Lawson, sent a copy of Cross's letter to all objectors, the local councils and other interested parties. On 7 July Lawson had to put pen to paper again to everyone saying 'I have been asked to write to all objectors to advise you that Mr Leaker has had to withdraw from the inquiry, and a further Inspector has now been nominated and appointed to sit in his place.'

The Inquiry eventually reopened on 27 September. Another three months delay. This delay and more could have been avoided if the DoT had implemented the Government's undertaking to adopt the Franks Committee recommendations, and the report of the 1985 Public Inquiry proceedings had been sent out to interested parties for correction – Inspector Leaker would not have 'expressed an opinion' at that stage and could therefore have properly and speedily dealt with the 'missing' evidence and taken note of any identified factual errors in his subsequent conclusions.

As it was, the additional delay gave all the groups and organizations, including the Countryside Commission and the Winchester M3 Joint Action Group time in which to consolidate their position, and to raise funds.

Another important consideration was that the additional three months enabled Winchester Council to complete the process of formally reconsidering its support for the Department of Transport Cutting route. This process of reappraisal had begun earlier in the year following my original 'toe in the water' motion to Winchester Council, which had paved the way for members to look again at the DoT proposal for completing M3. The formal announcement from Government that the Inquiry was to be reopened had provided the essential peg on which to hang discussion within the Council.

A report had been prepared by council officials, and the matter placed on the agenda. The Planning Committee met on 6 August 1987 and agreed 'that in view of the increased interest in the possibility of constructing a tunnel...and the Countryside Commission alternative for using the bypass all councillors [not least because of the significant number of new councillors elected in May] should receive a full presentation of the principal alternatives and that following these presentations the (Planning) Committee on 17 September, should reconsider the Council's stance.'

Winchester Council appointed Scott Wilson Kirkpatrick (SWK), consulting engineers, to advise on the practicalities and costs of a tunnel option. The senior partner, Geoffrey Williams, lived in Beauworth, a picturesque village just outside Winchester. Williams was a distinguished member of the civil engineering profession, had served as Chairman of the Association of Consulting Engineers in the mid-1980s and continued to hold a number of senior posts within the profession. In the 1960s he had been responsible for the Hong Kong Harbour road tunnel. In 1987 he was responsible for the Geotechnical and Structural Certification of the tube tunnel at Conwy in North Wales – the Conwy tunnel featured in the debate at the reopened Inquiry since the decision to tunnel under the Conwy had been taken, and justified, on environmental grounds alone.

Williams, the smooth boardroom operator, and the M3 Joint Action Group's tunnel expert, Thornton of Burslem Engineering Associates Ltd, a tough-talking Yorkshireman, were both highly professional, but their very different personalities provided a great contrast and balance at the Inquiry when the tunnel evidence eventually came to be presented. Williams was well positioned to present Winchester Council with details of the technical feasibility of a tunnel. He was thorough, convincing and local. The special Planning Committee meeting was held on 17 September 1987, just a few days before the Inquiry was due to reopen and many local people anticipated that Winchester Council, a statutory authority, would be withdrawing its support for the DoT route.

But I was now living on my nerves – for two years I had been backing the cause of Twyford Down and for the last twelve months or so I had spent huge amounts of time and mental energy nurturing support among my fellow councillors for our campaign. The prize – the formal objection of Winchester Council, which constitutionally represented the interests of Winchester and its residents – was by now tantalizingly near.

For reasons of both head and heart the objection of Winchester Council was very important to me. Of course, many other important organizations had by that time thrown their weight behind our objection – indeed it was ceasing to be just 'our' objection – it had become a national campaign, numbering among its supporters the World Wide Fund for Nature, all the major archaeological societies, environmentalists such as the wildlife artist, David Shepherd, and Miriam Rothschild, the scientist.

At a practical level Winchester Council's withdrawal of support for the Cutting would destroy, at a stroke, the Transport Department's claim that the Cutting route enjoyed 'public support' or the support of the 'local authorities'. It was simply unthinkable that a constitutionally elected local council objecting at Public Inquiry could be brushed off as a 'whim'.

But for reasons of the heart, too, it mattered to me deeply that Winchester Council objected to the Cutting route for Twyford Down. In part, no doubt, because Winchester was my 'home ground', but more deeply I cared that the ancient capital of England should not be failed by its twentieth century city fathers.

The tension and level of activity in the run up to the formal reopening of the Inquiry was substantial. But high on my worry-list was Winchester Council, and its deliberations. The Planning Committee would have to vote formally to withdraw support for the DoT route, and that decision would have to be put to a full meeting of all councillors so that the Council could ratify (or not) the decision. I was still counting heads, leaving nothing to chance, and David Croker (by then chairman of the revamped Winchester M3 Joint Action Group) rang round all our fellow councillors one more time before the Planning Committee vote. David was a member of the Planning Committee, I was not. But because of his dual role (councillor and chairman of M3JAG) he declared an interest and did not vote when the matter was finally put to the vote at Committee.

The Planning Committee met on 17 September 1987. Scott Wilson Kirkpatrick fielded their full team as consultants to the Council. The M3JAG group was represented by Richard Parker (who had become the Group's volunteer consultant engineer), Geoff Thornton of Burslem Engineering Associates Ltd, chairmen of the parish councils, and myself. The usual range of Council officials were present, including legal advisers and the chief engineer, David Marklew.

Councillor Patricia Edwards as Chairman of the Committee had kept her views on M3 pretty much to herself, but under her chairmanship the Committee considered the report by the Director of Planning, which ran to some ten pages. The Introduction of the report explained that its preparation 'had been delayed for as long as possible to take account of any new evidence...and prepared in parallel with the report of the Council's consultant engineers, Scott Wilson Kirkpatrick, who have needed all the time available to study and report upon such a major topic' and 'it has not been possible to take account of the consultants' findings in the preparation of this report or to make final recommendations.'

The conclusion of the officials' report read 'Subject to any advice that may be provided to the contrary by the consulting engineers (Scott Wilson Kirkpatrick) the Committee (should) adhere to its existing stance at the re-opened Inquiry...'. In the event, the advice provided by Scott Wilson Kirkpatrick was extensive, and convincing to the extent that the Committee decided it could no longer adhere to the Council's existing policy, and voted to recommend Winchester City Council withdraw its support for the Department of Transport Cutting route.

'Planners' U-Turn on Tunnel – M3 debate shock' reported *The Evening Echo* the day after the Planning Committee, describing the decision to withdraw support for the DoT route as a 'last gasp re-think which could have ominous consequences for the Inquiry due to start in ten days' (*Southern Evening Echo*, 18 September 1987).

There was just over a week to go before the full meeting of Council. But other shoulders were by now sharing the burden; Patricia Edwards, as the Chairman of the Planning Committee would be proposing her committee's recommendation to the Council.

When full Council met on 23 September 1987 there was only one item on the agenda. The public gallery was unusually crowded. Right up to the meeting there had been political comings and goings and attempts to water down the Planning Committee's recommendation – which would have reduced Winchester Council's revised policy to something less than outright opposition to the Department of Transport's Cutting route. Telephone calls were made to some of us suggesting amendments – weasel words which would fudge the issue. David

Croker and I kept in close touch and were confident that we should stick one hundred per cent behind the Planning Committee decision unamended. Sure of our numbers, I quietly refused all overtures to tweak it here or there 'just to make sure you don't lose the vote.' Only half-an-hour before the Council meeting I received one last-ditch effort to persuade me to back down – 'just a little, because support is dwindling' – but I knew that a substantial majority of my fellow councillors would support us.

Although some councillors did not share our views and still positively supported the Cutting route, and others did not feel that the issue justified the unusual, almost unprecedented, step of changing the long-standing policy, nonetheless opposition to the Cutting route with its high-level crossing of the valley was by that time firmly consolidated. As I left home that evening I was aware that there was a minority view that the Council should not change its policy but I was confident that we had overwhelming support. Council carefully debated the issue for several hours. If only so much care and debate had gone into the initial decision to support the DoT route all those years before!

'Council Backs Tunnel Route for M3' was next day's banner headline in the *The Evening Echo*, reporting that every shade of opinion on the proposed completion of the motorway had been canvassed. The policy change was decisively approved by 27 votes to 16.

David Croker and I had sat on our hands when an amendment proposing a route on the bypass was moved – the vehement, albeit localized, opposition to such a route was reflected in representation on the Council and any attempt to override that opposition would have pushed the Council back to supporting the Cutting scheme.

The morning after the meeting, the office door of the Council's solicitor, Meic Sullivan-Gould, proudly displayed our latest logo, 'Tunnel – It Makes Sense'. Seeing me in the corridor he generously said, 'to the victor belong the spoils' and the enormity of the decision began to dawn on me.

From the moment the City Council formally withdrew its support for the DoT route the energy and enthusiasm of its officers to implement the new policy transformed the campaign, bringing the manpower, expertise and a bureaucratic discipline that had been missing. A week later when the Inquiry reopened the full impact of Winchester Council's withdrawal of support for the Department of Transport scheme became obvious.

7

Reopened Public Inquiry in 1987

While the City Council had been going through the lengthy process of reconsidering its policy on the M3 route, other objectors had been organizing themselves. A different Inspector, Air Vice-Marshal Maughan, had been appointed and on 23 July 1987 held a pre-inquiry procedural meeting. In his notes of that meeting the programming officer reminded objectors that anyone 'intending to propose alternative routes would need to agree the details with the DoT by 14 August. A plan showing alternative proposals will be published in the press by 30 August.'

The M3 Joint Action Group formed a technical sub-group made up of four of our most appropriately qualified supporters, to produce the best possible alternative route going under the railway line and in a tunnel under Twyford Down. Richard Parker and Geoff Thornton, the two engineers, had many discussions with the Department of Transport's consultants, Mott Hay and Anderson, resulting eventually in the production of the new tunnel, low-level valley crossing, and under-rail alternative, known as JAG3. The importance of having your own professional advice to direct and focus the DoT's engineers at this pre-Inquiry stage cannot be overemphasized. At Winchester the issues were unusually complex, the topography, projected traffic flows and environmental considerations all compounding the difficulties of threading the motorway around Winchester; both the tunnel and under-rail crossing requiring very specific expertise.

At the end of August 1987 the local paper, *The Hampshire Chronicle*, carried pages of drawings, showing the various objectors' alternative suggestions for the route of the M3. Thirteen options appeared in all. JAG, Winchester City Council, the Countryside Commission and the South West Chapter of the Landscape Institute all proposed alternatives for the entire route from Bar End to Compton. Individuals and the two Parish Councils proposed partial alternatives or amendments to the DoT route.

JAG's representatives at the procedural meeting had requested, as respectfully as possible, that the new Inspector, Air Vice-Marshal Maughan should appoint a 'technical assessor' to assist him. We argued that the case for alternative JAG3 would include a great deal of highly technical information and that the interpretation of this information would inevitably become a major battleground between professionals representing the DoT and the objectors. We proposed that Inspector Maughan should be assisted by a technical assessor who would be able to provide an independent assessment of bored tunnel schemes, and the technical consequences of routeing the motorway under the railway line; we went on to say that, in the absence of such independent assessment, if the technical evidence presented by opposing parties was in conflict, the Secretary of State would have to rely upon his own staff for advice to resolve the position – the implication clearly being that the objectivity of such 'in-house' advice to the Secretaries of State might be compromised.

Inspector Maughan rejected JAG's request to appoint a technical assessor, saying, via the Programming Officer 'the issues would need to be explained in sufficiently clear terms so that they (are) readily understood and reported to the Secretaries of State....The Inspector did not believe the presence of an assessor would be advantageous.'

As it was, when the tunnel evidence was eventually put to the Inquiry in February 1988 many days were taken up with highly complicated and detailed technical presentations and argument, which most of us who were present had the greatest difficulty understanding; eventually Inspector Maughan was driven to ask the warring factions (three tunnel engineers) to try to come to some sort of agreement. A great deal of time, as well as objectors' and taxpayers' money, could have been saved by the simple expedient of the appointment of an assessor. Furthermore, it would seem likely that the whole of the Inquiry process could have been expedited by the presence of an assessor.

Structure Plan Inquiries (called Examinations in Public) have a panel of three 'Inspectors'. This would appear to be a considerable improvement on a single individual carrying the whole burden of an Inquiry.

The only person with whom the Inspector can have any direct contact during an inquiry is the Programming Officer. Obviously designed to prevent any suggestion of collusion between an Inspector and any party at the Inquiry, this slightly quaint arrangement does lead to communication problems. It is also odd that the programming officer is appointed from the workforce of the very office promoting the scheme.

At the M3 1987 Inquiry, Eric Lawson, the programming officer, went to considerable lengths to be seen to be totally independent of any contact with the DoT staff present at the Inquiry, which I am sure he achieved. But how difficult it must have been for him. Mr Lawson normally worked in the Department of Transport regional office in Dorking – the office behind the Cutting route proposal – and was a colleague of many of the DoT staff at the Inquiry. Because of his position he was clearly uncomfortable about talking freely to them. How much easier and more obviously fair it would have been if the programming officer came as a package with the Inspector from the Inspectorate division of the Department of the Environment.

There were also practical problems in the day-to-day running of the Inquiry, which is illustrated by an incident that occurred just before the Inquiry reopened. One day I received a telephone call from Lawson, who appeared to be in some distress. He seemed to be suggesting that my proposal to submit evidence on the change in public opinion did not constitute new evidence (as was required); I was sure that it did, and told him so, and suggested he should advise the Inspector. We then had a circular conversation: Lawson said it was not he who was saying it wasn't new evidence – it was the Inspector who had said that; but the Inspector could not say that to me! In an effort to blow the fog away I suggested that Mr Lawson should write to me explaining the problem. My file note then records, 'Mr Lawson said that wasn't possible – he could not write to me because he was only telling me what the Inspector had said, and the Inspector couldn't write to me because the only procedure for communication between the Inspector and an objector was on the floor of the hall!'

Thus, any communication between an objector and the Inspector has to use up Public Inquiry time at everyone's expense even while mere procedural issues are being clarified. Also, as will be obvious, the Inspector is in a very isolated position and does not have the benefit of being able to discuss the matters before the Inquiry, or the evidence, with anyone else at all. On the basis that 'two heads are better than one' this would seem to be an unnecessary handicap to Inspectors.

On Tuesday, 27 September 1987 the Inquiry finally reopened. The DoT had booked the largest hall in Winchester Guildhall with a capacity for 600, in response to the press and public interest in the M3 debate. Our supporters turned up in force and on the first day of the Inquiry the hall was full, which must have made no little impression on the Inspector, and certainly on the local press.

After introducing himself the Inspector asked for any initial submissions or comments, especially from the statutory objectors. Thus it was that Winchester Council's solicitor, Meic Sullivan-Gould, more or less opened the proceedings by announcing Winchester Council's withdrawal of its earlier support for the DoT Cutting and high-level crossing of the railway line.

The Hampshire County Council's representative then stated that the County's policy not only supported the DoT route but had moved from a position of neutrality to one of opposition to the tunnel, following the failure of a motion (proposed to the County Council by Ann Bailey, the county councillor for Compton and Shawford) to support a tunnel at a recent meeting of the County Council.

Meic Sullivan-Gould, well versed in local authority constitutional procedures, challenged the statement that the failure of a motion of support for the tunnel amounted to a decision to oppose such a solution. He pointed out that when a motion is put for debate, and lost, that does not cause any alteration to existing policy – the failure of Cllr Bailey's motion could only, he argued, mean a reversion to the status quo, which since 1985 had consistently been one of County Council support for the DoT, opposition to a route on the bypass and *neutrality on the tunnel*. This dispute gave rise to a great deal of argument, which rolled on for several days.

Sullivan-Gould had mounted a valiant and perfectly valid challenge to the County Council. The County Council's interpretation of the outcome of the debate seemed somewhat cavalier, and local authorities, clearly, have a responsibility to understand and work within the constitutional framework – especially those of the size of Hampshire County Council, whose budget is approximately £1000 million per year.

Faced with Sullivan-Gould's public challenge over what constituted Hampshire County Council's actual policy the County Council's representatives promised Inspector Maughan to come back to the Inquiry with clarification. The matter continued to resurface over the next two weeks until *The Hampshire Chronicle* reported, 'County Opposes M3 Tunnel and Crossing'. The report read, 'Hampshire County Council this week announced its opposition to...a tunnel...and a crossing under the railway at Shawford. The decision was taken behind closed doors at a meeting of the M3 Panel on Monday [12 October]. Members voted to exclude the press and public from the debate despite the fact that the meeting is normally open to the public.' The report continues, 'A County Council spokesman said the meeting had been confidential because legal advice was given to councillors about the inquiry which the Council regarded as semi-judicial proceedings. It would not have been in the public's interest for advice about different courses of action to be made known to other parties involved in the Inquiry, he added. The Council's change of stance was relayed to the public inquiry on Tuesday. The inspector...had asked the Council four times to clarify its position regarding the tunnel option...'(*Hampshire Chronicle* 16.10.87).

Hampshire County Council's support for the damaging DoT scheme was the source of considerable disquiet in Winchester. As the strategic planning authority for the area the County Council's support for the DoT scheme was a very important and persuasive factor. But, the County Council was now the only local elected body still supporting the DoT route.

Many employees of the County Council are residents in and around Winchester, and had personal views about the route for the M3. Some were even members of the M3 Joint Action Group, and there was much embarrassment about the role the County Council had played in supporting the DoT's routes for the M3, both the 1971 Water Meadows route, and the Cutting route.

Among the councillors on Winchester Council there was a fairly long-standing dissatisfaction with the way the Conservative-controlled County Council exercised its considerable powers. The County Council's persistent support for the DoT, contrary to the perceived wishes of the people of Winchester, served only to fuel this ill-feeling.

This was in part due to the fact that of the 102 councillors elected to the County Council only four represented Winchester. David Croker, as chairman of Winchester M3 Joint Action Group, argued that the County Council's overriding desire for early completion of the M3 link caused it to overlook other matters, such as the County Council's policy on conservation, heritage and the countryside, and that the failure to publicly discuss and weigh the balance of advantage of all relevant issues was a serious omission which undermined the value of the County Council's support for the DoT route. However, the County Council remained a supporter of the route, and no doubt provided considerable succour to the increasingly beleagured Transport Department.

The Government had reopened the Inquiry to hear evidence from English Heritage and the Countryside Commission and thus it was that on 27 September 1987 English Heritage had the unenviable task of being 'first in to bat'. Despite the critical role that English Heritage, and the archaeological impact of the DoT Cutting route, had played in the campaign to have the Inquiry reopened the actual presentation of English Heritage's evidence, and its formal objection laid before Inspector Maughan was low-key.

The official guardian of the nation's archaeology and Scheduled Ancient Monuments was represented by Dr Geoffrey Wainwright (at that time the principal Inspector with English Heritage), and by Mr Dai Morgan Evans, an Inspector of Ancient Monuments.

Geoffrey Wainwright opened by telling the Inquiry that the route proposed by the DoT crossed the richest archaeological landscape in the area and added: 'Our conclusion remains that this route will cause the maximum archaeological damage.' A statement which left no room for doubt, but tragically not made until many years of detailed planning had gone into the development of the Cutting route by the Transport Department. English Heritage and all responsible environmental watchdogs should have warned the Government of the damage its proposed route would inflict before ministers had put their names to the route.

English Heritage, and its absence from the previous Inquiry, were put under the microscope by DoT counsel, David Altaras, and there followed several hours of tedious, and at times slightly tawdry proceedings as Mr Altaras was trying to devalue the evidence being put forward by Mr Morgan Evans. This questioning, however, threw little light on the reasons for English Heritage's absence from the 1985 Inquiry. Inspector Maughan's Inquiry Report was later to précis English Heritage's evidence about this to the reopened Inquiry: 'With hindsight, it may be that HBMC (later known as English Heritage) should have recognized the rarity value of the archaeological sites to the east of St Catherine's Hill earlier, and when the DoT requested clearance in 1985 to work on SAM 273 and 543, tempered its advice to the Department of the Environment accordingly...'

What was clear was that the absence of any objection by English Heritage, or its predecessor, Historic Buildings and Monuments Commission, was interpreted as tacit support for the DoT route, and this in turn must have given the DoT confidence to pursue the route east of St Catherine's Hill over a period of years.

A bundle of correspondence was presented by the DoT, during the cross-examination of Mr Morgan Evans, disclosing the extent of discussions between the DoT and English Heritage over the period between 1983 and 1985. Interestingly, this correspondence appears to indicate that, after the DoT and ministers had put the Cutting route out for public consultation as the chosen option in February 1983, English Heritage wrote to the DoT in April of that year, saying 'We wish to point out that 2 Scheduled Ancient Monuments are affected by this proposal. These are Hants Nos 273 (Twyford Down Settlement site) and 543 (the 'Dongas' and Roman Road) 2 sites behind St Catherine's Hill; 273 only has been marked on the plan.' This letter (19 April 1983) enclosed '2 relevant site maplets', quite clearly showing the precise and extensive boundaries of the Scheduled Ancient Monuments. Despite the fact that English Heritage formally brought this information to the attention of the DoT, the DoT nevertheless published another public consultation document over a year later, in June 1984, again identifying the Scheduled Ancient Monuments only by large asterisks, though by now SAM 543 appeared. **The SAMs were still shown as unaffected by the road and no indication of the actual boundaries of the monuments was given, despite the fact the proposed road crossed both sites.**

Surprisingly, despite the importance of the archaeological evidence there was a curious lack of occasion during the presentation of evidence to Inspector Maughan by English Heritage. This was not a reflection of the quality of the case made by English Heritiage; neither Wainwright nor Morgan Evans left any doubt about the severe impact on the ancient settlement site on Twyford Down, or the old Roman Road, and the medieval trackways at the northern entrance to the Cutting. Maybe the lack of excitement was partly due to the fact that English Heritage deliberately played their presentation in a low key fashion – no counsel, no solicitors, no consultant engineer. Wainwright and Morgan Evans were simply two professional representatives of a Government environmental protection agency, giving professional evidence to an Inquiry. This contrasted with the atmosphere generated as the Countryside Commission team moved into the seats reserved for those presenting their case to the Inquiry, facing the DoT Inquiry team.

Jeremy Burford, QC, had been appointed by the Countryside Commission to steer the Commission's case through the reopened Inquiry. The team around him included consulting engineers, Halcrow Fox, instructing solicitor, Peter Wilbraham from Last Suddards, landscape consultant, Mark Lintel of Land Use Consultants and, of course, the Director of the Commission's South Eastern Regional Office, David Coleman. An impressive team by any standards, it was immensely reassuring to those of us who had been campaigning pretty much on a shoestring to see the Countryside Commission's concern about the damage to this part of the South Downs manifested in such an impressive group of professional witnessses.

The normal David (being any objector) and Goliath (the DoT team) situation at a Highway Inquiry was suddenly and rather dramatically turned around. It was evident that the presence of a Queen's Counsel, supported by such an expert team, resulted firstly in a polished presentation of the Countryside Commission's own case; it also resulted in an exceedingly thorough re-examination and reappraisal of all the evidence that had been put before the 1985 Leaker Inquiry. By means of quite extraordinarily tortuous re-examination of all the 1985 Inquiry documents, the submission of additional documents, such as the Minister's 1980 decision letter, and cross-examination of both his own and the DoT's witness, Burford extracted a great deal of detail and information. Burford's firm mastery of detail left the rest of us in the Inquiry feeling distinctly inadequate. No inaccuracies or inconsistencies by the DoT team were now allowed to pass, and there is no doubt that this very thorough reappraisal ensured that the DoT scheme was discussed comprehensively for the first time.

The Countryside Commission evidence was opened by David Coleman, the regional officer for the Commission in the South East Region. Coleman set out the policy background within which the Commission operates, the grounds on which the Commission based its objection to the DoT Cutting and Over-rail route, and the Commission's selected alternative method of completing the missing link in the M3 – a motorway on the line of the A33 Winchester bypass.

The Commission has a statutory duty to advise the government on proposals for developments in Areas of Outstanding Natural Beauty (AONB). Twyford Down and St Catherine's Hill comprise the western extremity of the South Downs, in the East Hampshire AONB. David Coleman referred to the national importance of the countryside through which the M3 would go, which contained many sites that had been designated because of their importance to the whole country. He said, 'The DoT's route will be an eyesore in this landscape. Breaching the Downs with an enormous man-made canyon so close to the natural route of the River Itchen would be entirely against the grain of the landscape.'

Mark Lintel, for Land Use Consultants, the landscape consultants retained by the Commission, presented more in-depth analysis of the impact of the DoT route upon the landscape of Twyford Down and St Catherine's Hill, and the Itchen Valley. Lintel drew attention, I think for the first time, to the damage, in landscape terms, which the embankments and Cutting would inflict on the Morestead Road escarpment, at the northern end of the route. In response to the Countryside Commission the DoT's team produced a number of new photomontages, showing the route from a number of new vantage points. By the time Lintel's evidence had been completed the Inquiry had received its most comprehensive account of the landscape impact of the proposed M3.

Having set out its objections to the DoT route so fully, the Countryside Commission moved on to promote its own alternative method of completing the missing link. Halcrow Fox, consulting engineers, on behalf of the Commission presented details of a route incorporating the A33 bypass, and passing below the railway line at Shawford. The Commission's alternative, which was known as CC1, provoked fierce opposition from a number of Winchester-based groups, from the residents of the St Cross area, and from Winchester College. The element to which they all objected was the retention of the M3 in the valley to the west of St Catherine's Hill – between the hill and the Winchester Water Meadows. Sadly, this responsible approach of constructive opposition, which led to the Countryside Commission proposing the economic and pragmatic alternative was years too late, and came at a time when the DoT had persuaded some elements of the public in Winchester of the benefits of a route behind St Catherine's Hill.

By 1987 the suggestion of consolidating the M3 in the valley between St Catherine's Hill and the Water Meadows prompted, and served as a focus for, support for the DoT's route, and from which the inference of opposition to the tunnel alternative was often drawn.

Sadly, too, the engineering details of the Countryside Commission route CC1 provided far too many details (bones) for the DoT's team of terriers to chew upon.

It is not clear why the Commission decided to make its appearance at the Inquiry with such a substantial team. It may be that the Commission's lack of input to the 1985 Inquiry left it feeling somewhat vulnerable to criticism, which it was determined to disprove, or it may be that the Commission took the view that the principles at stake at Twyford Down, in addition to the intrinsic landscape under threat, were so important, and could potentially be replicated elsewhere, that only the strongest possible team of professionals would be adequate. Undoubtedly the issues at Twyford Down were complex and the full understanding of those issues was considerably helped by the strength of the Commission's presence and presentation of its case.

It is interesting to compare the presentations made by English Heritage and the Countryside Commission to the 1987 session of the Public Inquiry. English Heritage provided low key evidence by two professional archaeologists who were confining themselves to the single issue for which English Heritage has responsibility – the impact of the M3 motorway upon archaeological sites – and standing back from the infighting on alternative routes, but were giving an analytical comment on the archaeological impact of the principal alternatives.

The Countryside Commission, on the other hand, extended its objection to the DoT route to a detailed presentation of its own chosen alternative. In so doing the Commission's team worried out of the DoT witnesses many details of the very complex DoT route: because of the thoroughness and professional expertise of the Commission's team the DoT were unable to brush these matters aside. Sadly though the Commission's alternative CC1 (along with another proposal for a route on the old A33 bypass, promoted by the South West Chapter of the Landscape Institute) proved to be the very threat (real or imagined) seen by so many Wintonians of the motorway being consolidated in the valley between the Water Meadows and St Catherine's Hill.

There was seemingly endless discussion, occupying days of the Inquiry time, about the details of the route CC1, its retaining wall, and the complexities of an under-rail crossing of the railway line.

Apart from the costs of such detailed discussion, and the many opportunities it provides for the DoT to undermine the validity of every alternative proposal, the only actual recommendation an Inspector at a Highway Inquiry can make is on the draft (DoT) schemes and orders before the Inquiry. It is not within the Inspector's remit to choose an alternative route, and thus it may be thought that objectors may be well advised to confine themselves to simply proving that the principle of an alternative is practicable and acceptable, rather than providing full details. However, it requires considerable skill (and no doubt a certain political cunning) for an objector to walk the tightrope of acting responsibly, proposing an alternative, but avoiding endless, and fruitless, debate on the details of some alternative proposal which may not arise until the detailed design stage.

Meic Sullivan-Gould, on behalf of Winchester Council, seemed to achieve this balance. Throughout his presentation of

Winchester Council's case to the 1987 Inquiry he reiterated that Winchester Council had appointed Scott Wilson Kirkpatrick 'to demonstrate the feasibility of completing M3 in a tunnel' and recommended the Inspector to 'accept the concept of a tunnel scheme in principle to enable an optimum route to be designed.'

Among those 'supporters' of the DoT Cutting route and counter objecting to the Countryside Commission alternative suggestion of a route along the old A33 bypass was Winchester College. The College had been a consistent supporter of the DoT route since the inception of the Cutting idea, and had opposed our alternative suggestion of a bypass route at the 1985 Inquiry. At the reopened session in 1987 Winchester College again appeared as a supporter of the DoT scheme, and as a counter objector to the Countryside Commission's proposal for completing the M3 link along the line of the old A33 bypass, despite promoting, during the 1970s, the suggestion of improving the bypass as an alternative to the earlier DoT proposal for a motorway through the Water Meadows.

Apart from its position as a landowner, the College is an integral part of the social and commercial fabric of Winchester. The College has substantial property holdings in the St Cross area of Winchester, as well as its landownership elsewhere. Founded in 1382 by William of Wykeham (once Bishop of Winchester) as an institution for the education of 'poor scholars' it became something rather more influential and has been prominent in national history as a result of its academic excellence and the influential positions achieved by its former pupils (known as Wykehamists) for several centuries.

In the 1970s the College was a key player in the Joint Action Group which fought off the DoT plan to put the M3 through the Water Meadows. Rumour has it that the College contributed substantial sums of money to the 1970s JAG campaign – some £60 000 was spent by JAG in that campaign – a huge sum of money in those days. During the 1976 Public Inquiry passions had run high at Winchester College as elsewhere in Winchester – the very start of the Inquiry was delayed by objectors so disrupting the proceedings as to prevent the Inspector from formally opening the proceedings.

The College's land holdings, which include property in the St Cross area, the Water Meadows between the College and St

Catherine's Hill, St Catherine's Hill itself and Twyford Down, ensured that it would be a key player in discussions of any route for the final M3 link in the vicinity of the College, and it was consulted by Mott Hay and Anderson (MHA) soon after their appointment to reappraise the M3 link in 1981.

During our own campaigning activities after the close of the earlier, 1985, session of the Inquiry and as part of our efforts to have the Inquiry reopened, Merrick and I recognized that the College was an important influence and explored how we might persuade the College to support our campaign. Merrick sought and ultimately achieved an interview with Lord Aldington, at that time the Warden of the College (the chairman of its governing body); I saw the Bursar of the College, Mr Vellacott. Unfortunately neither of us managed to bring about a change of College policy regarding the Twyford Down Cutting.

At slide presentations to local organizations, and elsewhere, a certain amount of discussion focused on the 'morality' of the College apparently accepting without public remonstrance the destruction of Twyford Down with its triple heritage designations. Twyford Down had been given to the College following the Down's purchase by benefactors 'to save it from development' in the 1920s. According to James Sabben-Clare in his book *Winchester College*, 'Twyford Down, and including the Hockley Golf Course, was put up for sale. An appeal to the Governing Body to try and secure it for the school had failed; the asking price was over £10 000 and they had no such funds available. A builder was already marking out the land in plots for development when two bachelor masters stepped in and bought it. They were Murray Hicks and Maurice Platnauer. They leased the land at no profit to themselves but considerable advantage to the College which enjoyed preferential rates for use of the golf course. Then in 1955 they handed the whole lot, now extended to about 500 acres over to the school, with the admirable proviso that the disposal of the rents was to be entirely at the Headmaster's discretion' (Winchester College, James Sabben-Clare 1981).

Certainly many people expressed the view that the College was being less than responsible and not providing much of an example of 'duty of care' in allowing the destruction of these scheduled sites within its ownership. On the other hand, Winchester College and some residents in the locality around the College, in the area of St Cross, took the view that any route in the vicintity of the A33 bypass was so totally unacceptable that any alternative would be better, despite College support for the 1970s campaign simply to improve the bypass. The College's evidence given to the 1985 part of the Inquiry had stated, 'It (Winchester College) therefore gives it support to the preferred route as this would be less environmentally damaging than any of the alternatives.'

For the reopened session of the Inquiry in 1987 Winchester College appointed leading counsel, Jeremy Sullivan QC. The College kept its case quite simple, and repeated that its support for the DoT route had been summarized at the earlier 1985 Inquiry – that the College's view was that the DoT scheme would satisfactorily provide for both through traffic and local traffic and that the DoT route would be 'the least damaging of the alternatives.'

The evidence, given on behalf of the College by Mr Robin Chute, the Estates Bursar, was summarized thus:

> I confirm that the College is a supporter of the published route and a counter objector to any route such as that proposed by the Countryside Commission and Landscape Institute to the west of St Catherine's Hill, and that any compensation receivable has not been considered as a factor in our decision. Our main support for an eastern route is as follows:
>
> (i)   Restoring the historic link between the College, its watermeadows and its Hill.
> (ii) Improving both the College's and the public's access to the Hill for education, recreational and social purposes.
> (iii) Removing the noise and visual intrusion of six lanes of motorway between the College and its Hill.
> (iv) Closure and filling in of the bypass.
>
> We are not unsympathetic to the responsibilities of the Countryside Commission in its regard to AONB in general, but object to their stance in this case, on the grounds of strong local historical circumstances.

At this Inquiry, because the College supports the Department's route, the College has not fielded a substantial team of experts, but if as a result of this Inquiry an alternative route is suggested which would involve the acquisition of College land it must be clear that, as at the 1976 Inquiry, the College would vigorously oppose any Compulsory Purchase Order and would be calling expert witnesses.

Burford, representing the Countryside Commission, pressed the College's witness on the matter of whether there were any restrictive covenants on Twyford Down, and received adamant assurances that none existed.

Quite clearly Winchester College played a pivotal role in the demise of the DoT's 1970s Water Meadows route. The extent to which the College was involved in the selection of the route through Twyford Down is far less clear. What is, however, quite clear is that the College subsequently became violently opposed to any return to a route along the line of the old A33 bypass.

The College stated that 'it has no objection to a tunnel alternative that provides for the bypass to be relandscaped, and that has no adverse effect on traffic movement in the south Winchester area.' Nonetheless Winchester College is recorded in the Inquiry proceedings as a supporter of the DoT Twyford Down route.

The M3 Joint Action Group presented its evidence towards the end of the Inquiry, and this was the highpoint for local campaigners. As part of its preparations for the reopened Public Inquiry the M3 Joint Action Group had engaged the services of Peter Towler, a barrister with chambers in nearby Southampton. Peter brought to the Group's cause a relaxed yet highly professional legal mind. His very real interest in the case we were promoting included a whole day spent walking the proposed route (somewhat marred by an unfortunate disagreement between his dog and the local farmer's collie-cross dog!) and many 'cons' – conferences with us, his clients. Towler's calm professionalism helped mould the M3JAG presentations into a cohesive whole without diminishing the individuality of our contributions.

Whatever the ambivalence the national landscape groups may have expressed as to the best route for the missing link in M3, there were very few doubts among Winchester's population, or its amenity societies. The **concept** of a tunnel attracted almost universal support, with local opposition from some residents in the St Cross area, and from Hampshire County Council. The merits of a tunnel and under-rail route were fervently expounded, leading Inspector Maughan to report later to the Secretaries of State, 'I have no doubt that it (JAG3 – tunnel and under-rail) goes further towards the environmental intentions of the 1987 Roads White Paper and local conservation policies and is the most environmentally sensitive of all routes before these inquiries, including the published route. It has attracted the highest degree of perceptible public support of any route...'

The M3 Joint Action Group relied upon the landscape evidence of the Countryside Commission, the Landscape Institute, the Hampshire Wildlife Trust, and English Nature, all of whom had given very full accounts of the special importance of Twyford Down, the Itchen Valley Water Meadows and the landscape setting which these combined to create for the historic city of Winchester. M3JAG felt no need to do more than associate itself with the evidence of those organizations.

The M3 Joint Action Group, having decided in principle that the only acceptable means of completing the missing link in the M3 was by means of a tunnel and with the under-rail route at Shawford, delegated the design of such a route to a small group of its members with the right qualifications. These three people, Colin Brooks (from Compton and Shawford Parish Council), Chris Gillham and Richard Parker, burned the midnight oil developing a highly refined scheme. Merrick provided advice and guidance on the landscape and Mark Sullivan, an independent specialist in Highway Inquiries, helped and advised. Sullivan had been offering Merrick invaluable advice for well over a year. With many years of experience, and an encyclopaedic mind, Sullivan was the bane of many a Highway Inspector's life but had been a source of considerable help and support to Merrick and me. Their scheme, known as JAG3, followed a similiar horizontal alignment to that of the DoT route betweeen Compton, south of Winchester, to the Hockley traffic lights. The vertical alignment was very different, starting off considerably lower than the DoT route and staying low to go under the railway by Shawford Junction.

Crossing the Itchen Valley Water Meadows at low level, rising slightly to cross the River Itchen and the canal, JAG3 descended into the Hockley Junction about 4 metres below the old bypass and entered twin bore tunnels in the area of the old chalk pit (see Figure 11). The tunnel was 1500 metres long and rejoined the already built M3 at the northern end of the gap in M3. The JAG3 tunnel would have been virtually a straight line compared with the wide arc of the DoT motorway. The vertical alignment of JAG3 had to allow for enough chalk overburden in Plague Pits Valley and thus dipped to a low point before rising towards the northern portals.

Both the tunnel and the under-rail crossing of the valley were technically complex elements in the scheme, though the under-rail crossing in JAG3 differed only slightly from that proposed by the Countryside Commission.

Burslem Engineering Associates Ltd (BEAL) were retained by M3 Joint Action Group following the earlier work BEAL had undertaken on my behalf some twelve months earlier. Geoff Thornton, BEAL's senior partner, worked closely with the 'technical group' in the design of JAG3.

Thornton's Inquiry evidence was detailed, and extensive. The DoT cross-examination of Thornton was more so, taking up hours and hours of Inquiry time – at no small cost to us in M3 JAG. Clearly it is necessary for an Inquiry to examine thoroughly alternative proposals, and the DoT's microscopic examination of Thornton's evidence on the method of construction of the JAG3 tunnel was well within the rules of the Public Inquiry game. But I do wonder whether a more adult approach to Road Planning Inquiries might not be in everyone's interest. As an example, BEAL presented evidence on tunneling through chalk. The evidence they presented was the same technical information they were at that time producing in connection with the A27 tunnel at Brighton. At the M3 Inquiry the DoT spent a great deal of time merely attempting to discredit this technical evidence.

After many hours of tortuous discussion of technical details the whole Inquiry seemed deadlocked, and Inspector Maughan asked the three tunnel experts, representing the objectors and the DoT to try to agree common ground to enable the Inquiry to move forward. After more than six hours they produced an agreed statement, which no doubt represented a compromise, that the tunnel would cost between 85 and £95 million and take between four and five years to construct. Both the cost and the construction time greatly exceeded M3JAG's professional advisers' estimates, but the gridlock at the Inquiry had obviously to be resolved. Geoff Thornton is a highly experienced tunnel engineer, with more than twenty years of practical experience in constructing tunnels. During the Inquiry there was an almost theatrical contrast between this Yorkshireman, and Geoffrey Williams, the senior partner in Scott Wilson Kirkpatrick, retained by Winchester Council. Both men knew the subject of tunnelling inside out, knew what they were talking about at M3 and came across as confident professionals. They also came across as genuinely excited at the concept of completing the M3 with a tunnel. The DoT team's response to these two tunnellers was lack-lustre and imprecise – and at one point embarrassingly inept, so much so that the DoT counsel sought an adjournment and repaired the damage to their team's presentation.

The M3 Joint Action Group's alternative JAG3 attracted widespread support. It was a sensitive solution to the conundrum. In his report on the 1987 Inquiry, Inspector Maughan later wrote that it was 'with great reluctance' that he had been 'forced to conclude' that he was 'unable to recommend JAG3 in favour of the DoT scheme' primarily because of the increased cost and longer construction time. But the hours of work which BEAL, Colin Brooks, Chris Gillham, Richard Parker and Merrick had put into the design of JAG3 enabled the campaign for Twyford Down to offer this practicable and environmentally sensitive alternative to the Cutting route for the remaining four years of the campaign.

Professor Martin Biddle appeared on behalf of eight archaeological groups including the influential Prehistoric Society, while giving further archaeological evidence for M3 Joint Action Group. A substantial part of Professor Biddle's evidence concerned the dispute between English Heritage and the DoT as to who should fund archaeological rescue work precipitated by road schemes. At that time (1987) the DoT gave English Heritage in the order of £100 000 a year to spend on rescue archaeology and the DoT had consistently refused to increase this amount, despite the fact that private developers were required to contribute vastly greater sums for rescue archaeology.

Biddle concluded his evidence to the Inquiry with the ringing words, 'The archaeological importance, known and potential, of this area [Twyford Down] is however not only remarkable; in one vital respect it is exceptional – perhaps unique: it provides a thriving modern city with a visual perspective reaching deep into its remote past so that here, perhaps alone in modern urban England it is possible in the course of an hour or so to walk from the twentieth century to the prehistoric past, or even glance from one to another in the course of a moment at work or at school. Such a setting for Winchester is beyond price.'

Winchester Council had made similar points, referring to the lost resource that would result from the M3's destruction of Twyford Down. Both Winchester Council witnesses and I had emphasized the potential of St Catherine's Hill, Twyford Down, and the Water Meadows as a heritage, tourist and local resource within easy walking distance from the Cathedral, Wolvesey Castle and the heart of England's ancient capital. The concept we promulgated was of the creation of a heritage area by the reconstruction of part of the Iron Age village on Twyford Down, together with the St Catherine's Hill Fort, and the scenically and ecologically rich areas of the Water Meadows and Plague Pits Valley. The damage and loss caused by the M3 construction is there for all to see. However, the lost potential of a unique area in southern England, of national and international significance, has been sadly underemphasized. Such a project would indeed have provided the City of Winchester with an unmatchable asset, which it can never now recover.

Throughout the 1980s the most obvious shortcoming of the A33 Winchester bypass was the junction at Hockley – the infamous Hockley traffic lights (Figure 15). Once the M25 was opened Hockley was said to be the only signal-controlled crossing between Southampton and Edinburgh – no wonder it proved, on occasion, such a notorious bottleneck.

Both the City Council and M3JAG spent some time proving that a temporary flyover at Hockley to remove these traffic lights would be cheap, and practicable; it would ease the bottleneck and the political pressure created by the traffic queues at peak times.

In 1976 JAG's suggestion of a grade separated junction at Hockley, as an interim improvement, had been fiercely opposed by the DoT, and the Hampshire County Council. The County Council's closing submission to 1976 Inquiry Inspector, Major-General Edge, throws some light on this: 'The most likely interim measures would be junction improvements (at Hockley) in order to reduce the lengthy delays which are experienced at busy periods. Yet...for the purposes of COBA (COst-Benefit Analysis) the removal of junction delay costs amounts to a very substantial part of the total benefits of the scheme. In an era where public expenditure is likely to be closely scrutinized the effect of carrying out desperately needed interim measures may well mean that the construction of the rest of the scheme shows

Figure 15 The notorious Hockley traffic lights, looking south towards Shawford and Compton.

up so poorly in cost-benefit terms that it can claim very little priority nationally in the allocation of whatever funds are available...'

Despite the recommendation of Inspector Edge in 1979 (he had overseen the 1976/77 Inquiry) that an interim improvement at Hockley be provided, the DoT steadfastly resisted this obvious temporary palliative measure, thereby condemning motorists to some further 15 years of frustration and inconvenience, while the highway authorities shed crocodile tears about the problem, but giving ample opportunity for reflection on the need to do something about the Winchester bypass.

The Maughan Inquiry proved no exception to the rule in those days that COBA, the computer tool used by the DoT to assess the benefits in economic terms of road-building schemes, would again feature prominently. Regarded as the terriority of 'boffins' even by experienced engineers and planners, COBA is highly theoretical and complex. It was, however, a critical factor in the decision-making process because, in order to obtain Treasury authorization for a road scheme, the DoT had to show that the scheme was good value for money, that is 'COBA positive'.

Thought by some to exemplify the Wilde definition of a cynic, as 'knowing the price of everything, and the value of nothing,' COBA takes no account of environmental considerations. Its use and accuracy have been challenged at many Inquiries and, though now largely discredited, COBA has remained a continuing thorn in the side of environmentalists and objectors at Inquiries.

The M3JAG challenge to the DoT's COBA figures for the tunnel/under-rail alternative was undertaken by Richard Parker. He and Peter Towler spent a fruitful day playing the DoT at its own game, leaving most of us quite out of our depth! An Inspector has no remit to consider alterations to Government (Transport Department) policy and thus Parker made no attempt to dispute the principle of the absence of environmental considerations in COBA, since any such discussions would have simply been ruled out of order.

The DoT analysis showed JAG3 tunnel/under-rail was COBA negative at −£21.35 m, assuming low growth in traffic. It is interesting to note, however, that the DoT's own route was marginally COBA negative assuming low growth, showing up at −£0.51 m and on high growth at +£8.99 m – hardly a ringing endorsement in cost-benefit terms, which may account for the persistent claims by the DoT that the scheme had been chosen on 'environmental' grounds (until it became untenable to persist with that pretence in the face of the belated outcry from the environmental organizations).

Parker pointed out that the 1987 Policy for Roads in England had attempted to introduce, in policy at any rate, a more balanced approach with regard to the environment, and that in the current (in 1987) roads programme some 10 per cent of the schemes had a negative COBA in the interests of environmental relief . He further argued that the already completed sections of M3 from London to Winchester had been built at a comparatively low cost. In cross-examining the DoT Project Manager on Policy, Towler uncovered the interesting fact that no COBA had been undertaken (or at any rate published) for the M25 – policy requirements had apparently overridden COBA.

Parker argued that the Government had shown itself prepared to devote substantial funds to achieve its transport objectives, while recognizing the landscapes through which they pass and that COBA need not be decisive. At Winchester the environmental gains greatly outweighed the economic disadvantage and a negative COBA was justified. Parker quoted various examples such as the tunnel at Conwy, costing some £154 m, and the cut and cover tunnels at Epping, saving a cricket ground.

Ultimately Inspector Maughan was to report, in his conclusions, 'I do not consider the provision of tunnels at extra cost for environmental reasons in other road improvements, or the policy decision taken in respect of the M25 can be taken as precedents for Winchester. In my view the [M3 at Winchester] has to be justified on its own merits...'

A number of other objectors, especially Robin McCall, the elder statesman of Winchester, made impassioned pleas that it was unreasonable for the final three-mile link in the M3 chain, acknowledged by all as the most sensitive and complex pinch point, to be self-supporting in COBA terms. The M3 was always intended as a strategic whole, providing the final link from London and the North of England to Southampton and the South Coast. As such, any COBA analysis should reflect the cost of the route as a whole.

The DoT's habit of identifying strategic routes, but breaking these down into more digestible lumps for decision, is obviously not very 'strategic' in its approach, though may well be expedient. It is certainly a continuing source of concern to many outside Government. At Winchester the final link was always going to be expensive – threading the motorway through such a highly complex landscape less than a mile from Winchester Cathedral resembled passing a camel through the eye of a needle. As Robin McCall argued, the M3 meets a national rather than a local need and thus the cost of the Bar End to Compton section should be costed as part of the whole, in which case even allowing for JAG3 the cost per mile would have been about half that for the M25.

The DoT rebuttal of Parker's evidence on economics highlights another nonsense in the Highways Inquiry process. Following conventional opening paragraphs, it says, 'The COBA results are shown below for the Published Route and for JAG3 for both the DoT's estimates of cost and opening date, and M3JAG estimates. As there will be at least 3 years delay in implementing JAG3, compared with PR, it is important to take into account the lost benefits in earlier years as a result of this delay...'

On the one hand, 'delay' in implementation of an alternative is, in theory, not allowed to count against that alternative route during its evaluation at the Inquiry; but, on the other hand, the Inspector will be browbeaten with all the problems associated with an alternative – and the delays inherent in abandoning the Transport Department's chosen route and starting the whole selection process from scratch. The 1987 Inquiry at Winchester was no exception – Inspector Maughan in the conclusions to his Report of the Inquiry to referred to 'the serious consequences of delay' as one reason for rejecting our JAG3 route.

A quite extraordinary paragraph appears in the DoT rebuttal to Richard Parker: 'The COBA printouts indicate higher benefits to JAG3 compared with PR in 1995, but in that year only. This is due to an overestimation of benefits in the opening year of JAG3 in order to preserve the correct accident rates on all links in the COBA network.'

The 1987 Public Inquiry finally closed in March 1988. A vast amount of technical evidence had been given; some 600 letters had been received by Inspector Maughan, in addition to the formal appearances at the Inquiry by 34 objectors to the scheme, and other organizations such as British Rail.

The essence of hundreds of hours and acres of paper making up the objectors' case can be distilled from the closing address, given on behalf of Winchester City Council, by Sullivan-Gould. 'Sir,' Sullivan-Gould commenced, 'it is difficult to see how, in the light of the new evidence, the Department's proposed solution to resolving the problem of bypassing Winchester and completing the M3 between London and Southampton can be found to be acceptable. In terms of policy, in terms of environmental impact, and in terms of public acceptability the preferred route fails to resolve the conundrum.'

He continued, 'It has been remarkable just how much new evidence has come forward at this part of the Inquiry, and just how much of it, despite a valiant rearguard action by the DoT, is of compelling weight in relation to the non-acceptability of the preferred route.' Proceeding to examine policy, environmental impact and public acceptability in turn, Sullivan-Gould said, 'The need for a motorway, and indeed the need to remedy the environmental detriment which the current Winchester bypass does, is not disputed. However, the DoT solution is not the only possibility, and it has been established that it is practicable to avoid extensive damage to the AONB, to the SSSI and to the SAMs. The DoT can no longer argue, as it did in 1985, that its route accords with the objectives of Government policy...the City Council urges that the Secretaries of State should accept some further delay and some additional cost in finding the right solution. The DoT route was always a compromise and is now demonstrably an unacceptable compromise. There is a feasible solution based on a tunnel, a low-level crossing of the Itchen Valley and a bridge under the railway line...if Conwy Castle is worth £177 m then Winchester is certainly worth £85–£95 m, and to protect and enchance the environment for ever it is worth the additional wait. However, much depends on political will...'

Sullivan-Gould's opening paragraph ('it is difficult to see how in the light of the new evidence, the DoT's proposed solution... can be found to be acceptable') seen in the light of the eventual outcome of the Inquiry begs the question, often asked by road campaigners, does an Inquiry alter anything?

The Maughan Inquiry nonetheless had consumed vast resources. Financially, the DoT's costs are unrevealed, but the M3JAG spent some £30 000 on professional fees alone, despite very favourable charge out rates from BEAL and Towler, and despite professionals, such as Richard Parker, giving their time and expertise voluntarily, and taking no account of the volunteer labour force who undertook every other aspect of the campaign from research to photocopying, from lobbying to press liaison.

The City Council paid out some £20 000 in fees; officer time, and administrative back up for the City's case, has no figure put to it. The Countryside Commission spent some £150 000. In the crudest possible terms it could be reasoned that there were never less than four objectors in the hall at any time – many, many days this number was exceeded. Assuming that these were professionals whose charge out rate in the real world would be about £150 per hour, a vast cost is quickly incurred. That is in financial terms alone, and gives no indication of the dedication of the volunteers, and the strains such dedication put upon family, job, or the individual themselves. One day, apologizing to Sullivan-Gould for failing to stay for an extended session during which the City was presenting evidence, I explained that I'd promised to be home, and thought I was in danger of having a tunnel but no husband!

The families and employers of all the leading campaigners were immensely forgiving and supportive, but upwards of five years left its mark, yet, without exception the campaigners echo Sullivan-Gould's final appeal to Inspector Maughan, 'Winchester is Worth It'.

8

March 1988 to 1989 – The transition from local campaign to national environmental issue

The close of the Public Inquiry in March 1988 saw many of us exhausted, leaving us with a huge backlog of tasks. It also left the M3 Joint Action Group (M3JAG) with substantial debts. Membership of the group included two Parish Councils, whose only income was from the rates (now council tax) and who have a duty to explain to the district auditor how public money is spent. Of the other members, the only organization with funds and a legal status was the prestigious Winchester Preservation Trust. The group itself had no legal status and thus any member could be held 'jointly and severally' liable for debts incurred by the group.

The Public Inquiry had dragged on longer than any of us anticipated, being spread over six months, and the costs of some £20 000 incurred had far exceeded the money raised by the Action Group. The financial realities soon brought us all down to earth, despite a slightly euphoric feeling that we had put forward a compelling and justifiable alternative which befitted Winchester. At that time the Joint Action Group debts of £7000 seemed a great burden and it was with some desperation that Action Group members organized fund-raising suppers and events in the best parish tradition. Slowly the funds came in, gradually diminishing the amounts owed on the final accounts (thankfully always on the low side) to the professional advisers we had commissioned.

In and around Winchester support for a tunnel as the best solution to the conundrum of linking the two parts of the M3 more or less stabilized. Later efforts to persuade the Hampshire County Council to add its support, and thus influence any ministerial decision, proved fruitless.

In 1988 the threat to Twyford Down and the historic landscape backcloth to Winchester had received minimal coverage in the national media, although the local papers, radio and television had been saturated with the various twists and turns of the story.

But public interest in the environment was by now creeping up the national political agenda. In 1987 the report of the Bruntland Commission on the environment had triggered public debate on all environmental issues. John Hanvey, chairman of the Harris Research Centre, had identified this trend towards public interest in environment as a political issue while he was overseeing our Public Opinion Survey project in 1987, when 40 per cent of those questioned had indicated that environmental considerations would alter their choice of route for the motorway. In the summer of 1988 MORI started monitoring 'environment' as an issue in the key surveys 'Most Plus Other Important Issues – Trends'. By November 1988 these surveys showed that 11 per cent regarded environment as an important issue – more so than Defence, Foreign Affairs, Northern Ireland, or the Common Market.

On 27 September 1988 Margaret Thatcher delivered her remarkable and unexpected speech to the Royal Society. 'For generations we have assumed that the efforts of mankind would leave the fundamental equilibrium of the world's systems and atmosphere stable. But it is possible that...we have unwittingly begun a massive experiment with the system of the planet itself.'

Environment rocketed up the political agenda. Overnight it became respectable, though not obligatory (unlike Law and Order) for loyal Tories to care about the environment. Before the Thatcher speech on environment, among my fellow Conservatives at the City Council my well-known monetarist, free market approach to most issues had shielded me, and the Twyford Down cause, from the then conventional prejudices about 'lentils and rope sandals'. In Conservative circles elsewhere we had worked hard to emphasize the realistic basis of our cause – 'Government abusing its own laws' and 'no private developer would be allowed within sight of Twyford Down' normally made our point.

But suddenly in 1988 we could discuss the ills of the DoT route through the Down in purist environmental terms. The awful environmental impact of the route, and its proximity to one of the jewels in England's crown, presented huge potential, which we were determined to exploit.

Three years earlier Merrick and I had embarked on the campaign pretty much on the basis that there was everything to gain, and nothing to lose. In that time, though, we had invested huge amounts of our own, and our families', resources – time, energy, and of course money. The campaign had now developed its own momentum, and when we faltered, or felt like throwing in the towel, others were there to drive it forward. In 1988 we had nearly every national 'green' organization on our side, we had massive public support locally in Winchester and we knew that the arguments against the DoT Cutting route, and the advantages of the low-level tunnel had been very well argued to the Inquiry. Apart from the need for Government to swallow its bureaucratic pride, and for the Treasury to swallow the increased cost of a tunnel, there was every reason to expect that the Inspector would reject the DoT proposal to route the M3 through Twyford Down and over the railway line.

The dramatic increase in the importance of environment as a political issue served only to increase our hopes of success. But in November Merrick heard disturbing news. Apparently Inspector Maughan's Report of the reopened Inquiry, and his recommendations, had been received by the Department of Transport. Slowly the contents of the Report leaked out to us; it seemed to be very bad news with the Inspector apparently acknowledging the shortcomings of the DoT route, the advantages of a low-level tunnel but rejecting any alternatives or amendments in favour of the Cutting and over-rail route.

For the time being we kept the news to ourselves – we had no proof and for us to speculate in public seemed pointless. There was no indication from Government, the DoT, or MPs that the report had been received by the Government. But our quiet confidence of the summer was shaken, and we began again to bend the ear of every politician to whom we could gain access.

Sadly, once again, we were disastrously late. The paramount need to reach ministers much earlier in the Governmental decision-making process was subsequently explained to me by a very senior civil servant: the key thing is to get ministers, not MPs, involved at a very early stage – before the DoT (or whichever department is originating a proposal/policy) goes 'public' to other Government Departments.

In March 1989 the local *Hampshire Chronicle* carried an exclusive article, leaking substantial parts of Inspector Maughan's report. Customarily *The Hampshire Chronicle* does not name the journalist responsible for the reports, and this one, headlined 'No to tunnel, as cutting route finds favour' was no exception. But we knew it was the work of Jon Valters, who had been with the paper for some years, and covered the 1985 Inquiry, the publicity surrounding our campaign for the reopening of the Inquiry and the reopened Inquiry itself in considerable depth. Jon Valters was very thorough and his reports always proved accurate. Indeed, the pages of *The Hampshire Chronicle* provide a remarkable record of the campaign for Twyford Down. *The Chronicle* report stated:

> The M3 Inquiry Inspector is backing the DoT's cutting route through Twyford Down and has rejected calls for a tunnel. His confidential report, which is not due to be made public until July, recommends that the government adopts the DoT's proposals, even though he accepts that the tunnel scheme is the most popular and the least damaging to the environment. In his report, details of which have been passed to *The Hampshire Chronicle*, Air Vice-Marshal Maughan...says he does not feel it is his duty to recommend a scheme that would cost the Government £80 million or more.

The cat was well and truly out of the bag. Once more it seemed as though all the rational effort had been for nothing. But no decision had been announced by Government. The rest of the local media went to town, besieging Government press offices. *The Southern Evening Echo* reported, 'The DoT today refused to comment on the leaked report. But a spokesman confirmed the Secretary of State was by no means obliged to take Inspectors' advice. He said the DoT's most recent motorway decision – on the M40 in the Midlands – was in defiance of an inquiry inspector's recommendation.'

Such comments were seized upon, and led us to redouble our efforts to make Twyford Down a national issue and shame the Government into saving the Down. It seemed incredible that a Conservative Government, so recently and magnificently 'greened' would want to be seen perpetrating environmental damage on such a scale, particularly if the Inspector had recognized the superiority of the tunnel solution but felt unable to recommend it on grounds of 'cost'.

The community of Winchester had, albeit belatedly, united to oppose the Cutting route. The scores of supporters who had contributed time and money to the campaign were not going to let go easily.

Alan Weeks, the then secretary of the M3 Joint Action Group commented, 'We feel this is a test case for the Government to see what their reaction will be because Winchester is unique.' As part of its fund-raising efforts the Action Group organized a public meeting in Winchester. Jonathon Porritt, director of Friends of the Earth, was the principal speaker. Merrick undertook the publicity for the event, and arranged the sale of the tickets. Some 600 people attended, packing the large hall, to hear Jonathon, as inspirational as ever, set Twyford Down firmly on the international environment agenda. The event proved a great success, both as regards press and television coverage, and financially.

Catching the mood of the time, *The Times* and the BBC PM programme ran an Environment Award. Nominations were invited for community projects which enhanced the environment. Dudley and Merrick nominated the campaign to save Twyford Down, but it was regarded as more of a political campaign than the type of practical project the judges envisaged. None the less, plenty of influential people had seen the nominations.

'£53 m Road Schemes Put Government's Green Policy On Test' read the headline on page 10 of *The Times* on 17 April 1989. Michael McCarthy had recently been made the paper's new environment correspondent. His finely tuned political antennae and instinct for a good story (in October 1991 McCarthy was to be given a national media award for his 'consistently keen political grasp of environmental matters and his news perception') picked up the potential conflicts between roads and the environment. On McCarthy's initial trawl through the various environmental lobby groups he had met with David Coleman, of the Countryside Commission. Coleman mentioned two road schemes which epitomized the damage roads could inflict on the environment – the A20 at Dover, and the M3 at Winchester. McCarthy's article started:

> The Government's green policy will be put to the test when road schemes affecting the White Cliffs of Dover and Winchester's last open hillside are decided. Both landscapes, celebrated, historic and beautiful, and designated in a variety of ways as of national importance are under threat. Decisions on their future are to be taken shortly by Mr Paul Channon, Secretary of State for Transport. Dover's cliffs, symbolizing for centuries England itself, face the prospect of a £24 million four-lane dual carriageway across their top, which the National Trust calls 'catastrophic'. Twyford Down...faces being sliced in two by the £29 million M3 extension...a development the Countryside Commission describes as 'devastating'. Both landscapes could be saved from serious damage if the Government were to discard the DoT proposed routes in favour of more expensive alternatives. Conservationists feel that the rapid rise of the environment as a voters' concern raises the political stakes involved in these two decisions.

This was precisely the type of coverage we hoped for, but appearing in *The Times* exceeded our wildest dreams. Winchester, whose population probably has a higher than average number of *Times* readers, began to hope again. Eight days later *The Daily Telegraph* carried a huge picture (Figure 7) of the proposed cutting through the Down with the headline 'Inquiry backs M-way through Bronze Age Village'. Charles Clover, the *Telegraph* environment correspondent, opened the piece, 'In what is likely to be one of the most controversial planning decisions of the decade, an inquiry inspector has recommended that permission be given to build an extension of the M3 through one of the most heavily protected landscapes in the country...and quoted Merrick, 'If this is confirmed by the Secretaries of State for Transport and the Environment, it will undermine the very fabric of [the UK's] conservation policy.' The article was completed with a picture (Figure 11), stretching across five columns, of the DoT photomontage of the M3 Joint Action Group tunnel as it emerged discreetly at the base of Twyford Down.

In the space of two weeks two major broadsheet newspapers had profiled the threat to Twyford Down, the *Telegraph* in spectacularly visual fashion. After four years the campaign to save Twyford Down had finally achieved national prominence.

The Twyford Down story had caught the imagination of not one, but two top national newspaper journalists. For the next three years Twyford Down was to retain the interest of these two men. Other papers, and the media, picked up the stories, but these two journalists led the pack – feeding off each other, yet competing to stay one step ahead of the other. A little like selling a house – what you really want is two keen buyers, pushing each other along – Twyford Down had managed to attract the interest of two top national journalists.

Nationally, the dramatic increase in the 'green' vote in the Euro-elections in June 1989, the publication of the revised National Traffic Vehicles Forecast, showing an acceleration in traffic growth, and the consequential anticipated demand for more roads provided the ideal context in which to set the M3 conundrum. There was widespread concern over the volume of traffic on our roads. Concern over the lengthening queues of cars, even on some of the newly completed motorways began to reach MPs' mail bags. The road lobby expressed continued concern at the length of time the DoT took to build new roads. At the same time environmental awareness reached an all time high in July 1989 when the MORI poll 'Most Plus Other Important Issues – Trends' survey recorded a staggering (in those comparatively early days of environmental awareness) figure of 35 per cent of the population rating environment as an important issue.

No one, certainly not the Transport Department, continued the pretence of denying that the Inspector's Inquiry report was with the DoT and by the early summer of 1989 we had learnt more about the contents of that report. Merrick had also heard disquieting rumours that the DoT intended to press ahead with the Cutting route.

After the Inquiry report was leaked to *The Hampshire Chronicle* earlier in the year Merrick had been told that Special Branch had been called in – though by whom I do not know – to track down the source of the leak. Bearing in mind the wide range of possible outlets for the information (such as the Inspectors' offices in Bristol, the regional office of the Transport

Department at Dorking, the DoT in Marsham Street, and the consulting engineers) this seemed something of an over-reaction – the more so in the context of the recommendations of the Franks Committee that Inquiry reports should be made available to all parties. None the less, apparently it happened, and apparently staff were moved out of various buildings in an effort to control or maybe identify the source of these breaches in security.

By midsummer, while we were awaiting a formal announcement of Government's decision, Merrick became convinced that his telephone was being tapped. I am afraid I didn't take the security angle very seriously. One June evening he called round to see me. I was distinctly sceptical about the involvement of the security services, but, in the best James Bond tradition, we went into the garden to talk. At the bottom of the garden, a safe distance away from listening devices he told me in the deepest confidence what he had heard: the Transport Department was commissioning a report for the Minister on the practicality of widening the M3 at Winchester to four lanes in each direction. This was one of a number of feasibility studies into motorway widening nationwide.

As part of the study looking at the feasibility of widening the M3 to four lanes, Kelsey Associates, the landscape consultants, had been asked to look at the environmental implications for the M3 around Winchester. During the Inquiries there had been internal discussion within the landscape profession, and its professional organization, the Landscape Institute, on the ethics and wisdom of the Institute involving itself in the M3 debate.

Some members of the profession were critical of Kelsey Associates for accepting the 'cosmetic' commission of producing landscape plans for the DoT's devastating route. But apparently for John Kelsey, the principal of Kelsey Associates, the four-lane study at M3 was nearly the final straw.

Kelsey's covering letter, enclosing his report on the M3 Widening Study stated, 'We feel bound to express disquiet that the landscape proposals presented to the Inspector and the public at large at the last two inquiries are inevitably going to be diminished, and made less robust and, in places, seen to be compromised as a result of highway widening. If a four-lane highway is felt by the DoT at this time to be a real future necessity we believe the whole matter should go back to public debate.'

Hardly a display of resounding confidence in the integritiy of the DoT proposals, Kelsey's letter was received by the consulting engineers on 14 July 1989.

We were deeply concerned, yet, at that time, in the summer of 1989, we had no proof of what was happening. We also feared an eight-lane tunnel would be technically difficult and prohibitively expensive and that this would be used to dissuade ministers from choosing the tunnel alternative for the M3 at Winchester.

As Merrick says now, 'The studies were commissioned and received by the DoT in secret, after the Inquiry report had been received, but before the final decision on the DoT route had been announced. This would not have been so important had the study been a straightforward audit of the DoT's proposed route, but the studies were not confined to the Cutting route. They looked at the implications of four lanes in a tunnel, and on the bypass. We have to assume these studies were important; why else would they have been done, and why wait for the outcome before making the decision on the route? If the studies were important then why were they not open for public debate, because they were clearly going to influence the decision. Our point is a simple one: either the Government confines all debate on technical issues to the Public Inquiry system, or it doesn't. If Government wishes to retain the freedom of taking new evidence any time it wishes, then it must abandon the pretence of the Public Inquiry system.' In July 1989 we were not able to go public on the story about the four-lane study since at that time we had no proof.

Soon, I was forced, however, to take Merrick's concerns about telephone tapping and surveillance a good deal more seriously. A friend, ringing from abroad to ask me to water her tomatoes, later commented that what she'd heard on the phone suggested to her that my phone was clearly being tapped. She'd had experience working with the security services and is a level-headed lady not given to dramatics. Then one day I received, in my view, proof positive. I'd been talking on the telephone late in the afternoon. Knowing I had to make one more call before an office closed I rang off, glanced at my watch – 5.25 pm – and thought I'd just get through before closing time. I picked up the receiver to dial the number to find the line quite dead. Thinking it had simply not cleared from the previous call I tried again – still dead. I tried again. Still dead. By then I was slightly desperate and muttering to myself went to check the other extensions to the phone.

The telephone rang – that's cleared it, I thought as I picked it up, to hear, 'Good afternoon, this is the telephone engineers. You have just reported a fault – no dialing tone on your line. It seems to be all right now.' I was nonplussed. I had not reported the fault – I couldn't. No-one else knew there was a problem, which anyway had only lasted a few minutes. From that time on the family accepted that our phone was tapped, and occasionally younger members of the family had some fun. I tried to ignore it, and hoped that our domestic trivia proved suitably boring to those who had the misfortune of monitoring our calls.

I have no idea of course who was listening in. It's easy to make the obvious assumption that it was one of the security services, but there may have been others. I wondered if I was becoming paranoid, whether I was over-reacting. But the incident caused me to recall, however, that, quite separately, three people in responsible positions had told me that the national security forces were opposed to a tunnel because of its vulnerability to sabotage. Clearly, the M3 was a strategic route to the south coast, so that may have been the case. If so, bizarre as it may seem, security concerns may have figured in the ministerial, or at least Departmental reasoning. Indeed, it may have influenced others' judgements – there are many military bases and defence establishments in the area.

Merrick and I however were by then operating on two levels – privately we had good reason to believe that the ministerial decision would favour the cutting. The public expectation was very different.

Some members of the Winchester Conservative Association were making pleas to the Prime Minister, Margaret Thatcher, 'As a party we have clearly taken a strategic decision to focus more on environmental issues. A consistent implementation of this is critical to the party's credibility' wrote the chairman of one local committee.

Sir Peter Ramsbotham, sometime ambassador to the United States, wrote to Prime Minister Thatcher on behalf of six of Winchester's great and good, including the Mayor and the Dean of Winchester Cathedral. Sir Peter's letter closed 'For twenty years successive governments have sanctioned piecemeal construction of the London to Southampton motorway, leaving Winchester's landscape caught betwen two fixed points on the roadmakers' map. Such a lack of strategic planning by the DoT has brought us to the present impasse – money versus the environment and the will of the people.' The Winchester establishment was finally nailing its colours to the mast – a pity it was so late in the day.

'Money versus the environment' was discussed in Professor David Pearce's book, *Blue Print for a Green Economy*, published in August 1989. The local press latched on to the story and ran a double-page spread on Twyford Down and the possible effect that a 'monetary' value on the environment could have had on the economic justification for the tunnel. It seemed to me that, since Twyford Down might have been developed by a private company for housing were it not for the protective designations (Area of Outstanding Natural Beauty, Scheduled Ancient Monuments and Sites of Special Scientific Interest) that protected Twyford Down, it was reasonable to promulgate the theory that the Down was worth roughly what the housing development would have produced. Commenting on my theory, David Pearce agreed that would be one technique for valuing the environment. Richard Parker, the consulting engineer, subsequently produced a COBA valuation of the JAG tunnel scheme incorporating residential values for the land; while the tunnel produced only a marginally negative result, the DoT Cutting scheme, using our revised criteria, came out massively 'negative' – that is, very poor value for money – and its construction would never have been authorized by the Treasury.

In November 1989 John Browne, the MP for Winchester, used Prime Minister's Question Time in the House of Commons to tackle Margaret Thatcher about the M3 route, 'Will she [the PM] assure the House that the Secretary of State for Transport will speedily be given sufficient funds to ensure that whatever route is finally selected, it will be friendly to the special and historic environment around Winchester, which is a national asset?' The Prime Minister replied 'The Secretaries of State for Transport and Environment are currently considering the Inspectors' Reports. I cannot anticipate what their decisions will be, but I know they fully understand the importance of environmental issues in cases such as this.'

We thought 1989 looked set to close with everything to play for politically. Then, a couple of weeks before Christmas, *The*

Times got wind of the secret Four Lane Study. Describing the secret
study as 'likely to reopen the 18-year battle over the motorway's
route in explosive fashion' the article went on, 'The affair presents
in an acute form the hard choice the Government will increasingly
have to make between economic growth and environmental protection, and is likely to set Cecil Parksinon's Transport Department
on collision course with Chris Patten's Environment Department.'
The article laid bare the political dilemma and the basic conflict
epitomized by the M3 at Winchester. There was therefore a very
real dilemma facing the Transport Minister, Cecil Parkinson and
the Government by the end of 1989.

Most people probably assume that Winchester is a true blue
Conservative seat, and that its member of parliament would
have carried considerable influence with the Conservative
Government. Sadly, this was not the case in the late 1980s. John
Browne, the member of parliament, had been the centre of most
unfortunate publicity. A very messy court case surrounding the
financial settlement which followed his divorce, coupled with
considerable unrest within the local constituency led the local
Conservative Association to go through a selection process for a
parliamentary candidate and in due course to choose a new candidate, Gerald Malone, to fight the next election whenever that
might be held. For some time we had an embattled member of
parliament whose energies were divided between representing
his constituents and defending his own personal corner. Even
though the local Conservatives had decided to have a different
candidate (who was almost certain to succeed as the next MP for
Winchester in due course), conventional and constitutional
courtesies still required that all communications to ministers had
to be via the sitting MP – yet the rumours and publicity were
such that, notwithstanding Mr Browne's work as a constituency
MP, there was decreasing public confidence in Mr Browne's
credibility as Winchester's member of parliament, and particularly in his influence at Secretary of State or ministerial level.

Increasingly concerned by the rumours emerging from the
DoT, which suggested a decision would be made in favour of
the Cutting route, I was anxious to be sure that ministers, of a
Government which in principle I supported, really knew what
they were about to decide, and also knew that there were alternative ways to complete the M3 motorway.

In an attempt to penetrate the inner circle of Government, I discussed our problems with John Hanvey, chairman of Harris Research Centre, who oversaw our M3 public opinion poll in 1987. For nearly twenty years, John was the Tory party's adviser on opinion research and undertook the party's private opinion polling. A life-long conservative he never sought a parliamentary career for himself, believing that using his considerable professional and intellectual talents to advise the party and a succession of Prime Ministers provided a real opportunity to influence events, opportunities denied to most MPs and even ministers. Modest and discreet, he was privy to many political confidences, working closely with the hierarchy of the Tory Party. He had a wicked sense of humour, and was always entertaining company. It may be a relief to many in public life to know that shortly before he died one of my sons asked, after hearing one of John's more outrageous anecdotes, if he kept a diary. Straight-faced John replied, 'No, I wouldn't do that. I just spread gossip.' But he was discreet about what he said, and it was never ill-humoured.

After our talk, John disappeared behind the scenes to talk to his 'contacts' . In due course he came back with fairly depressing news. John convinced me that the DoT's preference for the Cutting route would be given the go-ahead. Chris Patten (Secretary of State for the Environment) had his attention focused upon other policy issues pressing upon him at that time, most especially the catastrophic muddle the Government had created for itself with proposals to reform domestic rating and the introducion of the 'poll' tax, and Patten's battle to get his White Paper on the environment approved by the Cabinet.

John Hanvey felt that at least some at the top of the Conservative party were concerned at the political cost of pressing ahead with the Cutting route, but the attention and energy being taken up by the poll tax and the environment White Paper meant that the arguments put forward by supporters of the Cutting route were not being challenged as in other circumstances they would have been.

By the end of 1989 the 'green' lobby had vastly increased its potential political clout, but it needed far more power if it was to become a major political force. Green groups often had conflicting objectives or remits – for instance the National Trust, described by *The Guardian* as 'the sleeping giant of the Green movement', attracted criticism from other 'green' groups for allowing fox-hunting on its land.

9

1990 Challenging the Government's decision

Cecil Parkinson, still Transport Secretary, celebrated the new decade with a long awaited report, 'Trunk Roads – England into the 1990s'. The report, published in February 1990, included details of more than 500 road schemes but with a package of initiatives to reduce noise levels and improve road landscaping, which prompted Labour's transport spokesman at the time, John Prescott, to describe the 'greening' of the roads programme as 'a political sham'. It also led *The Sunday Telegraph* to carry an article, 'Parkinson puts cars before green vote' and to a good deal of speculation in the press about the differences of opinion between the DoT and the DoE.

The Trunk Roads report carried a coded pre-announcement that the M3 Cutting route would be approved – estimating the cost of the Bar End to Compton section as £36 m. 'Tunnel dead and buried by DoT budget clue' read the headline in that week's local *Hampshire Chronicle*.

Merrick had been warned that the formal announcement of the decision was imminent. Apparently documents supporting the decision in favour of the Cutting were being prepared: photomontages showing a grassed-over Winchester bypass bold in the foreground, with the motorway snaking away high over the railway line at Shawford distinctly less obvious; a drawing which showed the full extent of the Scheduled Ancient Monument boundaries and the impact of the Cutting route – during the preceding five years the DoT had never produced (or at least published) this particular document; and a drawing that superimposed a cross-section of the smaller Channel Tunnel over our Twyford Down tunnel – implying, or at least inviting the inference that the Twyford Down tunnel wasn't just 'at the forefront of tunnelling technology' but was beyond anything previously undertaken. A formal ministerial announcement was obviously immiment and late on the night of Monday 26 February I was told it would be made the next day. There was a mad panic.

Over the next two or three years those of us at the head of the campaign developed a close working relationship with the press. We provided good footage (all for free) but without the media coverage we would not have had a campaign. A local BBC cameraman was heard to remark that we must have kept at least one of them in a job for three years! This close contact taught us a good deal about media management. I also learnt very quickly that those reporters who were any good at their job had a remarkable ability to sort the wheat from the chaff of information and stories.

That February evening I shared our plans to demonstrate in Winchester the next day with my particular press mentor. It was firmly pointed out to me that an assembled mass of slightly bored press would have been summoned to the DoT press conference in London. My mentor said, 'You must make your own decisions, but the press won't all jump on a train to Winchester.' Then I telephoned David Croker, and we decided to relocate our protest in London. We rang round and managed to muster a dozen hardy souls, including the two Parish Council chairmen, to make the trip to London the next day. One or two undertook to make banners overnight.

The next day, Tuesday, 27 February 1990, Winchester's MP asked a 'planted' question in the House of Commons; Cecil Parkinson and Chris Patten appeared at the DoT press conference held in the DoT's London headquarters, at Marsham Street. A grotesque 1960s building it is shared by the Department of the Environment (causing one Secretary of State for the Environment to say his office had the best view in London – because he couldn't see Marsham Street!) We stationed ourselves outside the entrance in the concrete wind-tunnel created by the buildings, and assumed that the press were cosily inside.

It was very cold, made worse by our own anger and tension. Eventually the press emerged from the press conference inside the building, giving us the bare bones of the decision and in the same breath asking for our reactions. It was our first experience of dealing with the massed media. Although David and I were to become the principal spokesmen for the campaign there were always others on hand, particularly the Parish Council chairmen, George Beckett and Chris Corcoran. We frequently discussed the emphasis we wished to put on developments, but never operated a system of rigid, pre-agreed statements. Despite the obvious dangers in such an undisciplined approach it seemed to work, with each of us coming at the arguments from our own special perspective.

In the biting cold we attempted to pump into the press the facts about the Cutting route, the intrusion of the motorway crossing over the top of the railway line as it went through the village of Shawford, and the damage the decision would inflict on the Government's green credentials.

David Croker was quoted at length in *The Times*: 'We shall be taking legal advice and while it is regrettable that the action will result in further delays, the issue is of such overwhelming importance in the process of decision-making, as well as environmental protection, that a long legal battle is now inevitable.' Despite the cold David had managed to say it all.

I remember being pressed by the BBC on how far we would take the fight, and saying through chattering teeth, 'Until we win.' When I got home the family, who had seen the broadcast, quizzed me about that. We'd really very little idea about a legal challenge, with its financial implications and we'd certainly not seriously discussed the practicalities. Although we thought we knew what the decision was going to be we had no proof, and until we had the text of it before us no one could make any judgements as to the viability of a legal challenge. Merrick was away in Switzerland at the time of the announcement but now says, 'Although we'd been well informed, I don't think we were prepared. Somehow I always believed we would prevent the final act. When the decision was made it just did not seem possible that we had failed to stop the decision.'

One way or another the message we all tried to send that February afternoon in London got across – the national papers exploded in condemnation. 'Downland M-way decision provokes uproar' read The *Guardian* headline. 'Motorway to split protected countryside' read *The Daily Telegraph* under the infamous picture of the proposed Cutting, alongside the DoT's picture of the restored bypass with its Letraset daisies. Somewhat disingenuously the DoT route had been subtitled 'Restoration of the Countryside Link' in the press package.

'Motorway Madness' read the first leader in *The Times*, 'Cecil Parkinson...has made the wrong decision over the M3 extension round Winchester...[it]...is as extreme and irreversible an act of environmental spoiling as can be imagined. The conclusion must be that the Government's stated commitment to the preservation of the natural environment can in principle always be over-trumped by the need for an improved transport infrastructure and considerations of finance. The economy, and not the environment, is the greater imperative...The Twyford Down campaigners were riffling through the adjectives of outrage yesterday to condemn Mr Parkinson's decision, but the most damning thing to be said about it is that it is thoroughly dated. It is not the sort of decision secretaries of state should even be considering in 1990...' (*The Times* 28.2.90).

The law allowed a six-week period within which to seek judicial review of the decision. Not a long time when you consider the daunting list of tasks facing us:

1   The several hundred pages that made up the Ministerial announcement and the Inquiry Inspectors' reports had to be assimilated and a judgement made as to whether those documents provided grounds for a legal challenge to the decision. We then needed informed legal opinion on the basis of our lay interpretation of the issues.

2   Supporters of the campaign, local groups, and in particular the Parish Councils needed to be told about the issues and any possible action.

3   If there appeared to be reasonable grounds to challenge the decision in the courts we would have to decide in whose name that challenge be issued.

4   Dominant over all was the question of money. How much would the initial advice cost us, how much would a full challenge cost, how could it be paid for?

There was enormous enthusiasm in Winchester, and especially in the villages of Compton and Twyford, to pursue any legal move that could still, however belatedly, stop the DoT building the Cutting route. We identified a range of possible grounds for challenge – especially the unpublished feasibility study looking at the possibilities of making the M3 into four, rather than three, lanes, on the route through or beneath Twyford Down. In time legal advice whittled the potential grounds for challenge down to that issue, on which the UK lawyers remained keen, and to the possibility of challenging the Government on its failure to implement in UK law the European Commission Directive requiring Environmental Impact Assessments for major construction projects.

After exploratory talks with lawyers the full implications of a legal challenge gradually sank in. We were told the costs would be extremely high – maybe £50 000. An application for judicial review would have to be brought by one or more individuals, or possibly the Parish Councils. Since the Joint Action Group had no legal status it could not apply for judicial review. If three or four of us took the action we would be jointly and severally liable – that is, any one of us could theoretically be landed with the whole cost.

After many soul-searching hours and discussing every conceivable angle a consensus developed that the best combination to formally challenge the decision would be the two Parish Councils, with David Croker, Merrick and myself. That was the easy bit. There were obvious financial implications for us as individuals, and for our families' assets. The Parish Councils had different problems, but none the less severe. *The Times* was to describe our challenge as 'an act of faith' and I suppose it was – by us, and by our families. There was so little time in which to make a decision that inevitably we took a chance on coming out of it all with our families, our homes and ourselves more or less intact.

Chris Corcoran and George Beckett, the two Parish Council chairmen, David, Merrick and myself met at 6 pm every Friday evening throughout the six months leading up to the hearing. We called ourselves the M3Five (with apologies to Enid Blyton). We normally met at home, and only on the rarest of occasions was the meeting allowed to go on beyond 7 pm. We always had coffee, sometimes cake if the kids had left any, and when we were down, or if we had something special to celebrate, a glass of wine. The meetings were absolutely confidential. Alan

Weeks, who'd been secretary of the Joint Action Group in 1976
and again in 1987 came to our meetings to take the minutes,
unless told to put his pen down! The next week Alan brought
the minutes to the meeting, where they were quickly read,
handed back to him and destroyed.

The Joint Action Group (JAG) had exhausted its resources in
meeting the costs of the presentations at the Inquiry. None of
the members wanted to stand by and watch the Government
destroy Winchester's heritage, but nor did they have the sta-
mina or will to embark on an unknown and obviously risky
venture. For the present, the JAG continued to meet. It offered
support to those of us about to embark on the legal challenge,
and members of the Group were always on hand to help with
the multitude of ancillary tasks and research with which we
needed help. What it could not offer was finance.

It was Merrick who had the brainwave which was to lead to
the formation of the Twyford Down Association. He realized
that we had to harness the potential national implications of the
M3 route if we were to extend our power-base and fund-raising
potential. His philosophy was centred on the premise that the
heritage designations, such as Sites of Special Scientific Interest,
and the Scheduled Ancient Monuments which supposedly protected Twyford Down were part of the United Kingdom's conservation and landscape protection legislation. If these national
protective designations were so spectacularly ignored at
Twyford Down, what chance had people elsewhere in the UK
of securing protection for their areas?

Merrick suggested a Twyford Down Association, which
could, and he hoped would, attract support from all over the
UK. Clearly, the Association's first task would have to be the
defeat of the DoT Cutting route, but after that the Association's
continuing activities would be positive – a management plan, a
heritage site, partial reconstruction of part of the Iron Age
Village perhaps.

There were obvious problems in setting up yet another organization, but the benefits far outweighed any initial misgivings.
Under the presidency of Professor Martin Biddle, the Twyford
Down Association went on to attract wide support, both locally
and nationally. Three supporters in the public eye, Miriam
Rothschild, Fellow of the Royal Society and wild-flower garden-
ing expert, Jonathon Porritt, the environmentalist, and Maldwin

Drummond, a deputy lieutenant of Hampshire and Countryside Commissioner, brought substance and credibility when they agreed to become vice-presidents of the new Association.

As soon as the concept of the Association and its objectives had been agreed by the principal people, Merrick produced a promotional leaflet. The finished product was professional and produced to a very high standard. We did not skimp on the printing costs and it showed. We needed to show we meant business and the leaflet projected that message.

In full colour, the leaflet's cover showed an evocative photograph of Twyford Down set on a matt black ground; the only text on the front was the Association's objective, 'To secure, in perpetuity, the conservation of Twyford Down for the enjoyment and education of future generations.' Inside, the leaflet set out the strategy for achieving the objective – to raise financial resources to support the legal challenge, assist in securing an environmentally sensitive route for the M3 and extend the boundaries of the protected areas of St Catherine's Hill and Twyford Down. The centre pages of the leaflet explained the history of the Down and described its landscape, nature conservation and historic protection measures covering the Down. The back page of the leaflet carried the infamous picture of the Cutting, and invited contributions to the Association.

The problem of financing a legal challenge was both enormous and immediate. We had to submit the initial application for judicial review within six weeks of the decision at the end of February 1990. We needed money, or at least promises of it, urgently. The first two or three months were a considerable act of faith by all parties to the legal action, including the solicitors, Hammond Suddards from Leeds. None the less we decided to go ahead with the challenge because it seemed that there was no other way to save Twyford Down.

Merrick put forward a deceptively simple fund-raising proposal which had two key activities: a direct mail campaign and a series of lectures, using his slide presentation. The novel element in the fund-raising campaign was the use of a Standing Order Mandate to provide a mechanism to raise substantial resources as painlessly as possible. Merrick assumed that the process in the courts would take a year, and that we would probably be given eighteen months to pay off any resulting costs. We settled on a fixed term for standing order mandates of 30 months. We needed 600 people to sign a monthly order for £5 over the 30 months to raise £90 000. It sounded simple, and like most great ideas it was. We anticipated there would be some shortfall if the standing orders were stopped before the full 30 months, for whatever reason, but cash one-off donations given would offset some of those losses.

Merrick launched the first of the direct mail shots by writing to all 2500 members of his professional body, the Landscape Institute. We knew they would understand the issues, but could not judge the response. In fact it was nothing less than fantastic: £35 000 was pledged within the first few weeks. Merrick says he will never ever forget the response from his colleagues – people from all over the country who presumably had never seen Twyford Down contributed handsomely. Local people in Winchester contributed privately to the appeal. Many of our staunchest supporters over the years were local government officers, politicians and civil servants who did so privately and must remain anonymous, but their support sustained us through many difficult times – thus their contributions are inadequately acknowledged.

One day we received a hugely generous personal gift in a five-figure sum and the next meeting of the M3 Five cracked a bottle to celebrate. Yet of the hundreds of letters, donations and offers of help the most memorable to me remains the one which dropped through our letterbox one day – a simple, anonymous card, depicting rolling downland with two one pound coins sellotaped inside. The message explained that the gift was all the unemployed donor could afford, and he did not want to give his name so as not to put us to the trouble of thanking him for such an insignificant contribution to our efforts. Such gestures kept us going through some of the more difficult times we faced over the months ahead.

Merrick then launched into an intensive series of lectures. These lectures were made at the homes of sympathetic people who perhaps hosted a cheese and wine party for their friends. Merrick says these presentations were designed to inform rather than raise funds, though this aspect was invariably covered towards the end of the evening. Some £20 000 was raised from these 'events'.

Sometimes there were unexpected spin-offs from Merrick's lectures, most notably when he addressed the Green Society of Winchester College. Famous for producing leaders in all fields of our national life over the centuries, many College pupils are confident and able. The Green Society definitely didn't like what was being threatened for the Down. Its chairman at the time, Dominic Holdsworth, a senior pupil, was galvanized into all sorts of activities in support of the Down.

Dominic lent Merrick the book of old boys' addresses. A member of the Action Group used a computer programme to read the tiny, and tightly bound book, and produce addressed labels. The old boys of Winchester College (known as Wykehamists – after William of Wykeham, the bishop who founded Winchester College in the fourteenth century) all received a letter, written jointly by two of their peers, Tony Paterson and Dominic Holdsworth. The response from the Wykehamists was tremendous. They contributed about £25 000, but they also wrote letters – very erudite letters, from impressive addresses – to the DoT and to ministers – often on first-name terms.

Our activities, focused on constructing a realistic challenge in the High Court, and raising the money to finance the case, began to take some short of shape. Hammond Suddards, our solicitors from Leeds, were putting together the formal papers. In our ignorance about the procedures we had not initially understood that the judicial review proceedings would be dealt with by **written** affidavits, submitted in advance, each side responding to the other until each party felt they had no further arguments to place before the court, and that at the hearing itself only the barristers representing the two sides would be involved. This came as something of a relief, though in the end I think we all found it extremely frustrating to have to sit on our hands in court while others spoke on our behalf.

Preparations for the case required vast amounts of time retrieving the source documents for much of what we were saying, briefing the solicitors, and in turn meeting with the barristers. Each time the sell-by date for submission of an affidavit approached the activity reached fever pitch. In those days the only member of the Group with a fax machine was Richard Parker. Reams and reams of messages, draft statements, corrected drafts, and copies of the DoT's own statements rolled out. We used to joke about wall-papering our downstairs loos with the old faxes, until someone pointed out they faded away in time.

The burden of stress and tension fell on our families. All five of us had 'daytime' jobs, we were all assisting Merrick in his herculean fund-raising efforts, Chris Corcoran and George Beckett as chairmen of the two Parish Councils had considerable responsibilities to those Councils, the legal paperwork had to be checked and agreed, offers of help had to be responded to, the press kept informed of events and many more tasks had to be done. It is surprising, perhaps, that we all remained friends! Mostly we kept our sense of humour and perspective, though I recall an occasion when there was a stupid muddle over a meeting with the solicitor. At the end of a long day all five of us went along to a Joint Action Group meeting to let them know how we were getting along. Someone made what I took to be a rather pointed comment about some practical arrangements which I'd failed to sort out properly and, I think for the only time, I lost my cool and threatened to walk out of the whole thing. In retrospect it was really very funny, though not at the time. I remember David Croker puffing furiously at his pipe, pacing round and round the table, and saying it was all awful, and Merrick, ever the diplomat, carrying on a conversation with someone else as though nothing was happening. When I got home Dudley, seeing my face, realized something was wrong and was instantly sympathetic – with the result I dissolved into uncontrollable tears. Jumping to the wrong conclusion, he asked if I had crashed the car; incapable of speech I shook my head and grew more hysterical, confirming his worst fears – 'Has anyone been hurt' he asked. By this time I could see the funny side and as the tears gushed forth, I gulped away in an effort to explain. Eventually I calmed down enought to tell him what had happened. I am sure all the others had moments of private crisis, though perhaps my response to the tension was typically female.

By midsummer the die was cast: a motion was filed in the Queen's Bench division of the High Court 'seeking to stop the routeing of the motorway through the Down' as the local paper described it. The fund-raising was progressing much better than we had dared to hope, giving us confidence that, given time, we would be able to pay our way.

There was a steady stream of publicity, including a rather splendidly titled article, 'Carved with a difference' in *The Countryman*. A throughly damning piece, it read 'When Parkinson bashes up a piece of countryside he sure gets value for money. But we must not blame Mr Parkinson alone.

Twyford Down has been trumpeted as a point decision for the two Ps – Parkinson plus Patten. Which is tragic, for it tolls the knell of Mr Patten's already tattered reputation as an environmentalist. When he came into his present office he was warmly welcomed as a green change from his predecessor; It turns out that, though he may be green at heart, he has not the guts to be green.'

The political dimension of Twyford Down was developing. At the end of June we received our first visit to the site by a leading national politician. Simon Hughes, the Liberal Democrat spokesman on the Environment, toured the route of the motorway, meeting local people (Figure 16). Apparently persuaded by what he had seen and heard, he made a lengthy statement to the press, supporting the legal challenge and promising to take the M3 issue into the European arena in Brussels. He concluded, 'Places like Winchester – and I come from a cathedral city – and the traditional values of a county like Hampshire stand as symbols that will be a great encouragement to people elsewhere.'

Twyford Down was rapidly becoming a symbol and we tried to capitalize on this. I don't think we ever imagined the High Court case would be influenced by the profile, but our fundraising was helped by the publicity and, although it was very unlikely that the Government would undergo some sort of Road to Damascus conversion, it remained a remote possibility that, for some reason or other as yet unforeseen, ministers could be persuaded of the advantages of altering the Parkinson decision. We had everything to play for, and nothing to lose, excepting possibly a lot of money and an ever increasing proportion of our lives.

The political silly season of August was drawing to an end, and the party conferences were about to get under way.

One of the longest established and most influential pressure groups within the Tory Party is the Bow Group. By good fortune the secretary of the Bow Group's Environment Committee at that time was Tony Paterson, one of the former pupils at Winchester College who had joined us in our campaign against the Cutting route. His family still lived near Winchester and he was an invaluable source of advice on how best to approach his fellow old boys of the College, and keen to bring about real changes in the Conservative Party's approach to 'green' issues. The Bow Group's Environment Committee was an influential ally.

Figure 16 National politician visits the site. Simon Hughes, Liberal Democrat spokesman on the environment, visits the proposed route. From left to right: George Beckett, chairman of Compton and Shawford Parish Council, Simon Hughes, MP, Tony Barron, Liberal Democrat candidate for Winchester (1992 General Election), Hampshire County Councillor Ann Bailey, David Croker and Janet Stobardt of Twyford Parish Council. *(Reproduced by kind permission of The Hampshire Chronicle.)*

David Croker had long been an active member of the Conservative Party, and an elected Conservative councillor for Winchester for more than ten years. He was a 'conviction' politician, inclined to offend his colleagues when he challenged conventional thinking, but deeply excited by the achievements of the Tory administration's early years in power after the 1979 election.

I had been on the periphery of national politics in London in the 1970s, and had been closely involved in Conservative politics in Islington, standing twice for election to the Greater London Council. Although I had never been active in the Winchester Conservative Association I had been a member of the constituency Conservative group while a Winchester City councillor.

Merrick was not an overtly political animal, and in any event his job as a senior employee of the County Council made involvement with any remotely party political activity absolutely out of the question. The two Parish Council chairmen, whatever their personal views, would quite properly not partake in party politicing – fortunately most Parish Councils have avoided party political groupings.

Thus it was David Croker and I who made the political running in the campaign. We decided to take the Twyford Down Debate right to the Conservative Party Conference in Bournemouth. We did not have access to the Conference Hall but planned to hold an evening fringe meeting at a nearby hotel. Our message was to be, 'We are Conservatives – we want Twyford Down to be a winner for our Government.'

Shortly before the conference I learned from the press that a ginger group, the Tory Green Initiative (TGI) had been formed and were planning a range of activities at the Conservative Conference. After a fairly long telephone conversation (the telephone was the campaign's lifeline, and the intensity of activity was reflected in some very high bills from BT, who were certainly beneficiaries of our activities) with the chairman of the new group, Nick Wood-Dowe, it seemed sensible to try to work with them, rather than hold competing events, so to speak. TGI had already arranged for a high profile debate on Roads and the Environment, with speakers from CPRE and Transport 2000, and Christopher Chope, the then Roads Minister. Nick suggested that the Twyford Down Association attend the TGI meeting, that David Croker make a programmed speech from the floor, and that our promotional material, which included the display-size versions of the principal slides from Merrick's presentation, be set up in the venue.

The night before the meeting I went down to Bournemouth to meet Nick Wood-Dowe and other members of his committee. I was saddened to hear that TGI had been put under quite a lot of pressure by some of the Conservative Party's administrators, and invited to remove the Twyford Down literature from their stall. I think that only served to stiffen their resolve, but they were anxious to assure themselves that we really were genuine Conservatives.

The next morning the BBC Today programme carried a large item on the news about how the Twyford Down issue was splitting the Tory Party during its conference week, and *The Times* carried a half-page article on our campaign and the forthcoming court case. It was an extremely well researched piece by Michael McCarthy, the environment correspondent, and covered all the essential information about our cause and the magnitude of the task before us. The large picture accompanying the article showed Merrick, David and myself, and a rather handsome cow, strolling through a field against a background of trees and the undisturbed Twyford Down rising up to the skyline (Figure 17). The article had obvious spin-offs, but unexpected ones, too. In particular it led, through a curious set of coincidences, to my being put in touch with the man who was to become one of our most useful contacts in Brussels, Niall O'Neill, who was working for JM Didier, a European consultancy.

That evening David and I, along with a handful of Winchester Conservatives, made our way to Bournemouth. Normally fringe meetings at Conference attract only moderate attendance. But we arrived to find a packed hall, TV and radio and the newspapers. Years later I met one of the 'political advisers' working for the Channel Tunnel. He had forsaken the hotel bars in favour of attending that TGI meeting because of its perceived relevance. The meeting itself was an interesting debate

Figure 17 Left to right: Merrick Denton-Thompson, Barbara Bryant and David Croker in front of the undisturbed Twyford Down and the old railway viaduct. *(Reproduced by kind permission of Times Newspapers.)*

with topical contributions. Christopher Chope was the last of the speakers. David Croker spoke shortly and well, hitting just the right notes of concern for the environment, and the Conservative Party's credibility. Unfortunately the busy schedule of Christopher Chope, the Roads Minister, only allowed him time to make his speech but not to stay for questions. Equally unfortunately for Mr Chope, the only issue the press seemed interested in discussing with him was Twyford Down. It probably was not the best way to go about making friends, but by that time I think David and I were inclinded to be a little selective as to which members of the Government we wanted as friends. We left Bournemouth late that night, aware that next morning we would be in the very different arena of the High Courts of Justice, accusing two Cabinent Ministers of making a decision unlawfully, and that we would be facing the full weight of the State, in the form of Queen's Counsel for the Government, junior barristers and the usual clutch of Treasury solicitors.

At 7 am the next morning, Wednesday 10 October, 1990, David, Merrick, and I met the two Parish Council chairmen, Chris Corcoran and George Beckett, on the platform at Winchester Railway Station to catch the early train to Waterloo. Our families and supporters were catching a later train in time to be in court for the opening of the proceedings.

In London it was a fine autumn morning and we walked across Waterloo Bridge, over the 'liquid history' that is the River Thames, on our journey to the Law Courts. That walk, and the coffee and croissants we consumed in a coffee shop on the way were the best part of the day.

We had arranged to be at the Law Courts in good time to meet the team representing us, solicitors, the QC David Mole, and his junior, Paul Lasock. Lasock had been brought in as the junior counsel to advise on the European aspects of our case.

Having navigated our way through the marbled maze of the High Court building to the courtroom allocated to our case and gone through the last minute details, we were shown where we could sit in the court, where the barristers would sit, where the other side would sit and where only the QCs could sit. It was a small court and was shortly to be crammed full – five of us, five of our lawyers, slightly more on the DoTs side, then our families, friends and supporters. A very large number of press, and rather a lot of other people then unknown to us, also attended.

After years of articulating our arguments against the Cutting scheme and what we saw as the DoT's cavalier approach to environmental information we had to sit silent, crammed like sardines on the court benches, while the barristers set out their case – precedent and case history seemingly everything. Even though we had known this would be the form it seemed a long way removed from the realities of the Down, and what had and hadn't happened during the various Inquiries. The judge, Mr Justice McCullough, seemed to have a fairly sound knowledge of Winchester's geography – apparently he had once been a circuit judge, sitting at the Crown Courts in Winchester.

The case had been expected to last for two days. It soon became obvious that this was optimistic, and the problems of continuing the hearing eventually led to the case running on till the following Monday.

It transpired that among the unknown crowd in the courtroom were representatives of other road campaign groups – notably from Oxleas Wood, where local people were opposing the East London River Crossing, and the M11. If nothing else, the High Court Challenge had physically brought us into contact with those other groups.

One of those present was Hugh Morgan-Thomas, representing the M11 group. A lawyer, and member of a local council in East London, he passed me a note – drawing attention to one of the finer details of the European Directive, and the somewhat muddled legal discussion taking place in front of us. At the next break we had a long chat, and I learned for the first time that the Oxleas Wood and the M11 campaigners had taken both those schemes to the European Commission on the grounds that the Directive on the need to carry out Environment Impact Assessments had not been complied with. Our case, of course, hung on whether the UK Government had properly transposed the Directive into national law, i.e. the Highways Act. Morgan-Thomas told me of the discussions they had had with Ludwig Kramer, the Head of DGll, the Legal Section in the Commission's Environment Department. His view was that the Commission were deeply concerned that the Highways Procedures in the UK might be contravening European legislation. Certainly the advice that we'd received from our own advisers on European law confirmed that view.

In Winchester we had already considered the possibility of a formal complaint to the Commission. Before the end of the High

Court hearing I think we had agreed that such a complaint should be made. It was a matter of tactics, though, exactly when and how to go about it.

Meanwhile, the formal hearing came to a close, with Mr Justice McCullough promising to produce his judgment as soon as possible – in ten days or so. It seemed an eternity and all we could do was to agree what action we would take, and prepare a press statement, for either of the possible outcomes – win or lose. As luck would have it, Mr Justice McCullough chose to give his judgment on 26 October – I had to leave the family on half-term holiday in France and come back overnight to be in court.

Reading his judgment, of some 20 pages, Mr Justice McCullough found against us on both of the grounds we had cited – the commissioning of the four-lane study, and the failure to comply with the European Environmental Directive – the court's sole function he said was to decide whether the Secretaries of State had misunderstood or misapplied the law in approving the Cutting scheme.

An important judgment in legal terms, and critical for the future of Twyford Down, it was nonetheless rather sickeningly undramatic. I think David and I had feared the worst – I am not quite sure why. Merrick and George Beckett were really shattered; I could literally feel George's anger boiling up, but Merrick was deeply disillusioned. His faith in British justice had taken a fearful blow.

Apart from losing the case we had costs awarded against us. Mr Justice McCullough offered the usual four weeks for an appeal but the DoT argued for two weeks only on grounds of urgency – or perhaps merely as a tactic to crush any possibility of our deciding to lodge an appeal. Eventually, after some discussion between the judge and Paul Lasock, the only barrister present to represent us, we were allowed 21 days in which to lodge an appeal – and that only after George Beckett had pulled poor Paul Lasock's coat tail to point out that the Parish Councils had to give several days' notice of any meeting, making the suggested 14-day period quite unreasonably short.

Our carefully prepared statements firmly fixed in our minds, we faced the media outside the Courts. So too, did John Browne, Winchester's MP, who had come along.

Nothing makes quite such good news as bad news – national TV and radio, Sky TV, and all the daily papers reported our defeat. David Croker was widely quoted: 'Anyone who wants to see how little regard for the environment this Government has can look here. These proposals are horrifying.' I remember Nicholas Watt, who was newish on *The Times* I think, steering me away from one of our opponents, the sight of whom was definitely interfering with my concentration, in an effort to get some lucid quotes from me – he seems to have managed, though I think the pent-up anger of sitting silent for the previous three hours showed through, 'We will pursue every avenue that is open to us to ensure that this environmental vandalism and bureaucratic corruption is stopped.' The options I floated included appealing to the Prime Minister's environmental conscience, an appeal through the Courts to the House of Lords, or taking the case to the European Commission.

So far as the first option was concerned, and however unlikely it may have appeared, the Prime Minister, Margaret Thatcher, was in fact already fatally wounded. A ballot for the leadership of the Tory party was to be held and the men were out buying their grey suits. Just over a week later *The Times* in its leader, 'Twyford Down But Not Out' (Figure 13) was also to appeal to her to intervene on behalf of Twyford Down, but only three weeks later she lost in the first ballot in the leadership election, and decided to withdraw.

Mr Justice McCullough's judgment was delivered on 27 October 1990: we had just 21 days to consider and action our next move. The decision on whether all or any of us should appeal against the judgment depended, first, on advice from the lawyers as to whether such action would be worth while, in legal terms, and, second, on an estimate of the financial cost. Our solicitors arranged to take counsel's opinion, but in the meantime all five of us met. Chris Corcoran and George Beckett were sure that, however reluctantly, their parish councils would vote against pursuing the action in the Courts. The financial stakes would be too great. The Parish Councils had arranged to hold meetings in the next week, but they both anticipated there would be no question of either Parish Council appealing. We all understood this, and had anticipated it. We became more convinced that the best way forward would be via a complaint to the European Commission.

The remaining three of us, David, Merrick and myself, were left in the unenviable position of knowing that if we did not appeal the Cutting route would almost certainly go ahead, but the legal advice was not optimistic about the success of any appeal, and the costs could be enormous. The fund-raising projects had been very successful, but much of the money raised would only come to us over the next two and a half years. We had not yet raised enough to pay our own costs, still less those of the Department. It seemed very unlikely that we could raise the additional funds necessary to sustain an appeal. And this would certainly be impossible in the next two weeks.

Merrick was deeply unhappy. Perhaps he realized more clearly than I that the moment the deadline for appeal had passed the DoT would initiate the preliminary work for the project, starting with the archaeology survey. However, all the legal advice we were able to obtain advised of the difficulties of any appeal. One by one we all came to the conclusion that the risks and disadvantages of appealing were formidable and were too great to justify such a stupendous commitment – not just from ourselves, but from our families.

For as long as possible we kept our decision private, parried questions from the press, and left the DoT to sweat on it. Within a day or so of the deadline for the appeal passing, the topsoil from part of Twyford Down had been skimmed off in preparation for the preliminary archaeological survey. The very visible scar on the face of the Down prompted many comments in and around Winchester; people thought that the work had started on building the motorway and already commented on the dreadful appearance of the landscape.

The principle of lodging a complaint with the European Commission, on the grounds that the UK Government had failed to implement the European Directive on Environmental Impact Assessments No. 85/337, had been agreed among the M3Five during the lull between the end of the High Court hearing and judgment being given in October 1990. Our solicitors, Hammond Suddards, had recently opened an office in Brussels in the skilled hands of Peter Kunzlik. We had first met Peter during the earlier preparations for the High Court hearing when he had advised on the European law. Peter held the view that there were issues at stake in M3 which would be of interest to the Commission, and that a complaint to the EEC would be a thoroughly worthwhile exercise. He gave us an estimate of the very modest costs involved if he were to be instructed by us to prepare a complaint. It was agreed that the complaint should be made in the names of the three individuals, David, Merrick and me, and that it was sensible to have the papers professionally prepared.

Theoretically any citizen of the EU may lodge a complaint with the Commission – handwritten on the back of an envelope, so to speak. In practice, though, it is obvious that the matters at issue will be better, and more quickly digested by Commission officials if presented in an ordered form, referring specifically to those issues relevant to the Commission's responsibilities.

We had heard of the problems being experienced by the M11 and Oxleas Wood campaigners in progressing their complaints with the Commission. A few days earlier one of our guardian angels had given me the direct line telephone number of Judge Ludwig Kramer, the German lawyer responsible for the Commission's environmental legislation. Early one morning I dialled the number, and luckily Judge Kramer answered the phone himself. I explained briefly who I was, and that David Croker and I would very much like to meet his officials to discuss our proposed complaint to the Commission. By then he must have heard about the McCullough judgment so widely reported in the press, and he immediately offered an appointment for a few days hence. And so it was that within days of receiving the UK court's judgment against us, David Croker and I were on our way to Brussels.

When we arrived at Kramer's office he greeted us with typical European courtesy – warmer and less formal than British courtesy, I think. He introduced us to the three members of his staff who were present, and then invited us to explain what had brought us to see him. The courtesy may have been warm and informal but the mind was razor sharp, and launching into our story David and I felt distinctly ill-equipped to make the best of what would presumably be at most a half-hour interview. Engineers have a reputation for resorting to plans when words fail them; I'd obviously learnt something from the many hours spent at Public Inquiries and I pulled out the DoT 1983 consultation document – with one Scheduled Ancient Monument omitted, and the other one shown incorrectly by an asterisk at a point just avoided by the motorway. The essential points of our case were easy to put over after that, and we soon came to the McCullough judgment.

One copy of the judgment had been passed to us in court for our own use only. The approved, typed version which could be photocopied and passed to other people had still not been received. Nonetheless, David and I were able to give a fair idea of what was in the judgment. Kramer was obviously keen to see the judgment, but as the copy we had with us was unauthorized, and for our personal use only, Judge Kramer felt bound by the legal conventions which required that he awaited the production of an authorized version, and we promised to send him a copy as soon as we received a copy which we were technically permitted to reproduce.

During our meeting with Kramer, it became clear that the Commission lawyers were having great difficulty in establishing when 'planning consent' is formally granted for a motorway under UK Highway Law, and its legal derivation. Back home we raised this with various officials and professionally qualified people involved in highway procedures. Apparently there was no easy answer and it seems almost as if it was taken on trust that it was when the Minister made a formal announcement. Dudley undertook to research the complex subject and within two weeks had emerged from mounds of documents with a step-by-step analysis through the various Highway Acts, Statutory Instruments and Crown Development procedures that gave rise to planning consent, and these we forwarded on to the Commission. By all accounts this issue had proved a time-consuming and frustrating hurdle to the lawyers attempting to make sense of the complaints from a variety of sources in the UK, and the UK Government's responses. Since so many people in the Member States seemed to have had the same difficulty it is perhaps hardly surprising that one over-worked lawyer in Brussels was perplexed. It certainly highlights one of the myths surrounding the Commission, because at that time Judge Kramer had a merely handful of staff to monitor and enforce the whole environmental legislature for a population of some 300 million speaking a dozen or so different languages.

David and I came away from the meeting confident that whatever might be the eventual outcome the M3 complaint would at least be thoroughly investigated by the law officers of the Commission. Over the next couple of years well intentioned people would offer to write a personal complaint to the Commission to add weight to the campaign. Invariably David would respond with Ludwig Kramer's plea to have a single coordinated complaint – otherwise the Commission, and in particular his department, would be using up valuable resources on duplicated replies. This arises in part from a strange quirk in the system, whereby the complaint remains confidential between the complainant, the Commission, and the Member State, in our case the UK Government. The Commission is in fact prohibited from sharing with others its correspondence with either the complainant or the member state. In time this confidentiality rule was to fuel the fire of rumour, allegation and misunderstanding that surrounded the proceedings between the Commission and the UK Government, and left us, as principal complainants, very much in the dark and clutching at straws.

After leaving Kramer's office, David and I retreated to the sanctuary of Peter Kunzlik's office, which was to become our base during the various forays we made into the Commission and European Parliament. We gave Peter the details of our meeting with Kramer so that he could incorporate what we had learnt in his preparation of our formal complaint.

By then it was quite late in the evening, so when the telephone rang Peter hesitated to answer it – but it was the Press Association asking about the purpose of our trip. David was guarded in what he said. The potential confrontation between the Commission and the UK Government on environmental protection in general and Twyford Down in particular was already being anticipated in some quarters of the press.

The overriding impression David and I took home after that first visit to Brussels (apart from memories of a dreadful sea crossing which left David keenly anticipating the coming of the Channel Tunnel) was how very approachable the so-called Brussels bureaucrats had proved. Both of us thought it exceedingly unlikely that ordinary members of the public would have been able to penetrate the British Civil Service so directly, and be treated in such a simple, but nonetheless businesslike way.

Having left the final production of the complaint to the Commission in Kunzlik's capable hands David and I reported back to Merrick on our trip. The workings of the Commission were quite new to all of us. We had attempted to interest Winchester's Conservative Member of the European Parliament (MEP), Edward Kellett-Bowman at various junctures, but without any success. Originally he had expressed doubts that the route of the M3 was a matter for him as MEP and referred us to our Westminster MP. The non-involvement of our MEP had resulted in a failure to mobilize such influence as the European Parliament might have been able to wield. By contrast, Peter Price, the Conservative MEP representing London South-East, the constituency in which Oxleas Wood was located, had been active on behalf of the campaign against the East London River Crossing for some time.

Therefore it seemed sensible for us to embark on lobbying in Brussels and the European Parliament. We had very little idea of where to start on such activity. Yet again we fell on our feet when I was given two more telephone numbers and just over a week later I returned home to Winchester after a full day's meetings in Brussels.

It was clear that there was considerable interest in the implementation of the Directive 85/337, which was coming up for its five-year review by the Commission; that Ken Collins, the Labour MEP who was Chairman of the European Parliament's Environment Committee, was already interested in the case of Oxleas Wood; and that Twyford Down might prove to be just the catalyst necessary to precipitate action by the European Commission to ensure that the Environment Directive was enforced.

Over the succeeding two years we endeavoured to leave no stone unturned in Brussels, and our activities received extensive media coverage. There was extensive press coverage as soon as we announced that we had formally submitted a complaint to the Commission. The possible legal intervention of the Commission provided all the national media with the basis for many articles, features and television programmes. We became very experienced interviewees, and were no longer surprised at the full-page features in the Sunday papers, magazine articles and media coverage in foreign newspapers and TV. Of course, the Commission were looking at a number of complaints against the UK Government in connection with the Directive 85/337 on Environmental Impact Assessments. We were fortunate in being able to work with the Oxleas Wood campaign, and others, in lobbying Members of the European Parliament, who tabled questions in the Parliament seeking information on the progress of our complaint. Unfortunately much of the activity of the

Commission was shrouded in secrecy, owing to the rules of confidentiality which exist between the Commission and the Governments of the member states. None the less we received indications of activity from time to time, as did the UK national press.

In the circumstances there was little we could do except keep the profile of the Twyford Down case high on the agendas of both the politicians and staff of the European Commission. The press and media interest clearly helped us in that respect. So too did our various supporters in positions of influence in the world of conservation, who missed no opportunity to draw attention to the plight of Twyford Down, and the implications its demise would have for other supposedly protected sites in the UK.

In the autumn of 1990 the Royal Society for Nature Conservation (RSNC) had produced a report on the health of nature conservation in the UK. The Prince of Wales, as president of the RSNC, launched the report with a video saying, 'Now we can go on nibbling away at the corners of our remaining unspoilt and valuable habitats, justifying our actions on the basis of economic necessity, or even personal convenience, but what will the overall picture be like in...50 years' time?' The Prince said that, according to Government figures, 687 Sites of Special Scientific Interest, or 14 per cent of the total, had been lost or damaged between 1984 and 1988. He added that a study by the Wildlife Trust showed that proposed road-building plans in the South East would destroy or damage 372 of the SSSIs in the next ten years (Figure 18).

In November 1991 the Prince of Wales put himself at the centre of the controversy between the Major Government and the Environment Commissioner, Carlo Ripa di Meana, which had followed di Meana's letter calling for a halt to a number of big engineering projects, including the M3 extension at Twyford Down. The Prince spoke out publicly, describing the European Commission's powers to assess the environmental consequences of a major construction project as an 'important building block for the future' and added 'I think it is important to recognize that in many areas of environment policy the European Community, as the only body in the world with a supranational authority to legislate to protect the environment, is ahead of the world.' The Prince made his speech when he was presented with an award by the European Environment Bureau in Brussels.

D.H. BRYANT   B.Sc., F.R.I.C.S.   Chartered Surveyor   Valuer

HRH The Prince of Wales
Kensington Palace
London W8 4PU   24th January 1991

Your Royal Highness

M3 MOTORWAY EXTENSION (BAR END-COMPTON SECTION)
TWYFORD DOWN, WINCHESTER

We were greatly encouraged to read of your reported comments concerning
the implications for the countryside posed by the current road building
programme of the Department of Transport and other public bodies who so
often feel exempt from the normal rules associated with this country's
conservation designations.

You may recall that I wrote to you on 22nd September 1987, since when
there have been a number of developments on the M3 debate.

In February 1990 formal decisions were taken by the Secretaries of State
to proceed with the route through Twyford Down and at high level over the
main London/Southampton railway line. In March, three local people
(including my wife) plus the Parishes of Twyford and Compton and Shawford,
sought a Judicial Review in the High Court on the grounds that European
Directive 85/337 (requiring the submission of an Environmental Impact
Analysis) had not been complied with. In the event the case was lost and
I am enclosing a copy of the transcript of the Judgement given by
Mr. Justice McCulloch on 26th October 1990 which may be of interest.
Whilst nothing in the legal system is certain (!) there is a body of
opinion that would have wished us to appeal against this judgement,
although as you will be aware, the costs of litigation are substantial
and, frankly, we as a private group (supported by two small Parish

hedgerows, birds and scenic beauty which contribute so much towards the
delights of this country. The great sadness appears to be the willingness
of public authorities to adopt the new green vocabulary, but to stand well
back from the cash commitment that is a prerequisite to preserving our
finest landscapes.

Whilst we know of your deep commitment to protecting the best of this
country, we equally realise the sensitive position which you hold in
relation to Government and Government policy. Nevertheless, we hope that
we might have your thoughts from time to time on the uphill battle to
protect this one small corner of Hampshire where the battalions are ranged
rather heavily against us.

Yours sincerely,

D.H. Bryant

ST. JAMES'S PALACE
LONDON SW1A 1BS

19th February 1991

From: The Assistant Private Secretary and Comptroller to T.R.H. The Prince and Princess of Wales

Dea M. Bryant,

    The Prince of Wales has asked me to write and thank
you for your kind and thoughtful letter about the
extension of the M3 motorway through Twyford Down.

    His Royal Highness has every sympathy with the points
which you make and hopes that you will continue the debate
on this most important subject. As you recognise, His
Royal Highness is unable to make any specific personal
intervention on individual road schemes, but has made his
views on the general principles abundantly clear, both in
private meetings with ministers, and in public. I enclose
a copy of the script of a video which His Royal Highness
made recently for the Royal Society for Nature
Conservation which encapsulates these views, in case you
have not already seen it.

    His Royal Highness has asked me to send you his very
best wishes.

Yours sincerely,

Commander Richard Aylard, RN

Figure 18 Concern at the impact of the 1989 Roads Programme was
widespread and came from the highest level. The opening and closing
paragraphs of a letter Dudley Bryant wrote to HRH the Prince of
Wales, and the reply from Prince Charles's office.

David Croker and I, visiting the Commission just a couple of days beforehand, had heard that the Prince of Wales had been due to visit the Commission's Environment section in person. A senior official in the Commission told us that the visit had been cancelled – he said he was sad as 'I, too would have liked to meet your Royal family.' I heard later that the Foreign Office had vetoed the Prince's proposed visit to the Commission – presumably because of the explosive political atmosphere generated by Messrs Major, Hurd and Rifkind following di Meana's public announcement of the Commission's decision to look further into the UK Government's implementation of the EEC Directive on Environmental Impact Assessments.

It was to be nearly a year before the Commission finally announced it would not be proceeding with the case against the UK Government on the M3 at Winchester. The opacity of the process does nothing to enhance the reputation of Brussels; sadly though, it is imposed upon the Commission by the member states. The Commission's involvement and the UK Government's response is discussed in detail by Peter Kunzlik.

10

1991 A viable alternative: the tolled tunnel

On 1 December 1990, the Dean of Winchester Cathedral, the Mayor of Winchester, the chairmen of the two Parish Councils, and Professor Martin Biddle, as president of Twyford Down Association, wrote to *The Times*, seeking a reversal of the Twyford Down decision. Writing as 'individuals and representatives of groups closely involved with Winchester and its surrounding countryside' they expressed their 'dismay that the Department of Transport still plans a cutting through Twyford Down...We also strongly oppose the government's proposal to extend the M3 on high level embankment across the Itchen Valley. The fine villages of Twyford, Shawford and Compton, which form the setting for the jewel of the city itself would be the casualties of this scheme...The intervention of the European Commission is currently being sought...However, we would most welcome a change of heart by our government; a change of heart which would...save the cherished countryside which adorns England's ancient capital.' The two most influential citizens of that ancient capital were making a plea to the new Major Government to think again.

Merrick, David and I took stock of the campaign. We had reluctantly decided not to pursue the legal challenge in the UK courts; our information was that the European Commission would certainly formally investigate our complaint; and crictically there was a new regime in control of the Government. John Major had become Prime Minister, bringing Michael Heseltine back into Government as Secretary of State for the Environment.

Publicly our campaign had become confrontational with the Government – well mannered but it could hardly have been considered conciliatory to take the Secretaries of State to court, alleging they had acted other than in accordance with the law. Privately in our dealings with politicians we had always empha- sized our anxiety for a responsible and speedy resolution of the dilemma, but in truth we had little more to offer other than that the Government's scheme was a lousy idea, and we had a much better plan, which the public much preferred, but which would obviously be much more expensive.

The situation was deadlocked, and the time seemed ripe to go easy with the stick and to introduce a carrot into the scenario. Or, put more elegantly in lobby language, to offer the Government a 'political win'. In front of Christmas log-fires we mused about the various possibilities. The chairman of the Winchester Young Conservatives had achieved some local pub- licity when he advocated a private tunnel to break the impasse, saying, 'The project [private tunnel] would then provide an ideal example of how private and Government money can work together in the development of our road network.' The idea seemed a good one, but neither David, Merrick nor I had any idea how to take it further. Yet again, it was a personal contact that provided the key – my eldest son Owen had recently started his first job, working for the magazine *NGO Finance*, and he thought he had met just the man to help – Christopher Ogg. Following a telephone call from Owen, Ogg agreed to drive down to Winchester and meet us all shortly after Christmas.

Christopher Ogg was something quite new to our campaign – described as a 'public affairs and marketing consultant'. He formerly worked in the Conservative Party Research Department, and as Research Director of the Association of Independent Businesses. He had also been a director of Dewe Rogerson, the parliamentary consultants. He was a convinced Conservative, but probably to the left of the party. Like so many others before and after him, he seemed to be taken with the cause of Twyford Down, and like those others he brought his own perspective to the problem, and gave freely of his particu- lar talents to help the Down.

Twenty-four hours after our first briefing meeting Ogg faxed through his one-side-of-A4 appraisal of the Twyford Down situ- ation. Ogg's advice, which resembled a crash course in political lobbying, started, quite correctly, on the premise that the situa- tion is 'only soluble in terms satisfactory to you by political as opposed to legal means. Our government has never responded well to adversarial opposition. Fighting you [TDA] in the courts is a zero cost option for politicians – very expensive for you [we had noticed]. The only cost politicians respond to are electoral costs.'

The note went on to reiterate what he had said to us, that he thought a possible solution lay in 'tying together two of the most powerful trends of the Eighties – popular capitalism and environmentalism.' Ogg's concept was that the Twyford Down Association 'should formulate itself as a trust, acquire the land by means of public subscription and possibly subcontract or lease the project for the tunnel to a construction consortium. The exact structuring will provide lawyers and bankers with hours of harmless amusement.'

It seemed that the predicted traffic flows on the M3 at Winchester – in excess of 80 000 vehicles per day – would ensure a rather healthy return to any investor, and from that earliest meeting we decided that Twyford Down, citizens of Winchester and environmental charities ought to be the principal beneficiaries of any surplus profits.

Ogg suggested that we run an advertisement in the broadsheets, aimed at widening support for a toll tunnel option – a sort of pre-share issue campaign. The copy Ogg drafted out for us read:

> This time it's history's backyard. The Department of Transport want to drive a motorway through a piece of your natural and social history. Twyford Down. Home of wild orchids, rare breeding butterfiles, site of an Iron Age village, and a Bronze Age burial mound, Celtic field systems. Somewhere the Celtic mists lay a ghostly finger on the present. And the Department of Transport want to whack a motorway through it. We're trying to find a better solution. Our lawyers have fought. But we have engineers and transport economists working on it too. Because responsible opposition means finding viable alternatives. If you believe the legacy of the past can and should co-exist with the needs of the present, please help us.

Sadly, the advertisement was never published as events overtook the planned campaign, but how well Ogg had grasped and articulated the essence of what we were about.

We had discussed at length how best to introduce the Government to our new proposal. Ogg had advised that the initiative should be floated privately with 'relevant politicians first – with a clear understanding that they could claim a substantial slice of the public credit.'

We still had to face the difficulties of a sitting member of parliament, whose local party had decided to select someone else to fight the next election, and a new prospective candidate, who could reasonably be expected to become the next member of parliament for Winchester, given the substantial Conservative majority in the constitutency. The invariable rule is that approaches to Government ministers must be made by the elected member of parliament for the relevant constituency. There are obviously sound constitutional and practical reasons for such conventions. For Twyford Down they presented yet another problem.

The in-fighting in the local Conservative Association surrounding the selection of a new prospective candidate had spilled over to Westminster, and to Conservative Central Office, where the rumours that John Browne, the present MP, intended to fight the next election as an independent candidate in Winchester were begining to surface, adding to the general discomfiture. What we faced was a difficult and unusual problem.

Whatever the rights and wrongs of the rumours surrounding John Browne, by the time we were considering how to present a possible political win to the new Major Government he was perceived as a political liability. Merrick particularly had found him helpful and cooperative in pursuing things with the Government, but it was by then nearly six months since the local Tories first decided they wanted a new member of parliament. The local Tory Association's annual general meeting was held on 25 March. Dudley and I went along – in the interests of our Twyford Down activities. Dudley came reluctantly, anticipating the usual boring tedium of AGMs. It turned out to be riveting entertainment, and quite the most extraordinary political meeting I have ever attended. The largest hall in Winchester was full, standing room only. The standard agenda was thrown out of the window under the early item of 'Minutes of Previous AGM' and a debate as to whether John Browne or Gerry Malone should be the next candidate for Winchester ensued.

The Peterborough column in *The Daily Telegraph* on 27 March 1991 reported, 'One of the nastiest rows in recent Tory history looks like flaring up again. Following tearful scenes at Monday's annual meeting at Winchester Conservative Association the de-selected MP, John Browne may reconsider his decision to bow out from politics...Browne supporters failed by 105 to 206 to pass a motion nullifying Malone's selection...'

Meanwhile, Ogg had been putting feelers out into the Conservative Party. From him I learnt the technique of faxing draft letters to the intended recipient's office to enable amendments before a final version is dispatched. In his initial soundings with the Conservative hierarchy Ogg made these principal points: 'Unusually for an environmental group the Twyford Down Association overlaps substantially in terms of membership with the local Conservative Party (a new phenomenon at that time, though only three years later the 1994 agenda of the Conservative Party Conference was riddled with motions critical of the road building programme). I have suggested that even at this late date it would make sense to seek a solution in dialogue rather than confrontation. I believe such a solution exists...but solutions cost money, and the polluters should pay. Precedents for tolls exist, of course, but as far as I am aware this would be the first ever instance of polluters paying for environmental damage literally on a "pay as you go" basis.'

David and I had an initial meeting with Gerald Malone, the new prospective Conservative parliamentary candidate for Winchester – the MP elect unless something quite dramatic happened. Malone seemed vastly relieved that we were coming up with constructive, if novel, suggestions rather than rehashing the old ground again. His view was that 'something new' was needed to reopen ministerial consideration of the matter. He readily agreed to meet with Ogg to hear first hand more details of the concept.

After a good deal of private discussion we were advised that the best way to progress our idea with ministers was via the Transport Secretary Malcolm Rifkind's political research adviser and Rifkind's parliamentary private secretary (PPS), Henry Bellingham. The PPS is a minister's ears and eyes in the Commons – the link with his parliamentary colleagues, aware of the requirements of the administration of Government business but not part of that administration. PPSs are chosen individually by ministers from the Government back benchers to assist them in their parliamentary duties. They are not paid a salary, are not formally part of the Government, but are duty bound to support Government policy.

The vibes reaching us from the political think-tanks and the Marsham Street HQ of the Department of Transport gradually took shape. It seemed that the political researchers welcomed the chance to examine the possibilities of using a 'free market' solution to resolve the Twyford Down dilemma. On the other hand, officials in the Department of Transport were pouring cold water on the idea at every opportunity.

Despite our efforts to get the Government 'locked into' the toll-tunnel solution, at least to the point of obtaining private ministerial commitment to exploring the concept, before going public on the project, rumours began to circulate. The local and national media detected something, and on 5 March Malcolm Rifkind announced that the West Midlands western orbital scheme could be built and operated by the private sector. Depicted by the press as representing the latest stage in the Government's attempt to recruit private capital into provision of transport infrastructure, the story focused the agile minds of some reporters upon M3 and Twyford Down.

Michael McCarthy, environment correspondent of *The Times*, pursued the story in earnest. He was given conflicting versions. The Department of Transport press office denied any knowledge of a privately funded solution. Others indicated to him that there was substance in the rumours. Pushed, we issued a press release setting out the essential elements of the concept:

> Environmental Group Propose City Solution to M3 Impasse. The Twyford Down Association has proposed to Malcolm Rifkind, that the long-standing controversy of the M3 around Winchester could best be resolved by a private sector initiative to build a toll tunnel under Twyford Down. Chris Patten [by then chairman of the Conservative Party] pointed the way on environmental issues by his statement that the protection of the environment has a price, and the Government's privatisation programme has demonstrated the rebirth of the private investor and the advent of the consumer-investor. As far as we are aware this is the first example of a community proposing a viable,

commercial capital market answer to an environmental issue.

Our initial workings suggest that on the tunnel pricing and traffic flow data available such a venture could be undertaken profitably and, by means of access to capital markets, allow our community not just to fund a solution, but to profit from one. We would anticipate some part of the profits being used to fund conservation work and a study of Twyford Down as a unique and precious historic and natural site. The Twyford Down Association has proposed to the Secretary of State that a full feasibility study be prepared for his consideration.

Armed with our press statement, and assured by both Ogg and me that we had indeed received encouragement that the concept was politically attractive, McCarthy went back to the Department of Transport press office, who firmly denied that there was any substance to what we were saying.

However, on 9 March 1991 *The Times* ran McCarthy's exclusive, 'Private Toll Tunnel Scheme Could Save Twyford Down – Malcolm Rifkind, Transport Secretary, is considering a plan for a privately funded toll tunnel that would save Twyford Down in Hampshire from destruction by the M3...The Twyford Down Association has proposed to Mr Rifkind that a feasibility study be prepared for his consideration, and members of the Association are likely to meet him later this month.' The report accorded exactly with what we understood – that the Association would indeed be given an opportunity to explain the privately funded tunnel concept to the Transport Secretary.

In any event the Conservative Government was already laying the ground for tolling as a method for funding road construction. Almost a year earlier Cecil Parkinson had unveiled a package of 'new initiatives for privately funded roads' and the Government's response to the consultation Green Paper of a year earlier, 'New Roads by New Means', said, 'The response to the Green Paper shows that our proposals for the further development of private financing of transport projects enjoys widespread support. My new proposals will provide additional opportunities for the private sector to add to Britain's transport network.' At the same time Parkinson had announced invitations to tender for the privately funded Birmingham Northern Relief Road.

In March 1991, when we were proposing a toll tunnel solution, The New Roads and Streetworks Bill was being steered through the committee stage of the parliamentary process by Conservative ministers. This was itself a fairly obscure Bill, and its progress was passing almost unnoticed. A mish-mash piece of legislation addressing some very practical details, such as a requirement for public utilities to consult with highway authorities before embarking on works on main roads, the other 'half' of the Bill was the legislative framework required to implement the 1990 Green Paper, New Roads by New Means (that is, private financing of transport (roads) projects).

The clause of the Bill on which The Twyford Down Association's proposal depended was Clause l(i):

> In this part a 'concession agreement' means an agreement entered into by a highway authority under which a person (the 'concessionaire') in return for undertaking such obligations as may be specified in the agreement with respect to the design, construction, maintenance operation or improvement of a special road, is appointed to enjoy the right (conferred or to be conferred by a toll order under this Part) to charge tolls in respect of the use of the road.

Following the public airing of our concept in *The Times*, other national papers picked up the story: notably, *The Daily Telegraph*, in its Spectator column, often regarded as the voice of 'thinking Tories', which said, 'It is a wonder that this never occurred to that archetypal Thatcherite, Mr Parkinson; or was he merely concerned, in the Thatcherite manner, to build a road and solve a problem with the minimum delay, regardless of the environmental consequences? If the toll tunnel is approved, it will be an example of the social market which – however ugly the phrase – deserves to be welcomed.'

Shortly afterwards, we were told details of when and where we were to be invited to make the presentation to the Transport Secretary – the date was 23 April, St George's Day. An auspicious date on which we hoped to launch our plan to save the landscape backcloth to England's ancient capital.

On 20 March, somewhat clumsily, John Browne, the MP, tabled a formal Parliamentary Question to the Secretary of State for Transport, to ask 'Will he seek funding from the private sector, to be repaid from tolls, in order to meet the incremental cost of building a tunnel to accommodate the proposed M3

Extension?' The written answer came from Roads Minister, Christopher Chope, 'No. We have no intention of reopening the joint decision by the Secretaries of State on this much-needed scheme which followed twenty years of debate and four public inquiries.' The precipitous posing of the question had provided an opportunity for the Department of Transport 'establishment' to take a definitive and public view in advance of our meeting with the Transport Secretary – the last thing we wanted, as this would make it more difficult for the Secretary of State to acknowledge or accept the strength of our case.

In time for the meeting with Malcolm Rifkind and his advisers, we had refined the essential elements of the embryonic concept of the privately funded tunnel. Merrick had secured a meeting with the Managing Director of the merchant bank, Baring Brothers, which had strong family connections in Hampshire. It became clear that given a political go-ahead there would be both interest and enthusiasm for the project from the financial institutions in the City.

On the morning of 23 April Merrick, David and I set forth for London once more from Winchester railway station, this time with television crew in attendance filming for a major feature programme about Twyford Down. The television crew and the three of us were met at the House of Commons by John Browne, MP, and Gerald Malone, MP-in-waiting to all intents and purposes. Someone unkindly referred to this as 'the John and Gerry act' since it was quite apparent that the two were involved, involuntarily perhaps, in a game of cat and mouse, considerably more ridiculous than the famous cartoon ever was.

Rifkind chaired the meeting with easy good humour. Our team consisted of the three of us, and Ogg, Browne and Malone were in attendance. Rifkind had the full works, Christopher Chope his Roads Minister (who said not a word throughout), his PPS Henry Bellingham, the Department's press officer, and a team of Department officials. We handed over the carefully prepared and professionally produced briefing notes, and then took the meeting through them. The package included the obvious pictures, of the Cutting and of the tunnel, a brief note on the background, and three pages on the privately funded tunnel and low-level route.

After setting out the policy and political background to our proposal the document went on to address some specific issues.

To forestall the suggestion that tolls equalled traffic queues we
had researched modern tolling technology in use on the Oslo
ring road in Norway and the Italian autostradas, which proved
that modern tolling technology was such that regular and
indeed occasional users would not need to stop or even slow
below normal motorway speeds at the tolls. We explained that
there were a number of possible tolling systems, including a
high frequency transmitter, electronic tagging, and a
'Smartcard' system. The final part of our submission examined
the legislative framework set by the New Roads and
Streetworks Bill. Our statement read:

> [The Bill] was drafted with the provision rather than the
> protection of an amenity in view, but the latter interpreta-
> tion does not appear to be precluded. Similarly, the Bill does
> not appear to preclude the community being regarded as a
> concessionaire for the purposes of a road scheme.

> The consultation phases [following the Green Paper] made
> it clear that the normal model envisaged was a private com-
> mercial sector initiative which, to date, has consisted of con-
> sortia of construction, engineering and financial interests.
> Our proposal envisages a similar consortium, but acting on
> the initiative of sponsorship of community interest which
> might themselves be organised as commercial entities.

> The Government's encouragement of the private
> investor's re-engagement in the equity market provides a
> powerful final strand – the mechanism whereby the com-
> munity could give effect to the proposal. A public issue,
> underwritten by the institutions, allows a market tool to
> create a bridge between a specific affected community, the
> consumer [who, following the precedent of other trans-
> port-related flotations, would acquire concessionary use of
> the facilities] and the commercial, technical and financial
> partners. Seen thus, it [privately funded tunnel] is a
> straightforward task of project finance, civil engineering,
> and corporate planning.

> Our initial soundings in the City, based on figures and
> projections available, suggest that were these indications
> confirmed in a full commercial feasibility study, there
> would be no difficulty in implementing the proposal. The
> Association proposes to sponsor such a feasibility study.

The Association's purposes in seeking this meeting, is to ask whether a feasibility study of a privately funded tunnel and low-level route, if prepared, would be considered by the Secretary of State?

The Department of Transport team raised the usual old chestnuts against the tunnel route, delay, the size of the tunnel bore, the extra time that would be taken to construct the tunnel, and of course some additional arguments about traffic diverting off the motorway to avoid tolls, and the extra land-take required to provide the toll booths, and considerable scepticism about whether financial institutions would want to become involved. I certainly came away with the feeling that the thinking of the Department of Transport, politically and administratively, for whatever reason, was stuck in a sort of time warp so far as M3 was concerned.

The concept we were proposing was certainly novel; if adopted it would have proved a considerable administrative inconvenience to officialdom, marking out new ground; set against that, it would have saved the national exchequer some £50 million (the cost allowed for the Cutting route in the Roads Programme), and created a precedent for the use of tolls to encourage the private sector to protect an amenity.

We came away from the meeting with Rifkind not entirely unhappy. The chance to achieve a solution to the dilemma at little cost to the public sector was exciting. There was extensive national and local coverage of our proposition and meeting with the Transport Secretary, but one local paper, *The Portsmouth Evening News*, put a different slant on the story.

'Tunnelled vision?' it read, 'It would be convenient for the Government if it could free itself from the tangle over Twyford Down. Even better if the campaigners could do the spadework and find themselves a developer prepared to build a private toll tunnel. So off they trotted from their meeting with Transport Secretary Malcolm Rifkind, their spirits lifted by his encouraging noises over the private tunnel idea. Encouragement costs nothing. Mr Rifkind has a cheek expecting these people to come up with their own feasibility study. Shouldn't that be a job for the Government?'

Less than two weeks later Christopher Chope was programmed to cut the first turf to mark the start of the archaeological dig on Twyford Down. The bland pre-released press notice issued by the Department press office, read 'Chope Starts

Twyford Down Archaeological Dig...Speaking at the dig, Mr Chope said, "This archaeological dig is a prime example of the importance the Department [of Transport] places on archaeological features when building roads"...' etc.

One local reporter subsequently gave me a graphic account of what actually happened. Apparently Mr Chope, his officials, and the local press had all trooped up on to the Down; Chope had done his piece and then announced that Rifkind had dismissed the toll tunnel option; it was a few moments before his words sank in, and then all the reporters had raced across the ploughed field to get to back to offices and telephones. Mr Chope was apparently basing his comments upon a letter from Mr Rifkind to the Winchester MP, John Browne. We had no knowledge of any of this and were taken aback and angry. Interviewed on local television that afternoon Chope said, 'He [Malcolm Rifkind] doesn't see any advantages in a toll tunnel over an un-toll tunnel and an un-toll tunnel was rejected...last year.'

Naturally, the national daily papers picked up the story. *The Times* on Wednesday 8 May carried the story, headed, 'Rifkind rejects private toll tunnel for M3 extension'. The article went on to say that Rifkind had rejected proposals from the Twyford Down Association in a letter to John Browne, Tory MP for Winchester, on the grounds that the toll tunnel would cause unacceptable delays and other problems. Mr Rifkind 'had been thought much more sympathetic to the idea of saving Twyford Down than his predecessor...'

John Browne faxed a copy of Rifkind's letter to Merrick, and reading the letter, signed by a Private Secretary in the Transport Office 'for Malcolm Rifkind (approved by the Secretary of State and signed in his absence)' merely increased our anger.

The next day, on behalf of the Twyford Down Association, I wrote formally to Malcolm Rifkind and to Michael Heseltine, and issued the letters to the press. The letter to Rifkind began 'We are unable to write formally in response to your Departmental letter of the 3rd [May] for although copies were made available to the press on Tuesday, your office refused to make one available to us. The letter bears the stark imprint of Dorking, an office irretrievably locked into the agenda of the '70s and in tone and content accords ill with your stated concerns for environmental sensitivity...Our greatest disappointment is that your Department seems unable to grasp the potential of the New Roads and Streetworks Bill as a powerful tool for environmentalism, seeing it instead as a blunt instrument for smash and grab capitalism by the Road Lobby.' My letter continued in increasingly crisp terms and closed with 'We can only hope that you will consider these comments as an honest and concerned commentary on the clear discrepancy between your publicly stated position on the environment and the desire of your officials to turn our heritage into a parking lot.'

We were angry, but so too were others. *The Portsmouth Evening News* described the 'Government's promise to consider a private toll tunnel for Twyford as hollow as the huge cavity which is now certain to be carved out to the Downs...In the space of a few well-chosen words written to Winchester MP John Browne, Mr Rifkind has effectively reduced some of Britain's loveliest countryside to rubble and concrete.'

Equally angry was Gerry Malone, the prospective Conservative candidate for Winchester, who issued a formal press statement headed 'Malone Raps M3 Bungle'. In an obvious effort to retrieve the situation Mr Malone said, 'I have read the full text of Malcolm Rifkind's response following the meeting with TDA members. While he makes clear that on the present evidence he sees no reason to alter the findings of the public inquiry, or delay progress on advance works, he [Rifkind] confirms: "I would, of course, be prepared to consider a feasibility study report if one is produced." That is very different from the impression given by the reported remarks of Mr Chope, which led campaigners to believe their proposals had been completely ruled out. If this was a failure of communication it should not have happened. After a detailed meeting with the Transport Secretary I would expect government to extend the basic courtesy of ensuring those making representations were told of the government's reaction before the response was placed in the public domain. I have written to Mr Rifkind expressing my dissatisfaction at the way the affair has been handled.'

Malone went on to say, 'Reading between the lines, the reply makes it clear that the feasibility study would need to present a copper-bottomed case...It is not Malcolm Rifkind's style to give false hope to campaigners who impressed him with their commitment to their cause and their manner of presenting it. I do not believe the TDA expected miracles from their first meeting with the Transport Secretary. But the Government [Malone's own party] could have closed the door completely. I am pleased Mr Rifkind has confirmed he is still prepared to be convinced.'

Poor Twyford Down seemed always to be caught between conflicting forces. The threat to, and ultimate destruction of the Down resulted from the conflict between the people of Winchester, who opposed the 1971 plan to put the motorway through the Water Meadows, and the pressure from commercial interests to the south of Winchester and the road lobby. Twenty years on, the pressures which finally did for the Down were bureaucratic inertia and reluctance to embrace new thinking, alongside hard-nosed right-wing Conservatives of the build-it-and-be-damned variety: pressures which were to overwhelm the hesitant new philosophy of a social market economy, the prospective MP's desire to at least see every possible alternative option fully explored, and the combined weight of the conservation movement in the UK.

As one of our more philosophical supporters wrote at the time, 'Government policy on transport is one legged. It concentrates huge bureaucractic resources on formulating plans [based on] dubious statistics purporting to suggest the supply of roads we may need. Demand on the other hand is left to the whim of all of us who have the means to put hand to ignition key. The result is a constant complaint that there is far too much traffic and that it is destroying our quality of life. There are two unmatchable marginal prices here. The marginal price governing our demand for travel is the amount of congestion, while the marginal price of supply is governed by Government's ability to outmanoeuvre the environmental lobby.'

'The intellectual argument for road pricing which would match supply with demand rationally – by money prices – has already been won, even I understand inside the Department of Transport. The problem is that no politician will risk trying this out. The perceived political risks of criticism from special interest lobbies far outweigh the dispersed benefits to all travellers. Given that the Twyford Down Association now suggest that they may be able to find private capital willing to support a private tunnel the Government should stand aside and let free enterprise get on with it' (Eben Wilson – March 1991).

Sadly, the Transport Department was locked into the interventionist philosophy of the 1960s and the Conservative Party (for the most part) was unable to admit that subsidizing road transport was distorting the market, resulting in demand-led road building at the expense of public transport and the environment. Only three years later, in October 1994, a Conservative Transport Secretary was to submit, finally, to the growing clamour from Treasury officials, environmentalists and health experts, when at the Conservative Party conference Brian Mawhinney indicated a shift away from road building saying, 'Our main priority now should be to manage our existing road network in the most effective manner.' It is an abiding sadness to those of us who tried to save Twyford Down that it takes so long to slow, and finally turn, the administrative and bureaucratic machine of Government. Our campaigning activities from 1989 onwards carried an almost unconscious motive that if we could only 'buy enough time' Government policy, or the Government itself might change and save the Down.

To go back, though, to late May 1991, our campaign to save the Down was becoming even more highly profiled. Our complaint to the European Commission had been lodged and we had good reason to believe the Commission would be pursuing the complaint, though its progress was shrouded in mystery. We also had political support to produce a 'copper-bottomed' case for a privately funded toll tunnel, and the general election was unlikely to be less than a year away. Labour politicians appeared to be increasingly sympathetic to the cause of Twyford Down and a Labour Government was seen as a real possibility. David and Dudley had had a private meeting with Joan Ruddock, a Labour spokeswoman on Transport, who had impressed them both with her grasp of the M3 problem and her willingness to resolve it if at all possible.

But certain elements in the Government and certainly within the Transport Department were determined to press ahead with the Cutting route and achieve a pre-emptive strike by getting machines working on the Down as fast as possible and so, in May 1991, began the archaeological dig through the Down.

We were dismayed but not deterred. There seemed every reason for carrying on with the privately funded toll tunnel, not least because if the Commission should put the UK Government 'in the dock' such an alternative would provide an acceptable ladder for the Conservative Government to gracefully climb down.

Having taken a decision to press ahead and produce a feasibility study in spite of the mixed messages coming from the Transport Department, we had to address two principal aspects of the privately funded toll tunnel project: the finance and construction. Discussions were held with a range of professional advisers – transport economists, merchant bankers, consulting engineers and lawyers experienced in setting up ethical investment schemes.

A problem soon presented itself – the 'chicken and egg' situation over finance of the ultimate toll tunnel project. Merrick set this out succinctly following one of his meetings with Barings, the merchant bank. Writing to thank the bank for its interest he said, 'As I mentioned in my previous letter, we are in a chicken and egg situation. The Government can be persuaded to adopt this solution for political reasons; part of the process of creating that political will is demonstrating commercial support; commercial people are not normally in the business of creating projects *ab initio* in quite this way, and as you pointed out, there is no guarantee that those who led to the project being created would be the commercial beneficiaries.' As it was, we obtained 'expressions of interest' from City institutions and concentrated on the production of a technical study of the construction of a tolled tunnel, and the forecast returns.

It was obviously important that the feasibility study should be carried out professionally to ensure that the results would be acceptable to potential sources of finance and to the authorities, and that it should include identification of the toll points, and the extent of the route to be constructed as part of the project, the engineering costs, the traffic levels, data on existing toll charges to set realistic levels of the tolls to enable an assessment of the impact on traffic flows, the benefits to users, and revenues and costs.

The Twyford Down Association had little enough money uncommitted; the costs of the judicial review were set to eat up every penny raised and more, though the appeal to the Wykehamists had been undertaken on the understanding that part of the money raised would be used for publicity and 'constructive' campaigning. We therefore had the means to pay a limited amount in professional fees towards the costs of the feasibility study, and once again some of our generous sponsors stepped in to top up the amount.

David Croker and I approached Scott Wilson Kirkpatrick (SWK), the consulting engineers retained by Winchester City Council to present the Council's case for a tunnel under the Down to the 1987 Public Inquiry, with a view to commissioning the firm to undertake the tolled tunnel feasibility study. Geoff French, one of the firm's senior partners, willingly agreed to meet us to discuss things.

Chris Ogg and I met Geoff French and Peter Guthrie, another SWK partner with a special interest in environmental matters in June 1991. It was a long meeting at which we discussed all the political ramifications of a toll tunnel, and tried to relay the comments made by Transport Department officials at our initial meeting with Rifkind in April. Once more I found myself explaining to professionals that the Twyford Down Association could only afford to pay the most modest fees for professional services. Yet again I was reassured and encouraged by the sympathy and enthusiasm of the reception given to us; the daily manna on which I, and I'm sure David and Merrick, survived was the support for what we were doing so freely given by a huge number of people from every level of society and representing almost all the construction-related professions.

Geoff French wrote to me the next day, confirming SWK's willingness to help by undertaking the feasibility study – at a give-away price. As French said, in something of an understatement, 'Given the likely readership of any feasibility study it will have to be a clear, well reasoned document. We are confident that we have the necessary expertise and contacts to produce the sort of...study you require...You will appreciate that our quoted price is significantly less than the full cost which we expect to incur, but it is proposed by us in view of your desire to keep expenditure to a minimum at this stage.' It's quite difficult to imagine a document likely to be subjected to more critical perusal.

We were delighted, confident that the study was in the hands of a highly respected firm, which was frequently retained by the Transport Department; SWK had a long-standing involvement with the campaign to save the Down by means of a tunnel and had strong local connections in Winchester. There was of course a good deal of work to be done, and once more Richard Parker came to our rescue, offering technical briefing to SWK.

While SWK worked on the study the tasks which faced us were firstly to keep Twyford Down high on the political and media agenda, and to attempt to persuade the Government to pursue the toll tunnel alternative.

In June 1991 the private toll tunnel project was formally launched at an early evening reception in the Athenaeum Club in Pall Mall in London, hosted by the president of the Twyford Down Association, Professor Martin Biddle, who spoke with his usual mastery of the subject and ability to articulate the issues. Politicians, including Simon Hughes, the Liberal Democrat Environment spokesman, the press and financial institutions were invited to a fairly stylish briefing in the splendid library of the Athenaeum. Merrick had produced a really superb display, graphically illustrating Twyford Down, the existing landscape setting and the scheduled sites. SWK came along to answer the technical questions on construction and traffic flows. The event was an unashamed public relations exercise designed to raise awareness and the credibility of the toll tunnel project, and of course the campaign generally.

Soon after the launch at the Athenaeum the Twyford Down Association took a display stand at *The Sunday Times* Environment Exhibition, which was held at Olympia in July. This was not a cheap exercise, and the Exhibition itself failed to draw the masses of public that might have been hoped. However, the Prime Minister, John Major, was the opening speaker at the conference session and Rifkind was to speak later. Also there were campaigners from Oxleas Wood. The Association's display was professional, though fairly simple, and must have been seen by rather a lot of officials and politicians, who might have preferred to forget Twyford Down.

Earlier in the summer, shortly after the Association's April meeting with Malcolm Rifkind, I approached some of my political contacts with a view to obtaining the Environment Department's support for the alternative option of the toll tunnel. The Association wrote formally to Michael Heseltine, then Environment Secretary, as did a number of our supporters, including Miriam Rothschild. The replies were sadly as inevitable and defensive as they were formal – this is a matter for the Secretary of State for Transport and so forth. Privately I discussed the problems with John Hanvey, the Chairman of Harris Research Centre, and an adviser to the Tory High Command.

Some private contacts were made and I know that our views were brought directly to the attention of the Secretary of State via colleagues who were 'close to him'. I was told by John that the formal replies would be rather 'po-faced', and rather more elegantly by one of our contacts that 'it is unlikely that this will produce a formal reply, but I hope it may help.' In his initial assessment of the political aspects of the toll tunnel alternative, Ogg had identified it as a concept which might well appeal to Michael Heseltine. Before the Transport establishment started to pour cold water on the whole idea we had harboured dreams of working with the Conservative Party to produce a package which could be unveiled at the Conservative Party Conference with a fanfare as an immaculate 'Tory' solution, and as the Government's own proposal to save Twyford Down and utilize market forces to work for the environment.

That pipe dream was not to be but I understand that Heseltine could see the concept as a political winner, and that he was interested in it. However, I also understand that the suggestion of the toll tunnel 'got blown out of the water' at the level of letters in the intra-governmental decision-making process – that is, during discussions between officials. We had never felt that Heseltine was happy with the decision on Twyford Down any more than his predecesssor, Chris Patten, from whom he had inherited responsibility, but among all the other problems Twyford Down did not feature as highly as we would have wished. Secretaries of State, like anyone in any organization, can only afford to make a nuisance of themselves on a limited number of issues and Twyford Down did not feature at the top of Hesletine's list of priorities on which he was prepared to instigate a Cabinet showdown.

By the middle of October we received further indication that the Major Government was fairly well dug in to pressing on with the Cutting. The Prime Minister's Private Secretary, William Chapman, replying to a letter from David Croker, wrote, 'Nevertheless...the Secretary of State is willing to consider a feasibility study on a toll tunnel option if the Association produces one. As you rightly point out, the Government does wish to encourage more privately funded road schemes. However, cost is not the only factor to be considered before such schemes are sanctioned. The Government must be satisfied that there are no overriding disadvantages which would make private funding unacceptable.'

On 17 October 1991, the campaigners from Oxleas Wood in East London were meeting the Environment Commissioner, Ripa di Meana, in his Brussels office. I was meeting Malcolm Rifkind's parliamentary private secretary to ascertain when we could present our feasibility study to the Secretary of State. At about 5.30 pm Brussels time the European Commission released the news that it had issued formal notice to the UK Government alleging failure to properly comply with EEC legislation on the environment. The effect of this action was explosive. We feared that the toll tunnel project was now unlikely to be considered as the British Government would be in no mood to look for a compromise solution. Sadly, a serious attempt at constructive opposition ceased to feature on anyone's agenda.

The UK Government had until 17 December 1991 to formally reply to the Commission, the Transport Department had invited tenders for a preliminary phase of the M3 contract in August, and it seemed increasingly likely that the Government was intent upon letting that contract, regardless of the EEC intervention, or maybe even because of it.

There was no response to our earlier requests for an opportunity to present the feasibility study to the Secretary of State, but that was perhaps not surprising in the wake of the continuing furore resulting from di Meana's intervention. Quite suddenly, at the begining of December, John Browne, our local MP, contacted Merrick to say that a date had been arranged for us to present the study to Christopher Chope, the Roads Minister, on 12 December. I don't think that by that time any of us had any hopes that the Government would do other than press ahead with the Cutting scheme, but the timing of the meeting, and the individuals involved certainly did not give us much confidence.

Nonetheless, on a dark December afternoon a posse of us set off for the Department of Transport, along with Geoff French from SWK, to meet Christopher Chope, the Roads Minister, and John Browne, our local MP, at the Department's London HQ in Marsham Street. Copies of the completed feasibility study produced by SWK had been dispatched to the Transport Department in advance. On arrival at Marsham Street we were signed in, and shown up to a meeting room on the 'ministerial' floor at the top of the 1960s concrete box. In addition to a team of officials from his own Transport Department, Christopher Chope was accompanied by a senior Treasury official.

SWK had been working away on the feasibility study: by the end of September it had been ready for presentation to the Secretary of State. Very much a preliminary study it was designed to enable the Government to say, 'yes, we can see the project is feasible, and financially viable, and we will work with you to take the project forward.'

The Secretaries of State in reaching their 1990 decision to build the Cutting route had referred to the Inquiry Inspector's conclusion that he was not able to recommend a tunnel – despite its environmental superiority and the fact that it went further than any other scheme to meet the Government's requirement of public acceptability – on the grounds that a tunnel scheme would cause delay in completing the M3 link, and at vastly increased cost.

The SWK feasibility study sought to show how a toll tunnel scheme could overcome both those problems. The conclusion of the opening summary read 'The toll tunnel option together with the provision of a temporary traffic improvement at Hockley Junction answers all the criticism previously made of the tunnel scheme. A tunnel would result in major environmental benefits compared with the published [Cutting] scheme and need not cost the Government anything.'

Hockley Junction is a case study on its own, and I will digress: A temporary flyover at Hockley to relieve the bottleneck had been the focus of much debate at the 1987 Public Inquiry. Although originally recommended by Inspector Edge in his 1976 Inquiry report (a recommendation apparently accepted by the Government), a temporary flyover was strongly resisted by both the Hampshire County Council and the Transport Department and was simply not complied with. The delays arising from the Hockley traffic lights, the only set on the journey between Edinburgh and Southampton, were the focus of much of the pressure for speedy completion of the M3 link.

It is not unreasonable to speculate that if Inspector Edge's recommendation had been implemented in 1979, or even later, the climate in which the debate on the missing M3 link took place would have been vastly different; there would not have been the element of desperation to get something done and the Cutting route through Twyford Down might never have been proposed. However, in 1991 the notorious delays at Hockley dominated much of the discussion of the M3. Christopher

Chope represented a Southampton constituency and was no doubt freqeuntly lobbied locally about the unreasonable intransigence of the people of Winchester throttling the economic life of Southampton. During the 1991 Conservative Party Conference that October the *Southampton Evening Echo* had carried a front page picture of Mr and Mrs Chope, in an open-topped carriage with the Blackpool Tower in the background, with the headline 'Hockley Jams Cost £1m a Month – M3 missing link must be started soon – Chope'.

While the statistical evidence to support £1m per month was not especially clear, we certainly realized the political imperative of 'something being done' about peak period delays and thus the SWK report addressed the practicalities of a temporary flyover as part of the toll tunnel package. The irony of the matter is that it was the intransigence of the Transport Departmment and the Hampshire County Council in refusing to construct the temporary flyover that caused 20 years of inconvenience to the travelling public.

The SWK study defined the reasoning behind the suggestion for a toll tunnel as follows: 'The purpose of charging a toll for the use of the tunnel would be to recoup part or all of the expenditure incurred by providing such a facility.' Geoff French I think saw some merit in the toll recouping the difference between the cost of the Cutting scheme and a tunnel.

The feasibility study showed that if a toll of £1 were charged for all vehicles the tunnel would break even within 15 years except in the case of high interest rates combined with low traffic growth assumptions (neither of which materialized over the next four years!). On low forecast National Road Traffic Figures a 24-hour flow of 73 526 vehicles was estimated in 1998. On high forecast this rose to 83 777, and up to an estimated 104 200 per day in 2007. The construction cost at 1991 prices, to include the Hockley temporary flyover, toll plaza and booths, was estimated at £100 m. SWK estimated a four-year construction period under a design and build contract.

The feasibility study proposed the introduction of a private bill utilizing the 'same procedure as adopted for the new Dartford Crossing, or utilizing the mechanism of the New Roads and Streetworks Act for a Toll Tunnel.'

The meeting at Marsham Street quickly dispensed with the formalities and some serious discussion took place. It was obvious that the officials present had done their homework on the study. Perhaps it was in the light of the general expectation that the Government was pressing ahead with the Cutting in any case, but I felt that there was an element of 'technical jousting' with Geoff French by the Transport Department team.

The arguments employed by the Transport Department team were subsequently confirmed in a letter from Chope: although the Government 'welcomes suggestions for private financing of road infrastructure paid by tolls it would expect a suitable alternative route to be available for those who did not wish to pay the toll,' it seems that the historic requirement that tolls could only be charged on esturine crossings had been abandoned but still an equivalent non-tolled route was required.

The deep-rooted opposition to any interim improvement at the Hockley lights was reiterated. The old arguments of the drawback to a tunnel were trawled over again – disposal of the surplus soil, the constructional delays and difficulties, the size of the tunnel portals (always misleadingly portrayed although evidence had been provided time and again that the top of the portals could be dropped). There was no dialogue on how we could collectively save the Government vast expenditure in an environmentally pleasing way – simply a case of public officials carrying out their duty to see us, and then moving on.

In the light of the public discussion on road pricing nowadays, the doubts expressed by the Treasury as to the possibility of charging for road use on a widespread basis seem a trifle lacking in vision (or honesty) only four years later.

Explaining the decision to rule out further consideration of a toll tunnel, Chope wrote 'The toll tunnel proposal does not overcome the principal disadvantages of the earlier tunnel scheme of cost and delay. The proposal does nothing to reduce the additional cost of a tunnel compared with a cutting and although a privately funded toll scheme would reduce the cost of road provision by the Government it would transfer the burden [to] the travelling public.' Coming from a minister who was widely supposed to be a pillar of the Tory right wing, such statements did seem a little surprising – road provision by the Government – a free service with no market checks or balances. By the end of that meeting in Marsham Street, I think it was quite clear to all of us that the toll tunnel was dead, and about to be buried.

Only days later the Transport Department announced that the contract for the preliminary works on the M3 had been awarded to John Mowlem Construction. No satisfactory explanation was ever offered by the Transport Department to justify the division of the works into a 'preliminary' and a main contract. Engineers have repeatedly told me that there was no constructional basis for this division, and the inevitable assumption must be that it was a political move with the aim of diminishing the possibility of influence from outside stopping the construction of the Cutting.

11

The 1992 General Election – Tactical voting and the end of the campaign

The Transport Department's announcement two days before Christmas, 23 December 1991, that the preliminary contract for the M3 Cutting route had been awarded to Mowlem, marked a turning point in the campaign to save Twyford Down.

In January 1992 the contract, in the sum of £1.3 m, was for advance works: it included the construction of an access track to permit demolition of two minor bridges over the London to Southampton railway line near Shawford and construction of two new bridges, one over the railway and one at Hockley. The new bridges were to provide access roads for use in the main M3 contract. Despite being only a very small part of the whole M3 link project, the contract was nonetheless a significant step, and presumably intended to be seen as such. Sadly, the contract involved the destruction of part of the Itchen Valley Water Meadows in the area between Hockley Junction and the River Itchen.

There was obviously now no chance of altering the Government's mind; there remained the hope that the European Commission would instigate legal proceedings, which would more or less force the UK Government to halt the construction; most important, a general election seemed increasingly likely before the end of the summer, certainly before the main contract would be awarded.

For some time Friends of the Earth (FoE), the green campaigning group, had been helping the campaign for Twyford Down. FoE and World Wide Fund for Nature had been the only national conservation groups to offer financial assistance, and practical help, to our campaign.

The Council for the Protection of Rural England (CPRE) had apparently seen the writing on the wall some time earlier. CPRE had mounted a national fund-raising campaign against the Government's road-building policy. The envelope containing the appeal was imaginative – the 'window' for the addressee was set in the 'cut' on the Down, taken from the Transport Department's own photomontage of the scheme. Inside the leaflet a number of threatened sites were depicted, including Twyford Down under the title 'Sacrificed'. Sadly, our campaign did not receive any of the proceeds from that leaflet appeal.

With the awarding of the preliminary contract and the consequential threat to the rare Water Meadows site, within one of the Sites of Special Scientific Interest, Friends of the Earth began to consider the possibility of organizing peaceful protests on the proposed motorway site. The purpose of any such action would be, quite simply, to shame the Government, and to create a climate of national and international awareness, highlighting the damage which the Transport Department's route would inflict on Winchester's landscape and on the sustainability of the UK's environment protection policies.

Andrew Lees, the Campaigns Director of FoE, was well aware of the political possibilities created by the expectation of an early general election. An environmentalist with an almost spiritual conviction, Andrew was an unusual combination of 'green idealist' and pragmatic wheeler-dealer on behalf of his beloved 'environment'. Following his premature death some years later it was said 'the earth never had a better friend.' Certainly for Twyford Down he proved that 'a friend in need is a friend indeed.' During January 1992 we had extensive discussions with Andrew Lees, and with Roger Higman, FoE's Roads Campaign coordinator, and Robin Maynard, their Countryside Campaign leader. It was quite clear that time was running out for Twyford Down. Although the intervention of the European Commission remained a possibility it seemed increasingly less likely, and we had nearly exhausted much of our energy and most of our resources. Andrew, and Friends of the Earth, brought us campaigning expertise and resources when they were most needed.

The Twyford Down Association had become the proud possessor (or at least occupant) of a tiny semi-basement shop in the centre of Winchester. David Croker had recently retired from his job with IBM, and formed The Green Business Company, which specializes in supplying environmentally friendly stationery and office equipment to businesses. The Association and David's company co-existed at No 10 Southgate Street, Winchester. Over the period of time in the lead-up to the general election and during the election itself the office in Southgate Street was to be invaluable. It is doubtful if the campaign could have functioned without this 'shop front' with its telephone and fax machine.

Towards the end of January we learnt that Mowlem were to start work on the site on Monday, 27 January 1992. We only received confirmation of the date the weekend before and, early on the Monday morning, a decision was taken that local people should mount a peaceful protest. The actual place where Mowlem were due to start work was known as Bushfield Roundabout, and was very close to the railway line at Shawford. There was a Hampshire County Council smallholding close to the railway line, near the water meadows, with a stupendous view of Twyford Down and the route of the proposed Cutting. The infamous picture of the Cutting was in fact taken from one of the fields on the farm. The tenant farmer, a Mr Windibank, ran the smallholding with a sideline in selling bags of potatoes and turkeys at Christmas. The access road down to Windibank's farm was to be well trodden by many of us and the media during the coming months.

David activated the Twyford Down Association's bush telegraph and arranged for the local county councillor, Ann Bailey, who represented Shawford and Compton division on Hampshire County Council, and representatives of the local communities of Twyford, and Compton and Shawford to be at the site by about 2 pm with suitable placards. We advised the local media over the weekend. On the Monday morning I contacted my guru in the national media who saw at once that while the work about to be commenced was minimal (only preparing a spot for the contractor's site hut, I think), it would be symbolic. By 2 pm the national media had dropped everything and were massed at the site by the Bushfield Roundabout. Somehow the word had got around Fleet Street (or Wapping) that no national paper with an environment correspondent could afford to miss this event.

There was a satisfyingly comprehensive coverage of the start of work in the national papers the next day. *The Daily Telegraph* did us proud with a huge picture of Judith Martin, a Winchester councillor, waving a banner across four columns of its front page with the headline, 'Twyford Down M3 work begins despite protest'.

A couple of weeks later Mowlem were scheduled to demolish the two small farm-track bridges over the railway line. Arrangements had been made with British Rail that for two weekends the main London to Southampton railway line between Winchester and Shawford would be closed for a twelve-hour 'possession' period to allow the work to be under-taken safely. FoE and the Twyford Down Association decided that this would be a suitable opportunity to mark opposition to the destruction of the Down and its landscape. The carefully organized and disciplined protest was to involve a small group of FoE campaigners occupying one of the bridges to be demol-ished. The intention was to remain on the bridge until legally required to move. It was a bright February day and the occu-piers were brought coffee and sandwiches by the locals. The work was due to start at midnight on the Saturday, and by late afternoon the police arrived. The FoE campaign leader, Roger Higman, and I, for the Twyford Down Association, were informed by the police that they had powers to ask us to leave the site, and were now doing just that. Within a few minutes our supporters had all vacated the site.

There were, however, other protesters in the area, who decided to go back onto the bridges later under the cover of darkness. A small number of them chained themselves to the machinery and were removed by the police. This incident marked a changing element in the overall campaign. Until the autumn, when the main contract was let, FoE and Twyford Down Association remained the leaders of the campaign setting the agenda for legal, peaceful campaign events, such as rallies, both on and off the site. But the more militant protesters who were present for the first time that Saturday in February, were to remain on the periphery, but were present at almost all sub-sequent events.

By the end of February the national media had detected that a change in the Twyford Down story was about to take place. Michael Dynes, transport correspondent and Michael McCarthy, environment correspondent of *The Times*, identified the coming change: 'An off-shoot of a militant American organization has become involved in the dispute over the M3 extention through Twyford Down. Their involvement has raised concern that violence may be brought into British environmental politics for the first time. Mainstream campaigners fear that...a confrontation with the police may be provoked by members of Earth First! David Garland, of Earth First was quoted as saying, "Environmental policies are not being carried out fast enough in Britain. Things have to be speeded up and the only way to do this is through confrontation".'

For the time being, however, FoE and the Twyford Down Association maintained control over the campaign. FoE decided on a symbolic occupation of the threatened Water Meadows site. Legally the Transport Department, and its contractors, were not allowed access onto the Water Meadows until a formal four-months notice, under the Wildlife and Countryside Act, had expired, permitting works to start. English Nature had insisted that the full process be gone through, resulting in the delayed access by the contractors to the Water Meadows site.

A brave band of FoE campaigners pitched camp alongside the Water Meadows, careful to avoid damaging the ecology they were fighting to save. The 'occupation' was launched with Merrick, Jonathon Porritt, and Andrew Lees of FoE being chained across the site. The weather instantly turned cold and wet, and local people fell into the habit of taking hot coffee and breakfast down to the site. FoE had no way of knowing how long they would have to sit it out on site before the Transport Department authorized the contractors to move in.

By chance my family moved house at this time. Added to juggling family, home and job with the usual campaigning was moving house. I did wonder what our new neighbours would make of the comings and goings from the Water Meadows. The small band of 'permanent' occupiers would come back to our new home for a bath, a rest and some hot food. The house was still undergoing building works, and the bathroom and loo had bare plaster on the walls. We used to joke that we kept it like that so that they wouldn't feel awkward in their muddy, chalky clothes.

The time dragged a little and, to keep spirits up and maintain an element of stylish humour, the FoE campaign leader, Robin Maynard, decided to hold a candlelight dinner in the Meadows. Formal invitations were issued to various members of the

Government, but fortunately none of them embarrassed us by accepting or turning up for the superb meal. The press, however, did and photographs in the local and national press (Figure 19) recorded one of our more light-hearted and eccentric efforts. Black-tie dress was obligatory, the table was laid with damask linen, and hot food and good wine were served. There was a nasty moment when a threatening phone call was received by David Croker's family, saying that someone would be breaking up the party. The police kindly said they would pop down if necessary and Robin Maynard kept his mobile phone switched on, but it all passed off quite quietly.

On 9 March Friends of the Earth decided that volunteer campaigners should chain themselves across the entrance to the motorway site at the base of Twyford Down near the Hockley traffic lights. A legal briefing was issued to the half dozen or so who volunteered. FoE emphasized that it would be a peaceful

Figure 19 Protesting in style. Dinner in the Water Meadows, March 1992. From left to right: Cllr Ann Bailey, a protester, Merrick Denton-Thompson, Ruth Evans of FoE, David Croker, chairman of TDA, and Robin Maynard, Countryside Campaigner, FoE. *(Reproduced by kind permission of The Hampshire Chronicle.)*

protest, and that the campaigners' argument was with the Government, and particularly the Transport Department, and not the construction workers on site, or the police. FoE formally notifed the local police station, and asked the police to contact the European Commission because of the possibility of the Commission putting the matter before the courts, 'before taking any steps to remove FoE volunteers from the site.'

Access to the site was obstructed while the Transport Department went through the necessary legal procedures to obtain an injunction against the volunteers chained across the site (throughout one very cold night, too). The injunctions, properly drawn up, were duly served on the individuals, who were then cut free by the police. The exhausted volunteers were taken to various local homes, bathed, fed and left to recover for 12 hours, and then they left the area. They could no longer legally go onto the area around Twyford Down and they left Winchester for the time being.

On 17 March 1992 the contractors moved onto the site. Robin Maynard had developed a working relationship with both the police and the contractors. We decided to hold one last massive local protest. The word was put about that we wanted people to come along and show the politicians the strength of feeling that existed in the local communities, as well as nationally. FoE organized the rally, informed the police (and the media) and arranged for a number of responsible people to be present.

The rally was held on a Tuesday morning in a normal working week. There had been a good deal of local and national publicity during the preceding weeks, but we were staggered at the number of people who came down to the Water Meadows, many with banners, placards, dogs and children. In the main those who came along were local people from Winchester and the villages of Compton, Shawford and Twyford. Local councillors, a vicar, housewives, old and young, joined the committed campaigners. It was a large and good-natured crowd. After a while a man, with a young child, stepped to the front of the crowd. Carrying the toddler on his shoulder he advanced towards one of the machines stripping the turf. The machine retreated and the press carried dramatic pictures of an ordinary man, with a representative of the next generation on his shoulders, facing up to the road-builders. The man, Mr Myddleton, came from a nearby village, and the action he took was completely spontaneous. It was a remarkably evocative act which left a lasting impression on all of us there who witnessed it.

Others followed where Mr Myddleton had led and soon the machines came to a halt, surrounded by a mass of largely middle-aged men and women. After half an hour or so the police asked us to move people back off the site, and particularly to make sure that the young children were kept well away. After a little while almost everyone had left the construction site. As the police said afterwards, 'peaceful protest is historically acceptable.' Many of us were desperately keen that the campaign should remain one of peaceful protest and that the wide-based support from across the community should not be eroded.

The events on the Water Meadows made a substantial impression on the media, who recognized that almost for the first time they had witnessed middle-class Conservative voters, retired military men, elected politicians and a younger, less conventional group, coming together in an alliance against the Government's road building campaign. It was the pearls-and-twinsets which surprised the media, not the more radical elements in the crowd.

While the FoE campaigners had been camped in the Water Meadows they were joined by a charming couple of travellers, Stef and Sam; Stef played a mandolin at a number of rallies, and they had entertained everyone with their music. With the start of the work on the Water Meadows FoE decamped, putting away their tents. Stef and Sam moved their Tipee Tent up into the Dongas area, on the north side of St Catherine's Hill. Remarkable for its deep hollow-ways, protected as an SSSI on account of the species-rich downland turf, the area seems to have been named the Dongas sometime in the last century. Merrick always maintained this was a product of Winchester College's colonial connections as donga is apparently 'a Matabele word meaning drainage channel.' Be that as it may, Stef and Sam set up home in the Dongas and were joined by one or two others. During a hot summer they remained there undisturbed, to be joined by many other travellers. The Cutting route was destined to pass through the Dongas area and eventually, after the main contract for its construction had been let, it was the refusal of these people to leave the site which precipitated the final phase of the M3 saga. The group of travellers called themselves the Dongas Tribe, a name which has stuck and has become a byword associated with travellers and road protests.

In March 1992 John Major called a general election, adding another dimension to our activities. The national public opinion polls were showing the Labour Party, led by Neil Kinnock, with a massive lead. For some time we had been aware of the possibility of a general election offering a different means to save the Down. Much of our activity had had the secondary objective of 'buying' time. The general election could hardly have been called at a time when media interest in the fate of Twyford Down was higher. By the spring of 1992 the start of construction work on the Down and Water Meadows was providing a convenient focus for the media. The threat to the Down had moved from the realms of discussion and plans, to a physical reality. By that time, too, it had become almost obligatory for anyone aspiring to 'green' credentials to refer to Twyford Down at every opportunity. What a change from four years earlier.

For some three years we had run what was, for an 'anti-roads' campaign at that time, a uniquely political effort to save Twyford Down: a fringe meeting at the 1990 Conservative Party Conference, the toll-tunnel proposal which was building upon new Conservative policies, and the involvement of the Liberal Democrat's environment spokesman were outward signs. Behind the scenes we had lobbied Secretaries of State, Ministers, Members of the House of Lords, and ordinary Members of Parliament. Government offices from No 10 downwards had been pestered by our supporters, some of whom had been at the same school (Winchester College) as leading members of the Government, and the great and the good had been peppering Government with personal letters.

In one sense the announcement of the 1992 General Election provided a platform for the culmination of our efforts. There had been gentle speculation, which we had done nothing to stifle, that the Twyford Down Association might put up a candidate in Winchester. Jonathon Porritt's involvement in the Twyford Down campaign had not passed unnoticed; he had left Friends of the Earth and there was some speculation that he might be seeking a parliamentary career. There were many of our local supporters who would have abandoned their traditional party allegiance and voted for the charismatic man who had been one of the first national environmental figures to take up the cudgels for Twyford Down. There was no doubt at all that if Porritt were willing to stand for parliament in Winchester he would have attracted huge support; the profile of Twyford Down would have been incredible. There was, however, a real problem in that if Porritt stood as an independent candidate he would have been fighting a 'single issue' campaign. However good for the profile of the 'single issue' in question, such candidates rarely, if ever, get elected and the long-term benefits to the 'single issue' are debatable since the tag of having been defeated at an election remains and can subsequently be used as an argument against the popularity of the cause. There was some unfounded speculation that Porritt could stand as the Liberal Democrat candidate, but that overlooked two problems – firstly, the Liberal Democrats already had a candidate and, secondly, there was absolutey no indication that Porritt himself had considered joining the Liberal Democrats and giving up his political freedom.

I had discussed the political dimensions with Jonathon Porritt. He was as well aware as we were of the potential offered by a general election when it came. With the increasing speculation that Major was on the point of calling a general election a number of us had discussed the various options available: putting up a local Twyford Down Association candidate; persuading a national figure to stand; supporting whichever of the national party candidates most fully supported the aims of the Association; putting up a sort of 'gadfly' candidate in the constituencies of, say Major, or Heseltine, or even Rifkind.

The Association discussed the issue a number of times and agreed that the risks to the longer-term credibility of our campaign involving an Association candidate far outweighed any publicity advantages. The situation in Winchester was already likely to be very confused with two 'Conservative' candidates standing – Gerry Malone, the newly selected official Tory, and John Browne, the incumbent MP who was intending to stand as an independent Conservative. The Liberal Democrats were considered to be very strong, despite having selected a county councillor from Alton instead of the Winchester-based city councillor, David Chidgely (to become MP for Eastleigh). It seemed clear to us that, however worthy, any purely local TDA candidate could not compete effectively in that type of arena and that the failure of such a candidate to get elected would do only harm to the cause of Twyford Down.

With the calling of the election some decisions had to be made quickly. The local press, and the environment correspondents of the national broadsheets were nosing around and seeking comments from David Croker and myself.

Both opposition parties had given undertakings to reconsider the Twyford Down Cutting route if elected to Government. On 4 March Ann Taylor, the shadow minister for Environmental Protection had written 'Labour believes that thorough Environmental Impact Assessments should take place on all major building projects, not least because that is a European law to which the British Government has agreed. Environmental considerations must be at the heart of all policy making. On coming into office, a Labour Government will halt the work at Twyford Down and also Oxleas Wood [East London River Crossing] so that full Environmental Impact Assessments can take place in line with commitments by this [UK] Government at an international level.' The Liberal Democrats had repeatedly criticized the decision to destroy Twyford Down.

Following a couple of councils of war between Jonathon Porritt, David Croker, and me, a strategy was developed, which we decided to call the Twyford Factor. In agreeing the strategy we worked on the assumption that it was very possible that the outcome of the election would be a hung parliament, and that each and every seat would be more than usually important to the Conservative Party managers. Our motives were positive – the promise of the tactical voting campaign might still just push the Government into pulling back from the final decision; if we failed in that objective, the national profile of the threat to the Down would be vastly raised yet again, and hopefully both the Liberal Democrats and the Labour Party commitment to reconsider the Conservative Government's decision on M3 would be consolidated so that, in the event of a Labour victory, or a hung parliament with the Lib Dems holding the balance of power, Twyford Down would be rescued.

Jonathon Porritt defined the Twyford Factor as an assessment of the national swing against the Tory Party, a calculation of the additional swing (and actual number of votes) needed (in each seat we decided to target) to get rid of the Tories, making the additonal percentage swing/votes the Twyford Factor.

The first step was to decide which seats to target. It seemed sensible to confine ourselves to the immediate vicinity of the M3 near Winchester. The possibility of extending the tactical voting campaign to any seat with a contentious road project was discussed, but we recognized that we did not have the resources to make any sort of a reasonable job of tackling such an extensive campaign. The advantages of extending the campaign were seductive – increased profile, and, because of the increased number of Tory MPs who would become vulnerable, increased pressure on the Government to change the Twyford Down decision even at that very late stage. But the disadvantages were obvious: loss of focus, huge additional organizational problems, and a commitment of time and resources which frankly we probably could not hope to cope with.

In 1992 the organization of a national network of anti-road project groups hardly existed. By the time of a possible 1997 General Election things will be very different. Alarm UK, a sort of national confederation of local road-campaigning groups has developed into an effective network. Admittedly, many of these groups may not see political activity as their prime function, but there can be little doubt that the network could be activated to provide advice and support on tactical voting campaigns, and that a general election would provide sufficient stimulus for this to happen.

Having identified the seats most appropriate to target we had then to approach the strongest opposition candidate in each of the constituencies (either Liberal Democrat or Labour) to become one of the 'Twyford Down' candidates. The Twyford Down Association and its allies would offer manpower, high-profile support from Jonathon Porritt and others, and any other support or resource which was either available or wanted.

It was also hoped that the Green Party candidates would be willing to stand down in those seats where a Twyford Down factor was being invoked. Ideally, of course, a tactical voting campaign involves all the opposition candidates agreeing among themselves which one has the best chance of succeeding and the others withdrawing. In reality that is extremely hard to achieve. To outsiders it may seem an obvious arrangement, but political parties have paid up supporters, people who have committed themselves over some time to supporting a particular political party. They may not be willing to be denied the opportunity to express that specific support at the ballot box. The national party organizations have other constraints – what such action might have on national credibility and the fact that they may get tainted, even if only by association, with some national policies at odds with their own policies.

We eventually agreed to target only Southampton Itchen, Christoper Chope the Road Minister's seat, and Winchester itself. There was only four weeks' notice of the election, and we opted for quality rather than quantity. In retrospect this was wise, as the amount of work involved proved considerable and I think a wider campaign would have stretched the resources beyond breaking point.

Privately I contacted Gerry Malone, by now the official Conservative candidate for Winchester, and asked that we meet to discuss Twyford Down, and its role in the campaign. A firm commitment from Malone, on behalf of the Conservative Party, to reconsider the Twyford Down route was what we were seeking. If this had been forthcoming we would have aborted the tactical voting campaign. Over a coffee I explained the situation to Malone. Quite straightforwardly he told me that the best he could offer us was a personal commitment from him to press the Government to consider a low-level crossing of the valley and to pass the motorway under the railway line at Shawford. Malone and I had previously discussed the largely unrecognized scale of the impact on the villages immediately south of Winchester, which would be caused by a crossing at high-level, and I don't doubt his concerns about the high-level crossing. Sadly, though, I had to say that his limited personal commitment would not be enough for the Association and its supporters.

With the landscape around Shawford and Compton now gigantically raised above the natural valley floor, many people now recognize that the high-level crossing of the valley and railway line is equally as damaging as the cut through the Down. Indeed, in terms of impact upon residents it is probably worse. The fact was, however, that the cut through the Down, coupled with the high-level route (using the spoil from the cut for the embankments) formed a complete package. There was no indication that a candidate's personal pledge in a campaign would be transformed into Government policy, and there was every indication that the Transport Department would fight tooth and nail to maintain the composite package. Almost a year earlier there had been confidential discussions on the possibility of breaking the scheme into two parts, with a view to the motorway being passed under the railway line at low level. These discussions had come to nothing. I, for one, judged that a year on, after the furore over the European intervention, there was absolutely no chance of a change to a low-level route. We now had nothing to lose.

I therefore told Malone that the Association would be running a tactical voting campaign in Winchester, supporting his principal opponent, the Liberal Democrat on the sole grounds of the preservation of Twyford Down and Winchester's landscape setting.

Personally, as a Conservative at heart, it was not a decision I took lightly. In the preceding two years, in all our dealings Malone had operated fairly and in a businesslike manner. As someone who had been closely involved in national and local politics, I had a great deal of personal sympathy for Malone and for the can of worms he seemed to have inherited at Winchester Conservative Association. Winchester was a plum seat to be offered, but it certainly did not come to him on a silver platter. It seemed to me that Malone had navigated a very level-headed course through the local shenanigans over John Browne. But these considerations, however, simply did not, in our view, compete with either the threat to the Down, or the huge public support that we had been given over so many years in the fight to save it.

By the middle of March we were just about ready to go public with the Tactical Voting Campaign. David Bellamy had agreed to join Porritt at the public launch of the campaign. Coordinating the diaries of Porritt and Bellamy was no simple task, and we decided to go for Tuesday, 20 March, at the Winchester Guildhall. We had just five days to organize the meeting, and publicize the event. We discussed the size of hall, and Porritt gave me firm instructions to opt for smaller rather than large, in view of the very short run-in time which left the promotion of the event to word of mouth. As it was, I had little choice because of the very short notice we gave the Guildhall and all we could get was a large hall. Jonathon Porritt need not have worried – the hall was packed, with Guildhall management staff turning people away because of Safety Regulations. Twyford Down, the General Election, Bellamy and Porritt proved a heady mix.

The confrontation between Ripa di Meana, the European Environment Commissioner, and the Conservative Government hit the headlines again on 18 March. Speaking in Brussels di Meana reacted angrily to the start of construction works on the Water Meadows. He said legal proceedings against Britain in the European Court 'certainly cannot be ruled out.' According to a report in *The Guardian*, di Meana went on, 'I told Mr Rifkind (Transport Secretary) that I was certain I could rely on his wisdom, his commonsense, and his respect for EC law. I shall certainly write to him now expressing my deep sense of disappointment at what has happened.' Any hopes we might have harboured that the Government would pull back were firmly killed by the obvious confrontation between the Conservative Government and the Commission. The General Election was being fought just before the UK took over the Presidency of the EU and in the run up to the Maastricht Summit on the future of the EU. Support for matters European was very lukewarm among the Conservative grassroots supporters, a fact of which the leadership of the Conservative Party and the Government were all too well aware. On pragmatic political grounds the Conservative Government could not afford to concede on Twyford Down by mid-March 1992. I was told by close contacts of Prime Minister Major, that when the European Commission entered the fray so publicly the previous autumn the fate of Twyford Down was effectively sealed. I can well believe that to be the case, but it is sad to reflect that merely by exercising the power vested in it by the UK Government, which had signed the Directive on Environmental Impact Assessments, the Commission unwittingly contributed to the destruction of Twyford Down. There is an African proverb to the effect that when the elephants fight the grass gets trampled upon – in this case it was part of England's landscape heritage.

The day after the extensive national coverage of di Meana's criticism of the Government, *The Daily Telegraph* and *The Times* carried another Twyford Down story.

'Tories run into motorway protest vote' ran the headline in *The Daily Telegraph*. Charles Clover, the paper's environment editor, wrote, 'The Conservative candidate for Winchester, Gerry Malone, sought last night to head off a planned anti-Tory tactical voting campaign over the controversial Twyford Down motorway project...An environmental campaign against Mr Malone is likely to cause further confusion in the Winchester constituency, where the resident MP, John Browne, has been de-selected by the Tories and is contesting the seat as an independent.'

The Times, in a long piece by Michael McCarthy, also reported the launch of the tactical voting campaign, and referred to 'The Twyford Factor, which gives the environment real political significance in the election for the first time, could be decisive both in Winchester, a once safe seat where the Conservative vote may now be split by the candidature of John Browne...and in Southampton Itchen, a Tory marginal held by the roads minister, Christopher Chope...'

At a packed meeting that Friday evening Professor David Bellamy and Jonathon Porritt were besieged by the press and local TV and radio. The agreed press release said, 'The Twyford Down Association is to launch a new tactical voting campaign in two seats, Winchester and Southampton Itchen. The Twyford Down Association has come to this decision in the light of the Government's continuing refusal to protect Twyford Down, one of the most important conservation and archaeological sites in Southern Britain.'

'On behalf of the Twyford Down Association, David Bellamy and myself,' said Jonathon Porritt, 'urge all Labour, Green and disaffected Tory voters to support the Liberal Democrat here in Winchester, and urge all Liberal Democrat, Green and disaffected Tory voters to support the Labour candidate in Southampton Itchen.'

Porritt continued, 'This Government has shown a total disregard for the environment, for the law and for the interest of local people. In normal circumstance we would be powerless to do anything more to protect Twyford Down; in a general election, people can make the ultimate commitment by using their vote wisely to demonstrate their contempt for this Government's action.'

So, the campaigners for Twyford Down were invoking the ultimate democratic process. The hard work started in earnest the next day. Twyford Down supporters put themselves at the disposal of the two candidates, John Denham in Southampton Itchen, and Tony Barron in Winchester. It was not until the Tactical Voting Campaign that we realized how much support we had in Southampton. We has assumed that people in Southampton who had to drive through the Hockley lights would be opposed to our campaign, but that was not necessarily the case. We should have mobilized that support in earlier years, but it was a tremendous help during the election.

One of our new found supporters in Southampton suggested that a letter be handed out to all the passengers on the rush-hour trains travelling between Southampton and Winchester. Passengers on the trains enjoyed a panoramic view of Twyford Down, and the proposed route. The suggestion was that the letter be distributed by volunteers who would board the train at Southampton and hand out the letters to all passengers. Hopefully, by the time the train reached Eastleigh, just south of the motorway site, all passengers would have received a letter and the volunteers would be able to alight at Winchester. A really excellent letter was drafted.

As this train takes you past Eastleigh towards Winchester, take time to look east, over the water meadows of the Itchen Valley towards St Catherine's Hill with its crown of beech tress and the beautiful downlands that surround it.

Just past Shawford Station you will see the Winchester Bypass below. This road is inadequate and has been for years. We would like to see the skills of planners and engineers of the Transport Department put to work to upgrade this road to motorway standards, but with a proper concern for the unique landscape it is traversing. But the Transport Department will not entertain these ideas. It is intent on creating an engineering triumph – a new motorway cut through virgin land. You cannot easily imagine what is in store...We are not Luddites. We see the logic of completing the M3. But it is possible to do so without the orgy of destruction that you will see unfolding before you [a reference to the work already being undertaken in the Water Meadows and the stripped topsoil on the face of Twyford Down]. If it goes much further it will be your daily journey will in future be marred by the thought that you could have added your voice to the many – and it could have made a difference.

What can you do? You can offer us help, support or donation...Also you can use your vote wisely. Vote for a candidate who will fight for the Environment rather than one who condones the Government's grotesque annihilation of this precious landscape.

Put an action to help, at the TOP of your list of things to do today. Generations depend on you.

The letter was signed by David Croker, as chairman of the TDA, but had been written by an ordinary voter, Dr Clive Bennett from Southampton. A small band of volunteers boarded the rush-hour trains and distributed the letters. The election campaign was by then more than half over – polling day being Thursday, 9 April.

The activities of the Twyford Down Association and our supporters in Winchester prompted a 'special' leaflet being produced by Malone and distributed in Compton and Shawford villages. In simple terms the leaflet set out again what Malone had initially said to me, which he had subsequently confirmed in a letter: take the motorway under the railway line at Shawford, not over it. As a damage limitation exercise in the rough and tumble of politics the leaflet was a sound piece of electioneering. But as any sort of commitment to the environment, or to Twyford Down, it left a great deal to be desired, and irritated many of our supporters. For consumption in the blue heartland of Compton and Shawford I suspect it may have worked.

We had been scratching around in our minds for a photogenic and apposite 'event' to attract attention to our campaign. The obvious thing was some sort of represention of the ultimate election symbol, a voter's 'X'. The idea was all right, but precisely how to present the symbol proved more difficult. Eventually it was decided that a sufficient number of people could form the shape of an 'X' on the face of Twyford Down, which had by then a huge oblong chalk scar where the initial top soil stripping and chalk excavations had taken place in the last two weeks. We had every indication that at least one, if not two, national newspapers and the television would take aerial pictures of the demonstration. Jonathon Porritt would come down to provide a focus for the event.

A group of our supporters worked out the number of people needed to produce a sufficiently large 'X' ; the idea was that 100 people would make a respectably sized arm of the 'X'. As a minimum, we needed 400 people on the site, and they would have to be marshalled on to pre-marked plots to ensure the 'X' was recognizable. One of our most loyal supporters, Chris Gillham, and his team worked out the dimensions, prepared the markers and promised to be on the site at crack of dawn on the morning of the demonstration so as to marshal the people onto the right spots in time for the fly-over by several press planes. A team worked from the TDA office in Southgate Street, telephoning all our supporters to come along. We had planned to run the demonstration on the Saturday. On the preceding Tuesday, when most of the arrangements were in place, our media guru pointed out that to get the national broadsheets we should run it on the Sunday instead. I am glad it wasn't me that told the volunteers everything they had done, including the hundreds of phone calls, had to be redone but they took it well, and re-cognized the sense of it. Somehow the arrangements all came together in time and so it was that on the last Sunday of the campaign, 5 April, several hundred people, dogs, children and musicians gathered on the brilliant white scar on the face of Twyford Down and were marshalled into neat lines. Looking at

Figure 20 Voting symbol on Twyford Down in April 1992. The voting symbol of an 'X' made up of hundreds of protesters, strictly marshalled into lines and holding white boards skyward. *(Reproduced by kind permission of Times Newspapers.)*

the photograph (Figure 20) taken from the air one can see what a very thorough job Chris Gillham and his band had made of marking out the 'X' and keeping us all in line. The picture of Twyford Down's Tactical Voting symbol appeared in full colour on the back page of *The Times*, prompting at least one very senior Conservative to say to me after the dust of the election had settled what good coverage we had achieved.

That election time rally and the photograph marked the end of an era. The end was very close for Twyford Down by that time. Taken on a brilliant sunny day, the photograph shows most of the Down untouched by the bulldozers. It may be my imagination, but looking at that picture now there is a curious air of calm, the lull before the storms perhaps; almost as if the picture were taken in an earlier age of innocence in environmental campaigning. There is an old-fashioned sense of order in the demonstration. The single police squad car, perched on a mound of chalk, was doing what the English police are best at – keeping a fatherly eye on citizens behaving in a harmlessly eccentric manner. Within months, very different styles of protest were to take place on and around the M3 works. Perhaps harmless eccentricity is now no longer enough, though that saddens me.

As does the thought that if those who seek to govern us had the courage to lead, the intelligence to embrace new concepts, and confidence to reconsider decisions, the disaffection with the democratic process which we witnessed at Twyford Down could have been avoided.

Speaking in Southampton early in 1992 the Roads Minister, Chope, said 'Ninety-three per cent of all journeys are made by car. Therefore we have to ensure we have a road infrastructure to cope with that demand.'

Just two years later, in October 1994, the Royal Commission on the Environment published its report on Transport, calling for a doubling of petrol prices and the halving of the UK road building programme. The report made headline news, with comments such as 'the end of the love affair with the car'.

Apart from a few squawks of protest from the British Road Federation, the Commission's recommendations prompted no outcry of protest. Even the Automobile Association was measured in its reaction, recognizing that the time for restraint had arrived. However, the Transport Department persisted in dragging its feet.

In April 1992 those of us campaigning to save Twyford Down were only too well aware that time had all but run out. The only real hope lay in a defeat for the Conservative Government on 9 April. The Labour Party were well ahead in the public opinion polls, and there was a general expectation that the best the Conservatives could hope for was a hung parliament. During the last week of the campaign some of the national papers published damaging reports of the increases in taxes that would result from a Labour Government, and support for Labour stuttered.

In Winchester it did not seem that John Browne, the independent Conservative, had made much impact on the campaign, and we judged that the Winchester result would reflect the national swing. Should there be a massive swing against the Conservatives and towards the Liberal Democrats it was just possible that Winchester would be lost to the Conservatives. But it was on the national campaign that we pinned our hopes.

In those last few days I was worried that, if the Labour Party were to be elected, Twyford Down could become a victim of the pressures on the new ministers and that the staff in the Transport Department would present their minister with a pile of files, marked 'decisions made' or something like that and that Twyford Down would be lost by default. With the help of Geoff French from Scott Wilson Kirkpatrick a briefing package was put together, which included details of a possible interim improvement: a temporary flyover to relieve the congestion at the Hockley traffic lights. This briefing package was sent off to John Prescott, then Labour transport spokesman, Ann Taylor, the Labour party's environment protection spokeswoman, and to Simon Hughes at the Liberal Democrat Headquarters. Our hope was that these people would be sufficiently briefed not to be pushed into a corner on taking office.

By election day itself there was little more we could do. The environment correspondents of *The Times*, Michael McCarthy, and *The Daily Telegraph*, Charles Clover, came to Winchester to cover the election results. Winchester was the only constituency to have a remotely green tinge to its campaign, and those two journalists had run with the Twyford Down story for three years.

As soon as the polling stations closed and the exit polls started to emerge it was apparent that the result nationwide would be much closer than anticipated. The first few seats to be declared confirmed this. It seemed increasingly unlikely that the

Conservatives would lose Winchester. By the early hours of the morning it was confirmed that the Conservatives would be returned to power, albeit with a very much reduced majority. The Southampton Itchen count came on to the TV screens just before the formal declaration – the candidates waiting for the result. The Labour Party candidate, John Denham, had taken the seat from the Conservatives by just 270 votes.

John Denham wore his green 'Save Twyford Down' badge alongside his official Labour emblem, the red rose. Interestingly the twin seat of Southampton Test, which we had not targeted, had been retained by the Conservative MP James Hill by almost the identical number of votes that Chope had lost by in his Itchen seat. Twyford Down had proved that tactical voting was a practical proposition – it was possible to influence an election result, and by extension a general election result on specific issues.

Across the country opposition supporters were licking their wounds, and the Conservative Party sat back on its haunches, parading another victory, though in truth the Labour Party had lost the election. There was talk of John Major, with his own mandate setting a new course of modern Conservatism, but while the nation at large came to terms with such an unexpected result in Winchester we now faced a bleak prospect.

The return of the Conservative Government to power signalled the end of Twyford Down. None of us believed that Chope's absence would make any difference to Government policy. There remained a faint chance that the European Commission would take action, but that seemed increasingly less likely as time passed.

Malone's strong core Conservative support in the constituency, and the assurances he had given personally to try to minimize the impact on the residents of Compton and Shawford, proved enough to see him safely home at Winchester. He had given a number of pledges during the election campaign, in particular to arrange an urgent meeting with the Transport Secretary and to press for M3 to go underneath the railway line, but I had no expectation that this was an attainable option any longer. The villages of Compton and Twyford had hope, however, and early mail in Malone's postbag carried requests for the promised meeting with the Transport Secretary as soon as possible.

Time seemed to drag, and it was not until the middle of June that a meeting with the Minister was arranged. The new Roads Minister was Kenneth Carlisle. Our hopes died very slowly, and once again we approached friends and studied biographies of the new man for straws to clutch at – Dod, the parliamentary guide, told us that Carlisle counted 'conservation and wildlife' among his interests.

Gerry Malone, who had arranged the meeting, asked that we submit our suggested 'agenda' of matters we would like to discuss. Chris Corcoran, chairman of Twyford Parish, George Beckett, the chairman of Compton and Shawford Parish, and I met to agree tactics on what we would like to get out of the meeting and how best to achieve that. David Croker was not directly involved as he had taken angry exception to Malone's modest stance on M3. In any event, as vice-chairman of the Twyford Down Association I was to be its representative at the meeting with Carlisle.

Unfortunately the coffee grew cold as we learnt that in addition to ourselves Malone had arranged for a representative of the St Cross Community Association to accompany us. Representatives of the St Cross area had been fierce in their criticism of our objections to the Cutting route, and vehemently supported the route. The inclusion of a representative of this group was quite unexpected. I could well see that Malone was honouring his election pledges, that he wanted the community he represented to bury its divisions over M3, but I did wish he had come up with a more sensitive formula for achieving this. I think we recognized that St Cross had particular interests and concerns, being close to the Water Meadows. Indeed we had felt that St Cross had failed to grasp the damage that the vertical alignment – that is, the height – of the motorway would have on its community.

We were given little choice but to go along with the arrangements and we set about preparing items for discussion, which included a number of matters relating to the 'approved works' such as proper liaison with the local communities, confirmation that the carriageway surface would be tarmacadam, to seek the Minister's agreement to putting the M3 under the railway line, and to discuss 'options' for the stretch through the Down. This last was hopeful, but I felt it had to appear if only for the sake of completeness, and the others were willing to humour me.

The meeting itself was nearly a disaster. Corcoran, Beckett and I travelled to London. We duly signed in (yet again) at the Transport Department in Marsham Street. On being shown into a waiting room on the ministerial floor near the top of the building we were met by the representative of the St Cross group. Chris Corcoran opened the conversation but within a minute it was obvious that there remained a yawning gulf between ourselves and Ann Jones, representing St Cross. By the time Gerry Malone arrived there was a distinctly chilly atmosphere, which he attempted to defuse. Unfortunately things only got worse.

The door opened and a cheerful, friendly Minister wished us all good morning, and invited us to come along to his office. There was an awkard pause – you could have cut the atmosphere with a knife. With some presence of mind Gerry Malone said, 'Minister, I am afraid we are not quite ready – could you give us a few moments more?' Bonhomously the Minister glanced round, said 'Of course, join me when you are ready' and left. He took his dismissal with considerable equanimity and not at all personally. Later, in the meeting, he came across as a straightforward man who did not feel the need to dissemble, and who had a real understanding of what had driven us over the years. Perhaps he guessed at the underlying tensions that we carried with us at the end of the campaign.

Left alone with his warring constituents, Malone set about retrieving the situation. After a while we came to a sort of understanding among ourselves and Malone suggested we really ought not to keep the Minister waiting any longer. Unfortunately, we had no idea where the Minister had gone, nor where we were meant to go. The corridor was empty. Trying not to look like actors in a French farce, we eventually found the Minister and his officials patiently waiting for us in a large meeting room at one end of the corridor.

Chris Corcoran, who had been the principal architect of our 'agenda' for the meeting, kicked off on the subject of the arrangements for keeping local residents informed during the construction of the motorway about road closures, night working and temporary alternations to footpaths, and access to their homes. Corcoran complained that arrangements that the Transport Department claimed to have put in place were inadequate, and were not working at all. The Minister asked his officials to comment. They implied that very extensive liaison arrangements were working well. Corcoran explained the problems experienced by the residents in more detail. The Minister very firmly told his officials to set up a new liaison arrangement which would satisfy the parishes. At the time Transport officials looked less than happy at the Minister's firmness. But the liaison meetings with the parishes have since proved invaluable in minimizing the disruption to residents.

Almost in passing we asked the Minister to confirm that the motorway would have the 'black top' (tarmacadam surface rather than concrete) which had been discussed at the 1985 Public Inquiry. During cross-examination at the Inquiry, Transport Department witnesses had agreed with objectors and the Inspector that black top would be far preferable. The officials said the type of surface had not been specified – it might be left to the contractors. We were staggered. The presumption throughout the extensive reopened part of the Inquiry in 1987 had been that there would be a tarmacadam finish rather than the more noisy concrete. That might be so, agreed the official, but unless it was 'confirmed in the Decision Letter [the formal letter setting out the Secretaries of States' decision]' there was no necessity for undertakings given at a Public Inquiry to be incorporated in the final contract. Curious how naïve one can be. I had always assumed that if a witness, speaking on behalf of the Transport Department, told an Inspector that a particular detail would be incorporated in a scheme then the undertaking would be translated into Transport Department policy. This is a deeply disturbing attitude by the Transport Department, and one which must be addressed by Government to ensure that the Transport Department honours commitments made at Public Inquiries.

So far as the M3 was concerned, though, by raising this point with the Minister and the local member of parliament we achieved not just conventional tarmacadam finish but the prospect of the new improved finish – though sadly in the event it proved unpractical for the M3 at Twyford.

Discussion with the Minister about the actual alignment of the motorway, both vertical and horizontal, was short-lived. He made it clear that there was no question of varying the decision to construct it in the Cutting. Gerry Malone asked whether the Minister would look at putting the motorway under the railway line and was gently but firmly told 'No'. Malone did not press the point and it seemed (as indeed one would expect) that he had raised this before the meeting, and that he was only confirming the negative answer for our benefit.

As an opportunity to invoke the authority of the Minister to make certain that local residents suffered as little as possible during the construction phases, the meeting was a considerable success. So far as saving Twyford Down was concerned, the meeting was a complete failure. As the culmination of ten years' campaigning it was a feeble finale, and exposed the nature of manoeuverings by Government and its Departments of State in this dreadful saga.

At the end of June, Friends of the Earth organized a march along the length of the M3 route. Designed really to be a focus for all Twyford Down supporters, it was an opportunity to pay their last respects to the Down. Although the European Commission had still not made a decision (or at least announced it) on whether to proceed with legal action against the UK Government for failing properly to comply with the legislation on Environmental Impact Assessments of major construction projects, there was a tacit understanding by the summer of 1992 that nothing could now save Twyford Down .

There was, however, an increasing awareness of the potential that Twyford Down offered as an example of the damage the road-building programme was inflicting on the landscape of southern England. The Royal Society for Nature Conservation had identified several hundred SSSIs threatened by the road-building programme. In Surrey the Devil's Punchbowl at Hindhead was threatened by plans to improve the A3, and campaigners there had recently 'borrowed' our idea of the aerial views of the 'X' demonstration and achieved excellent coverage in the press with a 'NO' produced by volunteers holding white boards skywards while standing in the formation of NO. Oxleas Wood in East London was still under threat, and the campaign there was gathering momentum with the support of the local Greenwich council at last helping those residents who had kept the fight going for so many years. Oxleas Wood was, of course, another of the cases cited by the European Commission in a letter of formal notice sent to the UK Government under Article 169 of the Treaty. We strongly believed that whatever the outcome at Twyford Down, the greater the profile it achieved, and the more the Transport Department was forced to justify its decision to press ahead with the Cutting, the better the chances of saving Oxleas, the Devil's Punchbowl and other special places. So the FoE rally in June was seen not as an empty gesture

Figure 21 The final mass march in June 1992. The procession of protest-ers snaking its way from Compton Down to Winchester, led by Jonathon Porritt. *(Reproduced by kind permission of The Hampshire Chronicle.)*

but as part of a much wider campaign to put an end to the mind-less destruction of an unchecked road-building programme.

A lone Scots piper led Jonathon Porritt and several hundred people the five miles from Shawford Down into the heart of Winchester on a brilliant Midsummer's Day (Figure 21). Using the side-roads as close to the route of the motorway as possible, the crowd stretched out of sight. Motorists, delayed while the march crossed junctions, mostly seemed to be sympathetic as the police shepherded us along. The march was designed to be a show of strength – if the generally regarded 'lost cause' of Twyford Down generated such controlled support, what could the Government expect eleswhere – in middle-class Surrey, or at Oxleas with a huge local population and so close to London?

On 31 July, the European Commission finally announced that it would not be proceeding with the case against the UK Government in respect of Twyford Down. Oxleas Wood remained on their agenda, and the Government was faced with continued pressure from the Commission regarding Oxleas Wood. The decision was announced by way of a press release.

It was the holiday season and I was on holiday with the family on the remote Ionian island of Paxos. Our particular bit of heaven, to which we retreat every year, Paxos' great attraction is the tendency of its telephone links with the outside world to simply fail. David Croker was informed of the Commission's decision but was quite unable to get hold of me. He managed to contact Merrick, and sent me a fax. The fax was brought up to me at our place in the olive groves by Yannis, a local Paxiot who had no idea that he was bringing 'the bad news from Brussels'.

David had written simply, 'The EC has let us down. Smacks of political intrigue. Am handling the press as best I can. At home from 7 pm Friday, all day Saturday. Sorry to spoil your holiday. David.'

I went straight down to the village and eventually managed to get through to David, who was pleased to talk. There was nothing more I could do, except wait a couple of days to read the English papers when they arrived on the Sunday. When I returned to England I found that a member of the Environment Commissioner's Cabinet had telephoned me at home the day before the formal announcement to let us know in advance, which was a kind thought.

Simon Hughes, on behalf of the Liberal Democrats, issued a stinging press release, saying that 'Today's announcement bears all the hallmarks of a rancid, grubby back-room fix between the Government and the EC to avoid embarrassment to John Major during his term as President of the Community.'

The Times carried the story under the title 'Fight to Save Twyford Down ends as Brussels drops action' following what the paper described as 'a change of heart in the Brussels bureaucracy'. Maybe it was that, but *The Daily Telegraph* (3.8.92) referred to 'The EC decision not to proceed with the case against Britain – made during the parliamentary recess and on the eve of the Commission's annual holiday – follows intense pressure from the Government which had allowed preliminary works to begin.' The article went on to quote Mr Michael Howard, then Environment Secretary, as 'welcoming the Commission's recognition that there had been no breach of EC law.' Howard added: 'On Twyford Down, for example, we have had twenty years of public consultation, including five public inquiries.' Yet another Government Minister peddling the same old misinformation – on Twyford Down there had been ONE Public Inquiry (admittedly it had been reopened and so had the appearance of two) but to suggest FIVE was grossly misleading and a ministerial gaffe. And that was not a one-off mistake – Ministers consistently referred to five Public Inquiries and 20 years of debate. At that time it was less than ten years since the Transport Department, in 1983, first mooted any suggestion of the Twyford Down route. In any event Michael Howard of all people should have known better. He has strong local contacts with both Hampshire and Winchester. Way back in 1976 Howard had represented the objectors at the Public Inquiry when they were opposing the Transport Department's first suggested route for the M3 – slap through the Water Meadows.

Between them David and Merrick coped with the press, who of course besieged them for comments. It cannot have been the easiest set of interviews. With commendable realism and honesty Merrick told ITV viewers, 'We've lost.' In terms of the preservation of Twyford Down Merrick was patently right and I believe that he was right to say so. It was not a popular message in all quarters.

There was widespread recognition, however, that the campaign for the preservation of the Down (though not the campaign for proper care of the environment in transport policy) had been lost. Mr MacGregor, the Transport Secretary, had said he was 'delighted' with the Commission's decision and that the tender for construction would be let as soon as possible (Figure 22).

A couple of weeks after the Commission's withdrawal a rather sad group of the Twyford Down Association met to discuss the future of the Association. The Association's 'single objective is to secure, in perpetuity, the conservation of Twyford Down for the enjoyment and education of future generations' was how we had originally defined the purpose of the Association when it was founded in the spring of 1990. The first step towards achieving that objective had been to raise funds to meet the enormous cost of the Judicial Review.

In January 1991 the Association held its first public meeting. Jonathon Porritt, a vice-president of the Association, and Martin Biddle, its president, had held the audience of some 600 people spellbound with their different but equally compulsive oratory. The broader objectives of the Association had been defined as 'to protect the landscape, flora and fauna and antiquities of Twyford Down and adjacent areas of Winchester's countryside'

Figure 22 The lost cause. Construction work well under way: excavation of Twyford Down about half completed. (*Reproduced by kind permission of The Hampshire Chronicle.*)

but inevitably the Association's activities had been dominated by the need to save Twyford Down and the raising of money to fund these activities.

The question facing the Twyford Down Association in August 1992 was whether the Association should now publicly concede defeat so far as Twyford Down itself was concerned, while using whatever resources it had, whether financial or in terms of manpower and experience, to help other threatened landscapes.

Obviously this was a matter which should be put to every member of the Association. David Croker, as chairman of the Association, sent a letter to all members, with details of a General Meeting which was to be held on 7 September 1992. We were all anxious that the positive role that the Association could play in helping others should be emphasized, and David's Report said, 'The Association has become synonymous with opposition to the Cutting; has gained widespread support internationally, nationally and locally; is seen as a responsible organisation...The Association could continue to try to influence the scheme by seeking amelioration of the effects, by influencing the management plan for the remaining downland and by seeking a protective role for the rest of Winchester's downland setting. The Association could also seek a wider role in advising and giving help to other campaigns in the south of England. Members are asked to consider the way forward.'

The meeting endorsed the recommendations of the Association officers and conceded the legal battle. Professor Martin Biddle, as president of the Association chairing the meeting, said, 'There are lots of battles left to fight and we have a chance of winning some of them, but by fight I mean acting within legal means. The member of your [TDA] committee will not wish to become involved in anything illegal, because that erodes the edges of democratic society.'

Some individual members of the Association subsequently took the view that 'direct' action was justified, though they have always condemned violence. This debate (literally Machiavellian) as to whether the end can justify the means, has continued, but the Twyford Down Association has not altered the policy adopted at the General Meeting in September 1992, just prior to Tarmac Ltd being awarded the main contract for the construction of the Cutting, and the subsequent events on and around Twyford Down.

The elder statesman of the Association, Robin McCall, once Town Clerk of Winchester and then a Freeman of the City (an honour given to very few), had been in failing health and mercifully did not live to see the demise of Twyford Down. In the last few months of his life he struggled to attend the Association meetings and offer his help and guidance to us all. Three days before his death he came to one such meeting. His frailty was alarming, but more easily than some of us, he was able to look the future fully in the face, and that dark evening McCall suggested the Association consider setting aside any surplus funds for long term investment. The vision that McCall offered was that the Association should be formed into a permanent Trust which would outlive all of us, with the objective of maintaining funds to pay for the restitution of Twyford Down by backfilling the chasm with chalk and making good the landscape whenever it might be that the motorway became obsolete – maybe in two or three hundred years' time.

12

Postscript

The most difficult question to answer about the whole Twyford Down saga is also the simplest – why did it happen?

Did we end up with a road destroying one of Britain's most precious landscapes because of a series of innocent but catastrophic mistakes? Because of some hitherto undiscovered conspiracy? Or because the political systems that were meant to protect the environment and produce reasoned and practical solutions failed completely?

Early in 1991 the Government's plan to destroy Twyford Down was seen by many environmentalists and the press as the epitome of the 'roads versus the environment' debate in the UK.

The European Commission was examining the British Government's implementation of Community environmental protection legislation at a time when the Major Government was trying to establish its 'green' credentials in step with the public's increasing awareness of man's threats to the environment.

In April of that year, Tom Burke was appointed as a special adviser to the Secretary of State for the Environment on 'green' issues. A leading member of the environmental movement, Tom Burke left the Green Alliance – the non-profit making organization concentrating on environmental policy and politics – to join Michael Heseltine's team of civil servants at the Environment Department. His 'poacher turned gamekeeper' position – as some green colleagues would have it – means that today he has a unique perspective on the Twyford Down saga.

In 1991, Burke was known as a frequent, and articulate, critic of the Government's record on the environment. Today, he says: 'The Major government's record on the environment is not particularly stunning, but is nothing like as bad as its critics make out.' But despite this favourable assessment of the Government's overall record on environmental protection, Burke remains highly critical of the trunk road planning process in the United Kingdom: 'The way in which trunk road planning has been executed in this country is profoundly undemocratic – it gives a pretence of allowing for local objection, but does not give the substance to that.'

Burke says that the roads campaigns of the late 1980s and early 1990s, and those of twenty years earlier in the 1970s, struck a deep chord in what he describes as 'our intrinsically democratic society'. People sensed that there was something 'profoundly unfair' about the process of trunk road planning and it appears to the people involved that there is an imposition by the State of an arbitary decision.

For far too long the system by which trunk roads get built in this country has been, says Burke, 'a very peculiar process which starts with a traffic study, which in turn creates a sort of corridor, and there is then an evaluation of whether that warrants a road.'

Burke adds that the planned road is then put into the roads programme and financially assessed – but by now it has developed a momentum of its own and by the time a minister, or anyone else, gets near to assessing the proposal it is difficult to stop. Burke says: 'Nobody goes back to unpick that work, and the environmental assessment comes at a still later stage.' He describes the trunk road planning process to date as the 'hi-jacking of the political process by a technical élite who were able to impose their will in a way that was almost impregnable to oversight by Parliament, or by the political process at all – I am sure that ministers, most of them, did not really understand what was going on half the time.' But once a particular scheme had the support of the Treasury as well as officials in the sponsoring department – Transport – opponents found effective campaigns very difficult to mount.

'Twyford Down came to be recognized as a turning point,' says Burke, 'because, first, the issue represents a sort of Tory mobilization – it was who was involved and where it was that mattered – at Winchester, in the heart of Tory southern shire country; second, it was very easy to conceptualize that something was being ruined and, finally, because of the very effective publicity machine that got into gear so that after a while it became all-pervasive.'

Burke was newly installed in the Environment Department in April 1991 when the Twyford Down Association met with the then Transport Secretary, Malcolm Rifkind, to explain their proposal to complete the M3 in a tolled tunnel under Twyford Down.

Before his appointment, Burke frequently lectured to industry on environmental issues and had written two books on 'green capitalism'. The Twyford Down Association proposal was built upon the concept of 'the polluter pays' which had been embodied in the Environment White Paper produced by Mr Heseltine's predecessor at the Environment Department, Christopher Patten.

'The cutting through Twyford Down is the wrong solution to completing the M3 motorway,' Burke says. 'We could have put a tunnel through, even at the last minute. A tunnel was a viable option, and frankly, in any conceivable way in which you use cost benefit analysis [the then method for assessing the financial viability of road projects] there is no doubt that the benefits to the country far outweighed the losses.' He adds: 'Ministers, including Michael Heseltine, seriously considered the tolled tunnel proposal. Officials advised that it would not work. I believe that advice was incorrect and was probably offered because of the fear of any delay which might lead to abandonment.'

That fear was certainly one of the reasons the pro-roads lobby – most notably the British Roads Federation – backed the notion of pushing ahead with the Cutting route. But today's BRF director, Richard Diment, shares at least some of the concerns about road projects and the decision-making system where sensitive schemes are concerned. But he insists that most are not controversial. 'For the vast majority of schemes, the procedures are working very well. The biggest problem is why the Department of Transport is not processing these schemes faster.'

Mr Diment argues that the road-building programme raises two separate but related issues. The first is how to ensure that good quality decisions are taken, that take into account local people's needs plus environmental and other issues. The second concerns the fundamental wisdom of building roads at all – and that is really a debate about the type of society and economy we wish to have in future. If we want economic growth, if we want to create more jobs, that implies increasing trade and that means developing a system that enables this to take place. Twyford Down was responsible for pushing these debates to the top of the political agenda, Mr Diment agrees.

The macro-economic debate is only just beginning. But on the first point, he says, lessons are being learnt. 'It is not necessarily the best solution to build at the minimum public cost; if you do, it is very difficult to build roads of anything other than the most basic standards. In 1990 it was not possible to convince the Treasury of that or of the potential political cost involved. But that argument is being won. For example, the A3 Hindhead bypass originally skirted the side of the famous Devil's Punchbowl in Surrey. Now it is going to be put in a tunnel. There are schemes where the minimum civil engineering solution is not acceptable and alternatives are going to have to be funded.'

Mr Diment added: 'There is no doubt that Twyford Down changed the nature of the transport debate in this country. It made the Government far more concerned about the quality of the proposals it is putting forward, and we and others like us have to demonstrate far more effectively the benefits of schemes and the cost of not going through with them. The end result is going to be more expensive roads. They are going to have to be built with more expensive materials, with extra measures such as acoustic barriers to reduce noise – and we will have to look at more use of cuttings and tunnels. But the Treasury is going to have to accept that it is right to bear these additional costs.'

Mr Diment also agrees with many of the Twyford Down campaigners that the quasi-legal nature of the Public Inquiry system is unnecessarily restrictive. 'The problem is that once the legal processes have rejected a particular route it is not easy to return to that decision. It may be that once alternatives have also been examined that the original idea – or a variation of it – is the best option. But it is very difficult to get it back on the agenda without huge delays and extra costs.'

The Government is currently looking at ways round some of these problems by experimenting in setting up round tables of local people to debate difficult road projects. The idea is that they can make recommendations about, say, the proposed route of a bypass and that as many local and environmental concerns can be taken into account as early in the process as possible. This is a good idea but is not an easy panacea. 'Round tables seem to work best when they start with a blank sheet of paper, but the trouble with that is that a blank sheet of paper can blight a very large area unless decisions are taken very quickly.'

In retrospect, he says, it is clear the tunnel under Twyford Down should have been studied far more seriously than it was. 'At the time we took the decision that politically it was a non-starter. But it may well have been the right thing to do.' He adds: 'I hope we have all learned something – about how the planning process can be seen to be fairer and how we design roads that are acceptable.'

Tom Burke says the campaign may have been defeated, but it was still a success in many other ways. 'Without the willingness of ordinary citizens to believe in the notion of democracy, and to try to make the system work, the flaws in the process would never have been exposed or so widely recognized. Although frustrating for the individuals involved, the layers and layers of accumulated orthodox and conventional wisdom that concealed the truth about what generated all these silly road schemes would not have been stripped away without the activities of these people, who took the time and trouble to do so. Thus, seen in the broader picture this campaign was absolutely invaluable in creating the possibility of a decent transport policy in this country.'

What is clear is that our Twyford Down campaign has changed the political landscape. What is not yet clear is to what extent.

Will the eventual results be reform or revolution?

Will the campaigning result in changes to the planning system, making it more democratic and responsive to local and national concerns? Or will it also be seen as a campaign that helped change society's attitude to economic growth and all that goes with it?

Part Three

The Lawyer's Assessment

13

The legal battle:
'an astonishing intervention'

The legal steps taken by the Twyford Down Association to challenge the legality of the Government's decision could be summarized very briefly. First, the Association sought a judicial review of the decision in the English High Court. When that application failed the Association lodged a complaint with the Commission of the European Communities on the basis that the UK had broken European Community law. The Commission investigated the complaint and decided to initiate an 'enforcement procedure' against the UK alleging that the Government had indeed broken Community law. Later, however, the Commission terminated that same procedure and so brought to an end the 'European' challenge to the project on Twyford Down.

Such a stark summary would, however, fail to give a true picture of events as they unfolded and of the political and legal context in which decisions were made. More important, it would not raise the questions which need to be asked as to failure of the current system to allow for effective enforcement of European environmental law or to allow even a minimum degree of transparency as to the way in which enforcement decisions are taken. Neither would it show the practical constraints under which the Twyford Down Association had to operate nor the role of the legal challenge as part of the Association's broader campaign to recruit the support of public opinion against the Twyford Down scheme.

For these reasons, and because Twyford Down has come to epitomize the failure of the system to protect the environment or to allow citizens an effective legal role in challenging its despoliation, the story of the legal challenge to the project at Twyford Down deserves to be told in greater detail. It is a story about individuals who took very great risks. It is about their determination to struggle within the law to stop the desecration of their local landscape and about the frustrations they encountered along the way. It is also a story about power politics and their impact upon the European legal process. Before embarking upon this story, however, it is first necessary to set the scene by explaining a little about the law in question.

'DIRECTIVES'

From a legal point of view the Twyford Down case largely turned upon European Council Directive 85/337 'on the assessment of the effects of certain public and private projects on the environment'[1] ('the Directive'). A 'directive' is, in effect, a piece of legislation enacted by the European Community and addressed to the Member States. It does not become part of the law of the Member States automatically but must instead be 'transposed' into national law by an act of the national legislature. In other words, a directive is an instruction from the Community to the Member States requiring them to change their own laws so as to come into line with the requirements of the directive by a stated deadline.

If the UK fails to bring its own law into line with a directive properly and in time, then, in certain circumstances, private individuals can rely upon the provisions of the directive in proceedings in the English courts notwithstanding the fact that it has not been properly 'transposed' into English law. For this to be the case it must be shown that the content of the directive is such that it is intended to confer rights upon individuals and that the rules which it lays down are clear and are not conditional upon further steps being taken at Community or national level. Where these criteria are satisfied a directive has what is known as 'direct effect'. That means that if a Member State fails to transpose it properly and in time, individuals can nonetheless rely upon its terms in the national courts as against the defaulting Member State, its Government, public authorities and certain other 'emanations of the State'. Such a right of action is allowed in order to prevent the defaulting State from benefiting from its own failure to obey Community law.

It is sometimes thought that directives are 'inflicted' on the Member States by 'Brussels' but it is important to realize that they are finally adopted as Community law by the European Council, which is composed of ministers representing the governments of each Member State. Indeed, the Treaty provisions[2] which allowed the Community to adopt Directive 85/337 were such that it could only be adopted by *unanimous* vote in the Council. Thus any Member State, including the UK, could have 'vetoed' its enactment. In no sense could it be said that Directive 85/337 was 'imposed' upon the UK.

DIRECTIVE 85/337

The purpose of this Directive was to establish a procedure to ensure that the environmental impact of major development projects is properly assessed before they are authorized. The Directive was notified to the Member States on 3 July 1985 and was to be transposed into national law 'within three years of its notification'.[3] English law should therefore have been brought into line with the Directive by 3 July 1988.

Directive 85/337 applies to two categories of project. Of these, one category (those listed in Annex I to the Directive) is automatically to be subject to Environmental Impact Assessment. Annex I lists, among other things, the '*[c]onstruction of motorways...*'. Thus, all things being equal, the Twyford Down project involving as it did the construction of an extension to the M3 motorway, should have been subject to mandatory Environmental Impact Assessment in accordance with the Directive. In order to understand what happened at Twyford Down, however, we need to look at the Directive, and at the way in which it had been transposed into English law, in a little more detail. We have to encounter what has become known as 'the pipe-line point' and to consider the very nature of Environmental Impact Assessment.

So far as European law was concerned, the Twyford Down Association's case depended upon two fundamental points. First, that the UK had wrongly exempted certain motorway projects, including the M3 extension at Twyford Down, from the requirement of Environmental Impact Assessment and therefore had broken Community law by failing properly to transpose the Directive into English law. Secondly, that the Government had also failed actually to comply with the Directive in the specific case of Twyford Down.

FAILURE TO TRANSPOSE THE DIRECTIVE – THE 'PIPE-LINE' POINT

As we have seen, English law should have been brought into line with the Directive by 3 July 1988. In addition, Article 2.1 of the Directive provides that

> *Member States shall adopt all measures necessary to ensure that,* ***before consent is given,***[4] *[projects subject to assessment] are made subject to an assessment with regard to their effects.*
> (emphasis mine)

According to the Twyford Down Association this meant that after 3 July 1988 development consent could not lawfully be granted in respect of the extension of the M3 at Twyford Down unless the environmental impact of the project had first been assessed in accordance with the Directive. This view was not, however, shared by the UK Government.

In fact the Government had sought to transpose the Directive into English law so far as motorway projects were concerned by means of the Highways (Assessment of Environmental Effects) Regulations 1988 (S.I. 1988 No. 1241). These Regulations inserted a new section, section 105A into the Highways Act 1980 ('the Act'). This new section would have properly transposed the Directive in respect of motorway projects except for the fact that sub-section 105A (7) provided that:

> *This section does not apply –*
>
> *(a) where a draft order or scheme relating to construction or a draft order relating to improvement [of a highway] is published before the coming into force of the Highways (Assessment of Environmental Effects) Regulations 1988; or*
> *(b) where the Secretary of State has under consideration before that date construction or improvement [of a highway] without an order.*

The Regulations came into force on 21 July 1988 (eighteen days after the deadline set by the Directive). The effect of section 105A (7) was, of course, to exclude the need for Environmental Impact Assessment in cases where the draft order or scheme was published prior to 21 July 1988 (and so was in the 'planning pipe-line' before the section took effect) even though development consent itself might not be granted until after 3 July 1988 (the final date for transposition of the Directive). The M3 project was such a 'pipe-line case' because the draft schemes and orders were published over a period between 24 April 1981 and 19 April 1985 (inclusive) although development consent for the project was not granted until 16 March 1990,[5] some twenty months after the Directive came into effect, on which date the definitive schemes and orders were published.

FAILURE OF PRACTICAL COMPLIANCE – THE SPECIFIC CASE OF TWYFORD DOWN

In challenging the Government's decision, whether in the High Court or at a European level, it would have been little use from the Association's point of view to complain that the Government had failed properly to transpose the Directive in the abstract. As well as arguing that the Directive had not been properly transposed with respect to 'pipe-line' cases in general, the Association had also to argue that its provisions had not actually been honoured in respect of the Twyford Down project. They argued in fact that the Directive had been infringed because information which should have been made available to the public by the developer had not been properly provided. This was, in particular, because such information as had been provided by the developer had been made available in dribs and drabs over an extended period and because a 'non-technical summary' of that information had not been made available to the public as specifically required by the Directive. To follow these arguments, and to understand the importance to the assessment process of the information to be provided by the developer, we need to know a little more about the nature of Environmental Impact Assessment.

ENVIRONMENTAL IMPACT ASSESSMENT

The Directive requires that an Environmental Impact Assessment

> *will identify, describe and assess in an appropriate manner, in light of each individual case and in accordance with the Articles [sic] 4 to 11, the direct and indirect effects of a project on the following factors:*

- *human beings, fauna and flora,*
- *soil, water, air, climate and the landscape,*
- *the inter-action between the factors mentioned in the first and second indents*
- *material assets and the cultural heritage.*[6]

The Member States were allowed either to integrate the making of such an assessment into their existing development consent procedures or to set up new procedures specifically to comply with the Directive.[7] Whichever approach was adopted, however, the national procedures were to comply with the rules laid down by Articles 5 to 11 of the Directive.[8] These lay down the procedures to be followed in the assessment process and involve four elements. First, the developer is required to provide certain environmental information about the project. Second, the information provided by the developer is to be made available to the public and to certain consultees. The public are to be given an opportunity to express an opinion before the project is initiated and the other bodies are to be consulted. Third, the information provided by the developer and that gathered in the consultation exercise are to be taken into consideration in the development consent procedure. Finally, having made a decision on the application for development consent, the authorities are to notify the public of their decision and the 'reasons and considerations' upon which it is based.

ENVIRONMENTAL INFORMATION TO BE PROVIDED BY THE DEVELOPER

Whenever a project is subject to assessment the Member State concerned must ensure that

> *the developer*[9] *supplies in an appropriate form the information specified in Annex III [of the Directive]*[10] *inasmuch as:*
>
> *(a) the Member States consider that the information is relevant to a given stage of the consent procedure and to the specific characteristics of a particular project or type of project and of the environmental features likely to be affected;*
> *(b) the Member States consider that a developer may reasonably be required to compile this information having regard inter alia to current knowledge and methods of assessment.*[11]

Notwithstanding the discretion of the Member States under points (a) and (b) above, the information to be provided by the developer must

> *include* at least:
> – *a description of the project comprising information on the site, design and size of the project,*
> – *a description of the measures envisaged in order to avoid, reduce and, if possible, remedy significant adverse effects,*
> – *the data required to identify and assess the main effects which the project is likely to have on the environment,*
> – *a **non-technical summary of the information mentioned in indents 1 to 3.***[12] (emphasis mine)

Thus the Directive provides that, where an assessment is required, the developer must provide an irreducible minimum of environmental information and must include a 'non-technical summary' of that information. The Twyford Down Association argued that the information which ought to have been provided by the developer with respect to the M3 project was flawed and that, in particular, no non-technical summary had been made available to the public. It argued that in such circumstances any assessment of the environmental impact of the project which might have taken place as part of the planning procedure (including the two Inquiries) could not as a matter of law amount to a proper Environmental Impact Assessment complying with the Directive. It was deficient, not only because the provision of a non-technical summary is expressly required by the Directive, but also because subsequent stages of the assessment process depend upon the information to be provided by the developer. If that information had not been properly provided, the subsequent procedures could not have been carried out properly. This was particularly the case with the processes of consultation and consideration.

CONSULTATION

The Directive requires Member States to ensure that any request for development consent and the information which the Directive requires to be made available by the developer are 'made available to the public' and that '*the public concerned is given*

an opportunity to express an opinion before the project is initiated'.[13]
The Twyford Down Association's argument was that if the
information to be provided to the public has not been provided
as required by the Directive any public consultation exercise
would be flawed and could not comply with the Directive. This
was based, in part, upon the notion that the purpose of the
Directive, in requiring that the prescribed information be made
available to the public, was not only to ensure that the public
could be alerted to the environmental impact of a proposed project but also to guarantee that the public could make their representations on a properly informed basis.

In addition to public consultation, the Directive provides for
consultation with certain designated authorities and with other
Member States. Although Member States are required to ensure
that the authorities likely to be concerned by a project by reason of their specific environmental responsibilities *'are given an
opportunity to express their opinion on the request for development
consent'*[14] they nonetheless retain considerable discretion as to
the scope of such consultation. They are to designate the
authorities to be consulted either in general terms or on a case
by case basis when the request for development consent is
made. On the other hand, although the Directive allows
'detailed arrangements for consultation' to be laid down by the
Member States themselves,[15] it nonetheless requires that the
information to be provided by the developer (information
which, as we have seen must include at least a non-technical
summary and other prescribed information) is to be forwarded
to the consultee authorities. Once more, if the developer has
failed to provide the minimum prescribed information (including a non-technical summary) this obligation cannot properly
be carried out.

Furthermore, where a Member State is aware that a project is
likely to have significant effects on the environment in another
Member State, or where a Member State likely to be significantly
affected so requests, the Member State in whose territory the
project is intended to be carried out must forward the information to be provided by the developer to the other Member State
at the same time that it makes it available to its own nationals.[16]
Such information is then to serve *'as a basis for any consultations*

necessary in the framework of the bilateral relations between the two Member States on a reciprocal and equivalent basis'.[17] If the developer has not provided the prescribed information, the Member State concerned will simply not be able to comply with its obligation to forward it to such other Member States as it thinks may be affected by the project.

CONSIDERATION

The information to be provided by the developer and the information gathered in the consultation exercises are to *'be taken into consideration in the development consent procedure'.*[18] Although the Directive does not expressly specify which body is to be required to take the information into consideration, it can reasonably be inferred that it is to be the authority which determines the application for development consent.[19] Nothing in the Directive in fact indicates the weight to be attached to the various environmental considerations brought to light by the assessment process, nor does it specify the process whereby the authority or authorities are to weigh them against other factors, such as cost. Nonetheless, as the Twyford Down Association argued, if the prescribed information has not been provided by the developer in the first place it is simply impossible for the authority to 'take it into consideration' as required by the Directive. In such a case the final assessment made by the competent authority itself as to the environmental impact of the project would fail to comply with the Directive.

REASONS

When a decision has been taken on a request for development consent, the competent authority or authorities are obliged to inform *'the public concerned'* of the content of the decision and any conditions attached to it and where the Member State's legislation so provides of *'the reasons and considerations on which the decision is based'.*[20] The detailed arrangements for the provision of such information to the public are left to be determined by the Member States,[21] but if another Member State has been consulted then it too must be informed of the decision.[22]

POSSIBLE LINES OF ATTACK

In summary, therefore, the Twyford Down Association's main argument was that the Directive had not properly been complied with because the prescribed information had not properly been made available by the Secretary of State for Transport (as developer) to the public; and, in particular, because no 'non-technical summary' had been published. The result was, in the Association's view, that the subsequent consultation and consideration of the environmental impact of the project did not itself conform with the Directive and so development consent could not lawfully have been granted.

Before we see how this and the Association's other arguments were put forward we need to know more about the legal avenues that were open to them. In fact two possible lines of attack were available. First, the Association could apply to the High Court to have the Government's decision quashed. Second, it could make a complaint to the European Commission. The Association needed to find out just what was involved in these procedures and had to make some important tactical and practical decisions.

AN APPLICATION TO QUASH

An application could be made to the High Court under Schedule 2 of the Highways Act 1980 to quash the decision of the Secretaries of State.[23] The most important practical constraint was cost. If an applicant for judicial review of a governmental decision fails he will normally have to pay not only the costs of his own solicitors and counsel but also those of the Treasury Solicitor acting on behalf of the Government. If an applicant fails he can therefore incur liabilities of several tens of thousands of pounds. Furthermore, although it is easy to imagine that the risk of costs will be shared among all of the members of a common-interest group such as the Twyford Down Association, that is not usually the case. A group such as the Association has no legal personality. In legal terms it is merely an 'unincorporated association' of its members. It cannot bring legal proceedings in its own name but only in the names of some or all of the individuals who are its members. The individuals in whose name the application is made are the ones who run the risk of incurring liability for costs. Furthermore, even before their application gets to Court, they will normally be expected to pay their own solicitors fairly large sums 'on account' to fund work in progress. From the solicitor's point of view this is only prudent. The solicitor will be concerned that private individuals launching significant litigation might, if an order for costs is ultimately made against them, be unable to pay for the work which they have done. This is especially the case where the solicitor knows that their clients do not themselves have sufficient liquid funds to finance the litigation but hope to raise the money by appealing to the public and to other environmental groups.

This all means that it is a frightening prospect for an individual member of a common-interest group to agree to act as an applicant on behalf of the group as a whole. It is a burden which few common-interest group members are prepared to shoulder. Those who do take it on do so in the knowledge that if their application fails financial support from the public, benefactors and other members of the group may well fall away, leaving them with a large personal liability which they may be unable to meet. The possibility of having to sell one's house to pay costs concentrates the mind. It is a risk which only the most committed and determined individuals will be prepared to take. Such were the individuals, Barbara Bryant, David Croker and Merrick Denton-Thompson, in whose name the Twyford Down Association's High Court application was actually brought. As we shall see, however, there can come a point at which the risks involved in continued legal action become too great even for such courageous people as these, so that critical decisions depended, quite rightly, as much or more upon the extent of financial risk to the individual applicants as upon their own view (or that of their lawyers) as to the merits of their case.

A EUROPEAN COMPLAINT

The other avenue open to the Association was to make a complaint to the Commission of the European Communities. At one level, the procedure for making such a complaint is straightforward. Of course, in a case such as Twyford Down, complainants may wish to have their complaint drafted by a lawyer to ensure that it is as strong as possible from a technical point of view. It is not necessary, however, for that to be the case. There are no special formal requirements. A simple letter setting out the grounds of complaint will do. The cost of making a complaint may therefore be negligible. It is enough that the complaint, in whatever form, shows a sufficiently plausible case that the Member State against which complaint is made has failed to comply with Community law.

Having lodged such a complaint the matter is then largely out of the hands of the complainants. If the Commission takes up a complaint it will firstly correspond with the Member State in question and seek its initial response to the substance of the complaint. If, having made such enquiries, the Commission believes that there may indeed be substance to the complaint it will try to resolve the matter by further discussions with national officials or ministers. If the matter cannot be so resolved, the Commission may proceed to issue a 'letter of formal notice' to the Member State in question formally setting out the grounds upon which it believes it to be in default and requesting it formally to respond within a stated period, usually two months. If the Commission is not satisfied by the State's response it can then issue a 'Reasoned Opinion'. This once more sets out the ways in which the Commission believes the State to be in breach of Community law and the steps required for the Member State to comply with the law.

The Member State is required to respond to a Reasoned Opinion within a stated period, again usually two months. If the Commission remains unsatisfied it can then bring proceedings against the Member State in question in the Court of Justice of the European Communities. The Reasoned Opinion serves as the 'indictment' against the respondent State in as much as the Commission may not rely upon grounds unless they were set out in the Opinion itself. If the Court finds against the respondent State it declares it to be in breach of the law.

Although we shall see this procedure in action later, certain characteristics are very clear. The making of a complaint need not be expensive. Furthermore, even if the complainants hire lawyers or other lobbyists to help put their case, the cost is unlikely to get anywhere near the cost of losing High Court litigation. More important, the financial risk involved is more controllable. The complainants only have to finance their own lobbying activities and are not at risk of having to pay the Government's costs. They are not obliged to hire lawyers or other lobbyists, but if they do so and exhaust their available funds they can simply settle their bills to date, withdraw any further instructions and carry on any further lobbying or public relations effort without the help of professionals. Indeed, in the mission to persuade the European Commission or to win the support of public opinion complainants themselves can, as in the case of Twyford Down, be consummately skilful. So far as public opinion or the need to convince the Commission are concerned, few if any of the things done by the professional lobbyist could not be done at least as well or better by well-informed, energetic complainants themselves.

If it is clear that the making of a complaint is cheap and relatively straightforward it is equally clear that any procedure initiated by the Commission is a matter between the Commission and the Member State in question. Complainants are not entitled to know what passes between them and if the Commission decides not to take up a well founded complaint, or to terminate its procedures at any stage, it is free to do so on whatever grounds it thinks fit and the complainant has no right of appeal or other legal redress.

Furthermore, in a case such as Twyford Down where the complainants argue that a procedure required by European law has not been complied with, all that the Commission or Court could require is that the correct procedure be followed. If having followed the correct procedure the Government were to come to exactly the same decision and confirm the route of the M3 through Twyford Down nothing in European law would stop them. Why then did the Twyford Down Association ultimately think it worth while to make a complaint? Partly it was because they sincerely believed that if the proper procedures had been followed public opinion would be better informed as to the environmental consequences of the scheme, so that it would have been politically difficult for the Government to confirm the route. Secondly, the making of the complaint and subsequent steps in the enforcement procedure were important elements of a campaign to recruit public opinion against the project and to make it politically difficult for the Government to proceed with it. The news media report events. The fact that the M3 project was opposed by local groups may have been locally newsworthy for a short time. But to gain access to wider public opinion by attracting nationwide media coverage over an extended period required a succession of newsworthy events. The making of a complaint 'to Brussels', the later issue of a Commission letter of formal notice and subsequent steps in the procedure would each be likely to hit the headlines. They would introduce to the general public the complainants' view that the Government had broken the law and as a result was threatening a site of the greatest environmental importance. There was, of course, one further reason for making a complaint. Whatever the limitations of the enforcement procedure from the complainants' point of view, a complaint would, if High Court litigation were to fail, be the only legal step available to them.

A QUESTION OF TIMING

Having decided to seek a judicial review of the Government's decision, having raised some of the funds necessary to launch such an application and having instructed solicitors as well as junior and leading counsel, one of the key tactical questions which had to be faced by the Association was whether to launch a complaint to the European Commission at the same time as bringing an application in the High Court or whether to delay a complaint and to make it only in the event that the High Court application was unsuccessful. It was in fact decided to postpone any European complaint until after determination of the High Court application. This decision, taken at a conference with Counsel, was largely influenced by a desire to concentrate effort and resources on the task immediately to hand. It also depended, in part at least, upon speculation as to a judge's reaction to the lodging of a complaint in parallel with the High Court proceedings.

There is, of course, no impropriety in challenging Governmental action in the High Court while at the same time complaining to the European Commission regarding any apprehended breach of Community law by the UK. On the other hand, the psychological response of a perhaps sceptical High Court judge, when asked to grant a discretionary remedy which would involve holding up a major infrastructure project, also had to be taken into account. It was at least conceivable that the judge would decline to accept the Association's contentions of European law, or decline to quash the Government's decision, on the basis that if he were wrong the issues involved would, a complaint having been made, be taken up by the European Commission thus reducing the necessity for intervention by the Court.

The assessment of a factor such as this is far from an exact science and it might equally have been that the lodging of a complaint in parallel with the Court application might, especially if the Commission were to take up the complaint in time, concentrate the mind of the Judge and dispel any suspicion he might harbour that the arguments of European law advanced were not substantial. There would always be the danger, however, that a sceptical judge might enquire, having been apprised of the lodging of any European complaint, whether or not the Commission had yet taken any steps to uphold the complaint. If the answer to such a question were to be negative it would hardly improve the credibility of the case. It would be little comfort to try to explain to the Judge that the paper mills of Brussels grind slowly and that although nothing had yet been heard from the Commission that did not necessarily mean that the Commission did not take the complaint seriously.

In the event, the decision was taken to keep the making of a European complaint in reserve in case the Court application failed. This would have one incidental advantage in that, if ultimately a complaint had to be made, it would be possible to show the Commission that the complainants had exhausted all possibility of redress in the English Courts. There is in fact no need to exhaust national remedies before complaining to the Commission. On the other hand, the fact that national remedies have been exhausted in a particular case makes it clear to the Commission that, if the complaint is well founded, the only possibility of ensuring correct application of European law would be through Commission action. This would be especially so if the English judge were to dismiss the High Court application, and so set a national precedent, on the basis of what the Commission might regard as an incorrect interpretation of the Community law in question.

In fact, however, the postponement of the European complaint until after determination of the High Court application may, with the benefit of hindsight, have been unfortunate. This is really a matter of speculation. Nonetheless, for reasons which could not have been foreseen at the time, the Commission finally took steps in response to the Association's complaint at a time of heightened political sensitivity when its freedom of action may have been limited by political constraints. It is just possible therefore that, had the complaint been made earlier, the

Commission would have intervened earlier, in less highly charged circumstances, and perhaps with greater effect.

THE HIGH COURT APPLICATION

The Twyford Down Association applied to the High Court, with others, to have the M3 scheme quashed on the grounds that the requirements of the Directive had not been satisfied. The application was heard and then dismissed by Mr Justice McCullough.[24] The applicants' arguments based on the Directive were rejected on four grounds.

JUDGMENT ON THE 'PIPE-LINE POINT'

The Judge first accepted the Government's argument that it was entitled to exclude projects such as the M3 extension which were in the planning 'pipe-line' before 3 July 1988[25] from the need for Environmental Impact Assessment. The Government had argued, rightly, that Directive 85/337, like all directives, left the precise form of transposition to be decided by the Member States. It then argued that, since the Directive itself did not provide for transitional measures to deal with pipe-line cases such as Twyford Down, it was permissible for a Member State to exclude them altogether from the need for assessment even though development consent in such cases might not be granted until after the deadline for transposition. The Judge accepted that contention and held that because of transitional difficulties the Directive could not be construed as applying to projects which were in the pipe-line on 3 July 1988.

In my view and (as it turned out) in the view of the European Commission, the Judge's conclusion on this point was wrong. Although he analysed some of the provisions of the Directive correctly he jumped to an erroneous conclusion. He started by analysing the provisions of the Directive and concluding, in my view rightly, that the Directive was intended

> to affect a process which of necessity, is of considerable duration, and...is to influence that process at every stage.[26]

He therefore ruled (again rightly in my view) that

> [t]o treat the environmental considerations in isolation or to begin to take them into account at any stage earlier than the earliest would run counter to the clear intention of the directive.[27]

The Judge drew from this the following conclusion, namely that in these circumstances

> *the absence from the directive of any requirement to implement transitional provisions and, if so, what provisions, is significant. Had it been intended that the directive was to cover pipe-line cases one would have expected it to have said so and to have stated how the gathering and consideration of the information was to affect the stages that had already passed.*[28]

In my view (and, as we shall see, in the opinion of the European Commission) this was a wrong conclusion. It seems to have been founded upon a fundamental misconception as to the nature of a directive. Article 189 of the Treaty of Rome provides that a directive

> *shall be binding, as to the result to be achieved, upon each Member State to which it is addressed, but shall leave to the national authorities the choice of form and methods.*

It was quite consistent with Article 189, therefore, for the Directive to prescribe in absolute terms a result to be achieved (namely, that from the coming into force of the Directive certain categories of project should be subject to assessment before consent is given) and then leave the method of achieving that result, including the method of dealing with transitional cases, to the Member States. In other words the choice of the form and method of transposition of the Directive in respect of 'pipe-line cases' was just as much a matter for the Member States as in other cases *so long as the requirement of the Directive is achieved*, namely that as from 3 July 1988 before consent is given to any relevant project it must first be subject to an assessment in accordance with the Directive. This is particularly the case since Article 2.2 of the Directive expressly states that Member States have a discretion as to whether they integrate Environmental Impact Assessment into existing consent procedures or into other procedures or into procedures established to comply with the aims of the Directive.

The difficulty with Mr Justice McCullough's view is further emphasized by the fact that the different Member States have different consent procedures not harmonized by the Community. Thus, for the Community to provide transitional provisions to be capable of being applied on the ground in the way His Lordship anticipated, it would be necessary to produce different sets of rules, each set tailored to relate to the different stages involved in the different consent procedures of the different Member States. Such a task would place a considerable burden on the resources of the Community institutions, especially the Commission. Indeed, since it would require a detailed knowledge of the different planning systems of each of the Member States, it is a task for which the national authorities of each Member State were best placed to accomplish.

Furthermore, for the Community to have prescribed detailed transitional provisions would have run the risk of pre-empting the Member States' discretion as to the choice of form and method of transposition of the Directive even in non-transitional cases. This is because, for a transitional regime in a particular Member State to avoid causing as many difficulties as it might resolve, it would need to bear a coherent relationship with the regime as adopted by that Member State for non-transitional cases. Thus, were a detailed transitional regime to be prescribed by the Community for each Member State, then, as a practical matter, it would be likely to dictate, or at the very least to restrict, the form and method of transposition to be adopted by that State for non-transitional cases.

A further objection to the Judge's ruling on the 'pipe-line point' is that it depends, in essence, upon the argument that the administrative and other difficulties which would have been entailed in applying the Directive to pipe-line cases were such that the Directive could not have been intended to apply to such cases. The weakness of that argument is twofold. Firstly, Leading Counsel for the applicants had argued that the difficulties caused by applying the Directive to pipe-line cases could have been largely avoided if the UK itself had legislated in a more timely manner to transpose the Directive. Indeed, the UK and the other Member States knew at least three years in advance that the Directive would require Environmental Assessment of certain classes of project to which consent would be granted after 3 July 1988. It would therefore have been open to the Government to deal with administrative or practical difficulties which might arise in the case of 'pipe-line' developments without seeking wholly to exempt them from the scope of the Directive. By taking such a course it could have dealt with any supposed transitional problems while at the same time honouring the UK's obligations. That a Member State might fail itself to think ahead and plan a smooth transition to the Directive's regime can hardly be a reason for implying into the Directive a potentially wide power of derogation for projects which were 'in the pipe-line' prior to 3 July 1988. This is especially since consent to such projects might not in fact be granted until months or years after that date.

The Judge himself accepted[29]

> *that legislation relatively early in the three-year period to cater for pipeline cases could have achieved much of what [Leading Counsel for the applicants] suggests.*

Nonetheless he held that application of the Directive to pipe-line cases would have led

> **even with transitional legislation,** *to disruption, duplication of effort, additional expense and delay.*[30] (emphasis mine)

It is hard to reconcile this thinking with the Judge's logic elsewhere in his judgment. As we have seen, he had earlier concluded that the Directive could not have been intended to apply to transitional cases because, had it been intended to do so, it would have provided transitional rules dealing with the difficulties of applying the assessment process to projects that were already in the pipe-line. Here, on the other hand, he is suggesting that transitional measures could not, in fact, avoid the difficulties to which he referred. The greater problem with this strand of reasoning, however, is that it is inconsistent with well established jurisprudence of the Court of Justice to the effect that administrative and practical difficulties which may be encountered in a Member State do not justify that State's failure properly to transpose a directive. This point had been canvassed in argument, but was rejected by His Lordship on the grounds that the authorities which had been cited, principally Case 8/81 *Becker v Finanzamt Munster-Innenstadt*[31] were distinguishable. In that case the Court of Justice had held that the administrative difficulties involved in applying an exemption from VAT arose from the Member State's failure to transpose the relevant directive in time and could not justify non-application of the exemption in that Member State. His Lordship distinguished the case, however, on the grounds that

> *It is one thing to bring tax provisions into force by a prescribed date; it is another to bring into force a series of provisions*

> *designed to influence, stage by stage, and at every stage, the con-*
> *duct of development procedures which are likely, by their nature,*
> *to be in train for months if not years.*[32]

Whether the Judge was justified in limiting the scope of the ruling in *Becker*[33] in this way is controversial. In my own view, however, the European Court of Justice, being more concerned than
the national judge with the need to ensure effective application
of Community directives in the face of prevarication by Member
States, would have been unlikely to accept the Judge's approach.

A further objection to the Judge's view is that Article 2.3 of
the Directive itself provides Member States with a very limited
power to exclude projects from the Directive, a power which is
itself subject to important safeguards.

Article 2.3 only allows Member States to derogate from the
Directive *'in exceptional circumstances'* so as to exempt *'a specific
project'* from the Directive's regime. Thus it would not have been
permissible for the UK to derogate under Article 2.3 in respect of
an entire class of projects (such as those where planning procedures were begun before 21 July 1988) as opposed to specific
projects in exceptional cases.[34]

Furthermore, Article 2.3 imposes important safeguards. It
requires that in exercising the power of derogation, Member
States must make available to the public concerned information
relating to the derogation and the reasons for it. It requires such
a Member State, before granting development consent in a case
where it has granted a derogation, to inform the European
Commission

> *of the reasons justifying exemption and to provide it with the*
> *information made available, where appropriate to it's own*
> *nationals.*[35]

The UK had not sought to exempt the M3 project (or for that
matter any other highway projects which were 'in the pipe-
line') from the operation of the Directive pursuant to Article 2.3.
Nor had it satisfied the safeguards laid down in connection with
such a derogation. Accordingly, to allow it to exempt an entire
and potentially large class of case from the Directive's regime (as
it purported to do in section 105A (7) of the Act) would not only
exceed the power of derogation allowed by the Directive but
would also nullify the safeguards in Article 2.3 itself.

Finally, the fact that section 105A (7) of the Act came into effect shortly after the deadline for transposition of the Directive casts a particular light upon the arguments advanced on behalf of Government and accepted by Mr Justice McCullough. It means in fact that the UK's purported derogation was more extensive than might at first sight appear. It will be remembered that the deadline for transposition of the Directive was 3 July 1988 and that section 105A (7) excluded from its application projects where the draft scheme or order had been made prior to the coming into force of the Highways (Assessment of Environmental Effects) Regulations 1988 on 21 July 1988. Thus projects where the draft scheme or order was published *after* 3 July but *before* 21 July 1988 would be excluded from the requirement of assessment by the transposing legislation, even though not only the grant of development consent in such cases but also the commencement of planning procedures occurred *after* the deadline for transposition. Such cases would not even have entered the planning pipe-line at the time when the Directive came into force, but would nonetheless be exempted according to the provisions of the transposing legislation which Mr Justice McCullough upheld. In such circumstances the Government's assertion and the Judge's ruling that section 105A (7) conforms with the UK's obligations under Articles 2.1 and 12 of the Directive cannot, with respect, be right.[36]

The Judge's ruling that 'pipe-line' cases could be excluded from the requirements of the Directive would itself have been enough to allow him to give judgment against the Association. He went further, however, and considered whether, if he were wrong on the point, it would make any difference to the outcome. He concluded that the applicants could not succeed for three further reasons; because, in the Judge's view, they had suffered no *'prejudice'* as a result of the alleged breach of Community law; because, as the Judge saw it, no breach of Community law had been proven; and because, even if Community law had been infringed, English law afforded the applicants no remedy.

NO 'PREJUDICE'

As we have seen, for private individuals to be able to rely upon the provisions of a directive in the English courts, certain criteria must be met. His Lordship was satisfied that they were indeed met in the present case. He had *'no doubt'* that the obligations

imposed by the Directive were sufficiently unconditional and
precise to be capable of direct effect and that the applicants *'were
amongst those whom the directive was intended to benefit.'* He
nonetheless concluded that no right of action could arise since
the applicants had *'not suffered as a result of'* the alleged failure to
implement the Directive.[37]

NO BREACH

The Judge then went on to hold that the applicants had, in any
event, failed to prove any breach of the Directive[38] on behalf of
the Secretaries of State. The Association had argued that there
had been no proper Environmental Impact Assessment of the
M3 project because the Secretary of State for Transport (as
developer) had not provided a non-technical summary of the
prescribed environmental information as required by Article 5.2
of the Directive. Indeed, no document purporting to be a non-
technical summary for the purposes of the Directive had been
provided by the Secretary of State. However, in the course of
the High Court proceedings, Counsel for the Secretaries of State
argued that the Inspector's Report provided after the 1985 local
Inquiry in fact constituted such a summary. It was, of course,
wholly artificial to regard such a report as constituting the
required non-technical summary. In the first place it was available only to those who attended the Inquiry and was not easily
accessible to all residents of the area affected. Secondly, it was
provided as advice to the developer rather than as information
provided by the developer himself. Finally, it could hardly be
described as a non-technical 'summary' of the necessary information since it was no less than 322 pages long. The Judge did
not, in fact, hold that the Inspector's Report was the required
non-technical summary. Instead, he held that the applicants had
failed to prove that it was not.[39] Accordingly he found against
them on the point.

NO REMEDY

Finally, the Judge held that, even if he were wrong on the earlier points, Schedule 2 of the Highways Act 1980 would afford
the applicants no remedy since such a scheme would be
quashed under that Schedule only where the applicants had

suffered *'prejudice'* and, in His Lordship's view, none had been proved.[40] Thus apart from the substantive points as to whether or not the Directive applied to 'pipe-line cases' and as to whether or not its provisions had been infringed,[41] the application failed because, in His Lordship's judgment, the applicants did not have any recognized interests which had been adversely affected by the alleged infringement of the Directive. What this means, of course, if the Judge is right, is that proceedings in the courts of a Member State are totally inadequate as a means of enforcing much Community environmental law. Dr Ludwig Kramer (Legal Adviser to the Environment Directorate General of the Commission – Directorate General XI) has himself succinctly described the problem as arising because

> *[e]nvironmental legislation affects each one of us; but at the same time, no group has a vested interest in seeing environmental standards actually applied. This becomes plain when we consider the question of who is affected by the disappearance of a species of butterfly or a bird's habitat, affected to an extent that he could take action against planned measures...*[42]

He might equally have asked, in the light of the Twyford Down judgment, who has sufficient interest to seek enforcement of the provisions of the Directive requiring provision of information to the public?

AN APPEAL?

The applicants and their advisers took the view that there would be strong grounds of appeal against some aspects of the judgment, in particular against the Judge's ruling that it was lawful to exclude 'pipe-line' cases from the requirement of assessment. Other arguments also looked promising. There is, for example, a rule of Community law requiring national courts to provide effective remedies for infringement of Community law and to ensure that national procedural rules do not make the vindication of rights conferred by Community law impossible. It could have been argued that the Judge's ruling that the applicants could not bring an action to vindicate the rights conferred upon them by the Directive because they had suffered no 'prejudice', was inconsistent with that principle. Similarly, the Judge's ruling that the applicants had not proved that the

Inspector's Report was incapable of being a 'non-technical summary' could have been challenged. This could have been put on
the basis that what is capable of amounting to a non-technical
summary is a matter of law for the Judge and that there was sufficient evidence before the Judge to conclude that the
Inspector's Report, being more than 300 pages long, was incapable of amounting to such a 'summary'.

It could not be said, however, that each of these potential
grounds of appeal would have been bound to succeed.
Furthermore, the lodging of an appeal would have exposed the
applicants to the risk of even greater liability in costs. This was
all the more so because the applicants' best hope of succeeding
would have been to persuade the English courts to refer the
questions of European law which the case involved to the
European Court of Justice. This might well have meant having
to appeal the case as far as the House of Lords and even then
there would be the risk that the House might refuse to make the
reference.[43]

Because of these uncertainties and the sheer expense of pursuing an appeal the applicants reluctantly decided that they
could not press their case further in the English courts. The only
other avenue open to them was to make a European complaint
and at the same time to continue their appeal to public opinion
in the months before the impending General Election.
Accordingly Barbara Bryant, David Croker and Merrick Denton-
Thompson instructed me to draft a fully reasoned complaint.

THE EUROPEAN COMPLAINT

The complaint was lodged with the European Commission on
19 November 1990. It argued that the United Kingdom had
acted unlawfully in purporting to exempt 'pipe-line' projects
such as the M3 at Twyford Down from the requirement for
Environmental Impact Assessment. It then alleged that the
United Kingdom had infringed Directive 85/337 in two ways
specifically in connection with the Twyford Down project. The
first argument was that the UK had failed to ensure that a 'non-
technical summary' was provided by the Secretary of State for
Transport as developer. Secondly, it alleged that the project
failed to comply with Article 5 of the Directive. The argument
was that Article 5 required not only that certain prescribed infor-

mation should be provided by the developer but that it should be provided in a comprehensive and self-contained form (whether in a single document or series of documents) and should be provided by the developer at an early stage in the development consent procedure. It was argued that such information as the Secretary of State had made available had not been so provided but had been produced in a piecemeal fashion over a period of several years so that no comprehensive and continuing document of record was available to the public throughout the planning process.

The difficulty facing this last argument was that the Directive does not expressly prescribe the form in which, or the time at which, the prescribed information is to be given by the developer. In fact Article 5.1 simply provides that the developer is to supply the information listed in Annex III *'in an appropriate form'*. Thus, although such information may be conveniently presented in a single 'environmental statement' the Directive does not expressly require that to be the case. Against this, the complainants argued that the requirement that the prescribed information be provided in a comprehensive and self-contained document or series of documents at an early stage in the consent procedure follows from a 'purposive' interpretation of the Directive. Community legislation must generally be interpreted 'purposively' and all that this means is that the contents of any piece of Community legislation must be interpreted so as to conform with the objectives or purpose of the measure as a whole. The objectives of Directive 85/337 are disclosed by its Preamble which, among other things, recites

> – [the]...*need to take effects on the environment into account **at the earliest possible stage** in all the technical planning and decision making processes* (First Recital);
> – [that the environmental assessment]...***must be conducted on the basis of appropriate information supplied by the developer**, which may be supplemented by the authorities and by the people who may be concerned by the project in question* (Sixth Recital);
> – [that]...*the principles of the assessment of environmental effects should be harmonised, in particular with reference to...the main obligations of the developers and the context of the assessment* (Seventh Recital);

– [that projects subject to assessment must as a rule be subject to] *systematic assessment*; and
– [that for projects which are subject to assessment], *a certain minimal amount of information must be supplied* (Tenth
Recital). (emphasis mine)

The gist of the complainants' argument was that if the environmental effects of a project are to be taken into account at *'the earliest possible stage'* in the technical planning and decision-making
process *'on the basis of...information supplied by the developer'*, the
developer should be obliged to provide the prescribed information in a complete form at the earliest possible stage.
Furthermore, if developers' *'main obligations'* (which must surely
include the obligation to provide the prescribed information)
are to be *'harmonised'* so as to allow for *'systematic assessment'*,
then the timing and method of provision of information by the
developer cannot be left entirely to the Member States' discretion.

It was further argued that Article 7 of the Directive also
implies that the information which the developer is required to
supply should be provided in a comprehensive body of information rather than on an ad hoc basis over a period of several
years. This was because Article 7 requires that the information to
be provided by the developer must be forwarded to other
Member States upon whose territory the project is likely to have
significant effects *'at the same time as it makes it available to its own
nationals'*. It was submitted that these words implied that the
information to be provided under Article 5 must be made available in its entirety to the public concerned at one 'time' and
must at the same 'time' be provided to the other Member
States.[44] Furthermore, if it was thought appropriate that information to be provided to other Member States should be provided at a single time, the same should apply to the provision of
information to the other consultees, especially to *'the public concerned'* by the project.

It is interesting to note that, when the Commission later intervened in connection with the Twyford Down complaint, it
based its criticism of the UK solely upon the absence of a non-
technical summary and did not take up the complainants' more
fundamental contention that the Directive requires that the prescribed information be provided in a coherent body of material
at an early stage in the development process. By taking this
course it was, of course, on safer legal ground than if it had

argued the more fundamental point, but its sole reliance upon the absence of a non-technical summary did allow its critics to characterize its intervention as being based on the narrowest of legal technicalities, a view which informed much of the public debate about the matter. This tended to overshadow the complainants' contention of principle that if the Directive was to work as intended, the public should have access to the prescribed information in an easily accessible and coherent form at an early stage in the development procedure. As we shall see, the Commission's approach also allowed it room to manoeuvre when it subsequently decided to withdraw from the case.

In fact, however, it was the Government's position, rather than the complainants', which really involved treating the Directive as a mere 'legal technicality'. The Government's contention throughout was that, even if no non-technical summary had in fact been made available to the public, the requirements of the Directive had as a matter of substance been satisfied. In its view, therefore, the substantive information to be provided by the developer under Article 5 had been made available, in one form or another, in the course of the Public Inquiries and planning procedures generally. Such an argument involves the view that the Directive is satisfied if the prescribed information is made available in dribs and drabs, hidden among thousands of pages of documentation generated over a period of many years. It involves regarding the provision of information to the public under the Directive as a purely mechanical process, which can be satisfied by a piecemeal and incoherent release of information and which can be divorced from the purpose that the provision of information is intended to serve, namely to inform the public of the main points of impact of the project in an easily accessible way, so as to allow it to have an informed view of the project and to bring its informed opinion to bear at a stage at which it is capable of influencing the decision-making process.

In fact, of course, nothing more clearly illustrates the unsatisfactory nature of the Government's approach than its suggestion, made in the High Court action, that the Second Inspector's Report could even be regarded as the required non-technical summary. When the Commission ultimately intervened in the case, by issuing a letter of formal notice to the UK, the letter (in language borrowed directly from the complaint) rightly rejected this contention out of hand. In the Commission's opinion the

Report could not be treated as the required summary because it had been provided as advice to the Secretary of State and not in order to alert the public, in simple and straightforward language, to the environmental impact of the project and because, although it had been made available to those who had attended the Second Inquiry, it had not been made more generally available to the public concerned by the project,[45] in particular those resident in the area affected by it.

ANTICLIMAX

The lodging of the complaint opened a new chapter in the campaign to save Twyford Down, with the three individual clients and other members of the Association once more submerging themselves in the task of drawing public attention to the threat hanging over the Down and to subsequent European developments. Theirs was a campaign of public speaking, of press briefings, of fund raising, of letter writing and lobbying. After the initial 'event' of submission of the complaint, however, there was a long and deafening silence from Brussels. Nothing seemed to happen. Despite repeated chasing, we did not even receive a receipt evidencing registration of the complaint until 6 February 1991 (nearly three months after the complaint had been lodged). At first we were told that the delay was caused by the fact that the complaint had been associated with a number of other complaints and was the responsibility of a single official in Directorate General XI, who was struggling to make progress because he was unfamiliar with the English planning laws and procedures involved. We do not know whether or not this was true, but as we shall see, we later discovered that the Commission deliberately delayed taking the decisive step of issuing a formal letter of notice with respect to the complaint (and the others with which it was associated) because of its anxiety to reach a negotiated solution with the British authorities. As the delay became protracted, we did not know and were not entitled to know what stance the Commission was taking nor what was passing between it and the United Kingdom Government. When the Commission did finally intervene, and Mr di Meana (the Environment Commissioner) was forced by political pressure to defend his action, the full picture became clearer. The description given below is based partly upon what we knew at the time and partly upon the Commissioner's later account of events. The background against which it must he understood was dominated from the beginning by the Government's determination to press ahead with the M3 project despite the lodging of the complaint.

THE PACE QUICKENS

According to the Commissioner's account, the Commission sent an informal letter to the UK Government on 26 March 1991 raising issues arising from the complaint. The UK responded on 21 May 1991 and Commission and UK officials met on 10 June. Only three days later, however, the Department of Transport published an invitation to tender[46] (the ITT) in respect of work to be carried out on part of the site, including part of the Itchen Valley (Winchester Meadows) Site of Special Scientific Interest ('SSSI'). This SSSI comprised an area of wet fen meadow which had been described by English Nature as being of *'exceptional richness'*. The 'preparatory works' to which the ITT related involved the construction of a bridge and the stripping of the vegetation and upper soil horizons of the meadow. The deadline for receipt of tenders was to be 20 August 1991. From then on the contract might be awarded, in itself a significant step.[47]

Merrick Denton-Thompson then wrote to the Department of Transport requesting them to delay further steps in connection with the M3 project, pending the outcome of the Commission's deliberations. On 1 August 1991, a Department of Transport official replied stating that

> [t]he Government has responded to [the Commission's] request for comments on a complaint that an environmental assessment was required before authorisation of the motorway proposal, in accordance with Directive 85/337...[w]e have received no further correspondence from the Commission.[48]

The reply concluded that

> [w]ork on the scheme, as you will be aware, is continuing.

A response from a different Department of Transport official dated 2 August 1991 made effectively the same points. It stated that a letter had been sent by the UK to the Commission *'refuting the complaint'* and that the fact that the Commission had invited comments on a complaint did not *of itself mean that there is any substance in the complaint or that the Commission will pursue the matter further[49]...[t]he Department sees no reason or justification for work on the scheme to be halted. As you will be aware, advance works are under way with a view to starting the main construction next year.*

Needless to say, the complainants alerted the Commission to the dangers posed by publication of the ITT for advance works on the site and transmitted to the Commission copies of the Department's letters, as evidencing the likelihood that damaging work would shortly commence on the site.

After the publication of the ITT, the Commissioner apparently received an *aide-mémoire* from Mr Rifkind and further exchanges, according to the Commissioner, followed.[50] We do not know the content of these exchanges. In response, however, to our representations to the Commission as to the danger posed by the Government's determination to let the advance works contract for the site, we did receive, on 29 August 1991, a fax from the Commission official dealing with the case indicating that the Commission had now decided to write a letter of formal notice (referred to as a *'letter under Article 169 of the Treaty'*) to the UK in connection, among others, with the M3 complaint. We also obtained from a Commission source a copy of the draft letter of formal notice itself. We were told that the letter had been approved by the college of Commissioners in one of their meetings, but had not yet been despatched. Needless to say, the fact that the Commission had stated that it would be taking the first step in an enforcement proceeding against the UK was of the greatest value. The press were briefed and the story hit the national headlines. A copy of the Commission's draft letter was also leaked to the press by, I believe, a source other than the Twyford Down Association. It provoked widespread media interest.

On 29 August, the same day that we received the Commission's fax, Merrick Denton-Thompson wrote once more to the Department of Transport, and to the Secretary of State for Transport personally, enclosing a copy of the fax and once more requesting that further progress of works on the site be halted pending the outcome of the Commission's procedures. Departmental officials responded by letters of 11 September and, on Mr Rifkind's behalf, of 17 September. The letter of 11 September said that *[t]he Department has had no communication from the European Commission [since 2 August[51]] and that therefore there is still no reason or justification for work on the scheme to be halted.*

The letter of 17 September replying on Rifkind's behalf was similar in tenor, saying that notwithstanding the indication received by the complainants from the Commission, the Government had not received an Article 169 letter from the Commission in respect of the M3 and that, as regards the complainants' request for work on the scheme to stop, there was nothing that could be added to the earlier letter. This correspondence also was brought to the attention of the Commission as still further evidence of the Government's determination to press ahead with the M3 works unless the Commission intervened.

The next step occurred in early September 1991 when 'rescue archaeology' work began on the site, as part of which mechanical diggers stripped the top soil off an area of approximately seven acres of land between the two Scheduled Ancient Monuments and from the monuments themselves.[52] Thus, by mid-September 1991, the Commission knew that the Department had consistently indicated its intention to proceed with the scheme, notwithstanding the Commission's investigation of the Twyford Down complaint and notwithstanding its indication that it would be sending a letter of formal notice in connection with the project. Furthermore, quite apart from what it may have learned from its meetings and exchanges with the Department, the Commission knew that so far as the Itchen Valley SSSI was concerned the contract award procedure had been commenced and that the contract could be awarded after 20 August. The position became more urgent on 1 October 1991 when the Department of Transport served on at least one of the owners of land comprised in the Itchen Valley SSSI two 'Notices to Enter'[53] which would entitle the Department or its contractors to enter the land, and so commence the works, on or after the expiration of 14 days.

Thus, so far as Twyford Down was concerned, the prospective letter of formal notice would have to be despatched by mid-October if it were to have any prospect of ensuring that the environmental effects of the project were assessed in accordance with the Directive, prior to the infliction of significant damage to the site. It was in fact despatched on the 17th of that month.

AN 'ASTONISHING INTERVENTION'

In the event, on 17 October 1991, Mr Ripa di Meana despatched not one but two letters. He despatched to the UK Government the Commission's letter of formal notice (which had previously been approved by the Commission as a whole). This alleged failure by the United Kingdom to honour its obligations under the Directive. It alleged failure in a number of respects to transpose the Directive adequately into English law. It argued, in particular, that the exemption of projects which were 'in the pipe-line' when the Directive took effect was unlawful. It also alleged that the UK had failed to ensure practical compliance with the Directive in respect of the Twyford Down Project and no fewer than six other projects, including two other major highway projects, the A406 East London River Crossing which was to cut through Oxleas Wood and the proposed Link Road between Hackney Wick and the M11.

So far as Twyford Down was concerned, the Commission's letter upheld the Association's contention that the UK had failed to ensure that a 'non-technical summary' was made available by the developer, the Secretary of State for Transport. As we have seen, it did not take up the Association's other argument, namely that all of the prescribed information should be made available in a comprehensive form at an early stage in the planning process.

The Commissioner also wrote personally to Mr Malcolm Rifkind, then Secretary of State for Transport, asking him

> not to proceed with work on these projects so that the environment will neither be lost nor damaged beyond repair.[54]

THE CRISIS BREAKS

Both letters were highly publicized and, on the eve of the Maastricht Conference, sparked an immediate crisis in relations between the Commission and the Government. They had been sent, in a highly publicized way, in the immediate run up to the Maastricht Conference[55] and their effect can only be understood in light of the political tensions within the Conservative Party and the highly charged political atmosphere in the UK which preceded that Conference. An additional irritant was the fact that Mr Major, then newly appointed as Prime Minister, was away from home attending the Commonwealth Conference in Harare, Zimbabwe, when the news broke. Thus, at his first Commonwealth Conference as Prime Minister, he found himself having to defend his Government's environmental policy to press and media journalists rather than being able to project his own political agenda.

This background in part helps to explain the vehemence of the Government's response to the Commissioner's letters, both as regards the intemperate comments made by UK ministers at the time[56] and as regards subsequent political developments. Mr Major himself was widely reported as having complained that the Commission's action was an *'astonishing intervention'*, that it had acted on the basis of

> *ill-founded reports and not facts and facts that were not discussed with the United Kingdom* [and that such an approach]...*has to be absolutely how the European Commission should not behave and I have told them so...*[57]

Mr Major did indeed write a well publicized letter to Mr Delors, President of the Commission, complaining about the intervention.[58] According to press reports, the Prime Minister's letter even warned that the intervention would make it more difficult politically for the UK Government to support economic and monetary union at the forthcoming Maastricht Conference.[59]

Criticism of the Commission's intervention focused on four points. First, that the Commission had intervened without having first properly discussed the matter with the Government. Second, that the Commissioner's personal letter to Mr Rifkind was unauthorized and that its disclosure to the press was in some way improper.[60] Third, that the two letters had been disclosed to the press before they had been despatched to the ministers concerned. Finally, in the words of Mr Hurd, the UK Foreign Secretary, that the intervention was an attempt by the Commission to interfere in the *'nooks and crannies of national life'* by trying to dictate to national authorities what field a new road should go through.[61]

In fact, although Commissioner di Meana's intervention, and its manner and timing, were no doubt embarrassing to the Government and, as it turned out, to the Commission, these criticisms were, as we shall see, unfounded. Furthermore, as we have seen, developments on the ground in connection with the

M3 project had significantly restricted the Commissioner's freedom of choice as to the method and timing of his intervention.

The intensity of the Government's response to the
Commissioner's intervention, and the tenor of Mr Major's letter
to Mr Delors, must have caused consternation within the college
of Commissioners. Indeed, within days I received a telephone
call from a member of Mr di Meana's cabinet saying that the college of Commissioners was to meet in Strasbourg later that
week and that members of the Commission were 'after his
blood'. I was asked to fax di Meana's cabinet any documents in
my possession which demonstrated that, contrary to its public
line, the Government must have known in advance of the
Commissioner's impending intervention. Having obtained my
clients' consent I duly faxed certain documents to Strasbourg.

Mr di Meana's defence of his position must have been convincing because the Commission meeting in Strasbourg
expressed its *'complete solidarity'*[62] with him. Interestingly, however, it did so in the absence of Mr Delors who, with Vice-
President Marin, was engaged elsewhere at the time.[63]

DISCUSSION WITH THE UK AUTHORITIES

The Commissioner took the opportunity to defend himself more
publicly when, a few days later, he addressed the European
Parliament's debate on Environmental Impact Assessment.[64]
According to Mr di Meana, the allegation that the Commission
had intervened without first discussing the facts of the cases in
question with the Government was quite unjustified. On the
contrary, he said that there had been a great deal of discussion,
including dialogue at the political level. The chronology of
events in respect of Twyford Down and the two other highway
cases covered by the letter of formal notice illustrates his point.
Apart from the initial exchange of correspondence between the
Commission and the Government which followed the lodging
of the complaints,[65] there had been extensive discussions over a
period of many months. The Commissioner revealed that the
formal letter had been approved by the Commission as a whole
on 20 March 1991, some seven months before its despatch, the
UK Permanent Representative (Britain's Ambassador to the
Community) being advised of the opening of the Article 169

procedure *'immediately'* afterwards. The Commissioner explained that the seven-month delay in despatching the letter had been caused by the Commission's determination to resolve the issues that it raised by dialogue with the UK authorities rather than by initiating the Article 169 procedure. He said that

> [i]n these seven months there [had] been numerous contacts with the British authorities at various levels, including the political one, to explore all possibilities of a non-legal solution.

As we have seen there had, in particular, been a meeting on 10 June 1991 between officials of the Commission and the UK Departments of the Environment and Transport. On 30 July 1991 the Commissioner had received an aide-mémoire from Mr Rifkind on the basis of which there were *'other exchanges of information and meetings as well as a long, direct telephone conversation'* between him and Mr Rifkind. This was followed *'at the beginning of September'* by a meeting *'at a high level between the two administrations'* attended by the Commissioner himself. Furthermore, on 16 October 1991, the very eve of the despatch of the Commissioner's letters, there was a further meeting between officials.

According to this detailed account of events, there had indeed been an extensive dialogue with the Government before despatch of the letters. To the extent that it conflicts with the Government's initial response to the intervention, the Commissioner's account is to be preferred. Such is the nature of the procedure under Article 169 that it would, indeed, be inconceivable for the Commission to despatch a letter of formal notice without first having discussed the facts of the case with the Government of the Member State concerned. Furthermore, the seven-month delay between approval of the formal letter and its ultimate despatch was consistent with an attempt by the Commission to try to resolve things by dialogue. It would, to say the least, be inconsistent with a picture of the Commissioner as indulging in hasty, precipitate action.

Furthermore, the Government had been put on notice of the likelihood of the Commission's intervention by a series of articles appearing in the British press from the early summer of 1991.[66] These articles, based on a leaked copy of a draft of the formal letter, accurately reflected the substance of the letter as it was ultimately despatched. Although the Government could not be expected to respond in public to such articles, it is inconceivable that the Departments concerned would not have taken up the matters reported with the Commission itself. After all, the developments in question included major infrastructure projects which were important elements of the Government's transport policy. The Government knew them to be politically controversial and that complaints had been lodged with the Commission. It would be strange indeed if it did not take up the press reports, or at least some of them, with the Commission and if further exchanges did not ensue. This is particularly the case because, as we have seen, on 2 September 1991 a member of the Twyford Down Association wrote to the Department of Transport and to Mr Rifkind enclosing a copy of the fax received from Directorate General XI, which in turn stated that a letter under Article 169 would indeed be sent to the Government in connection with the M3 complaint among others.[67] In such circumstances it beggars belief to imagine that the Department did not initiate a discussion with the Commission about the threatened action.[68]

IMPROPER PUBLICATION

Mr Di Meana also sought to refute the allegation that his personal letter to Mr Rifkind was in some way 'unauthorized' and its publication improper. That allegation, he said, stemmed from

> confusion between two completely separate acts that arises in the letter from Prime Minister John Major, a confusion that makes it possible to speak of presumed abuse of power on the part of a Commissioner.

He emphasized the distinction between the initiation of the enforcement procedure itself, a *'due act'* under Community law, and the writing of his personal letter to Mr Rifkind. The latter, he stressed, was a *'political gesture'* made by him personally and not in the name of the Commission. It was not, he added, *'a secret, confidential or private letter'*.

It is submitted that this distinction is fully justified and that (whatever the political effect of his personal letter and the publicity attached to it) the Commissioner was quite entitled to act as he did and that his personal letter did not need to be authorized by the Commission as a whole or by its President before despatch or publication. Furthermore, any other view would lead to the conclusion either that a Commissioner is entitled to express himself to Member States in contentious matters only in private; or that if he does so in public, it should only be with the permission of the college of Commissioners or its President. Any such a conclusion would be at odds with the everyday practice of Commissioners and would result in an unacceptable accretion of power to the Commission's President, allowing him to control the public stance of Commissioners within the scope of their portfolios. It would not sit comfortably with the duty of independence of the Commissioners. This duty is laid down by Article 157 of the Treaty of Rome itself, which requires Commissioners to be

> *completely independent in the performance of their duties* [and which expressly requires that]...*[i]n the performance of those duties, they shall neither seek nor take instructions from any government or from any other body.*

For a Commissioner to be prevented from public comment on a matter within the scope of his portfolio without the prior consent of the Commission as a whole or of its President would, above all, diminish the political influence of individual Commissioners by limiting their possibility of appealing directly to public opinion. In the environmental field, the responsible Commissioner's ability to enlist the support of public opinion to ensure national compliance with Community law is essential if he is to be able to prevent environmental degradation pending the outcome of enforcement procedures in environmental cases. It is, of course, true that once an action under Article 169 is actually commenced in the Court of Justice the Commission can apply to the Court for interim protective measures. The problem is, however, that the commencement of an action in the Court is only the ultimate step in what is in practice a lengthy procedure; during the period before that step is taken the Court cannot order interim measures and the Commission itself has no legal power to order that a site be preserved pending the outcome. These deficiencies in the enforcement procedure mean that an allegedly defaulting State might well be able to deprive such a procedure of practical effect by irreversibly damaging a site (and so presenting the Commission with a *fait accompli*) at a stage at which interlocutory measures are simply not available.

Of course, the Commission itself could reduce the possibility of such an outcome by speeding up its own investigations and deliberations, but some degree of delay is unavoidable because

Directorate General XI is short-staffed, because it prefers, if at all
possible, to resolve infractions by negotiation rather than by litigation and because of the need for letters of formal notice to be
scrutinized by the Commission's Legal Service. Nonetheless, in
light of the deficiencies of the enforcement procedure, it is
surely essential that the responsible Commissioner should have
the right, in his own name and at his own discretion, to appeal
to public opinion and so apply political pressure to prevent
damage to an environmentally important site before completion
of its procedures. Indeed, as Mr di Meana himself told the
European Parliament, he

> [knew] very well – and the British government [knew] it too –
> that at this stage of the violation procedure the Commission does
> not have the power to impose a suspension on the work, but
> everyone also [knew] that, at a later stage, namely that of
> recourse to the Court of Justice, [the Commission had] the option
> of asking the Court for an order to suspend the work. And in sim-
> ilar cases we have also turned first to the competent government
> authority to ask for respect of the procedures laid down in the
> environmental impact directive.[69]

The Commissioner responded to suggestions that he was victimizing the United Kingdom by pointing out that his personal
request to Mr Rifkind to suspend work on the projects was not
unprecedented and that

> [t]here have been similar requests in the past to other ministers,
> in cases where we could not yet use the available legal instru-
> ments [so that his conduct in this case was therefore] analo-
> gous with cases dealt with in the past in completely comparable
> ways and affecting almost all Member States.[70]

Thus, far from 'victimizing' the UK, Mr di Meana purported to
be acting in a well established way and in a way dictated by the
weakness, in environmental cases, of Article 169.

'LEAKS' TO THE PRESS

The specific complaint, that the Commissioner had publicized
his letters before they had been made available to the UK
Government, also seems to be without foundation.[71] According
to Mr di Meana the formal letter was sent by fax to the UK

Permanent Representative at 12.27 pm on 17 October. It was faxed to Mr Rifkind at 12.44 pm on the same day. Mr di Meana is reported as telling the European Parliament that the personal letter to Mr Rifkind was communicated to the UK Permanent Representative at 5.03 pm *'seven minutes after the communication to the permanent representative'*.[72] The press release was *'timed for 6pm'*. Of course, although this does show that the necessary proprieties were respected there can have been little doubt that the timing of the press release was calculated, as one would expect, to attract maximum attention as it was released in time to feature in the late evening news in the UK.

NOOKS AND CRANNIES

The final criticism, that the Commission's intervention was an unacceptable attempt to intrude into the nooks and crannies of British life by dictating the route of particular roads, was also without substance. There was, as the UK Government later accepted,[73] no question that the Commission had attempted to dictate the line of the M3 or of any of the other roads covered by the letter of formal notice. The Directive, and the Commissioner's intervention, were concerned solely with the proper application of Environmental Impact Assessment procedures and not their outcome.

Much of the criticism of Mr di Meana's intervention was based on a perception that its timing was inopportune since it embarrassed both the UK Government and the Commission itself in the crucial weeks before the Maastricht Conference. Mr di Meana could hardly have been unaware of heightened political sensitivity prior to the Conference. As we have seen, however, his timing was dictated in part by his desire to allow time (no less than seven months) to reach a negotiated settlement with the UK. As the Commissioner himself told the European Parliament, other factors ultimately forced his hand. By 16 October, it had become clear that, despite extensive negotiations, the Commission and the UK *'had failed to achieve a rapprochement in [their] position'* and Mr di Meana was so advised by his Director General.[74] The Commissioner recounted that

> *in the meantime we were thrown into a state of increasing tension due to numerous parliamentary questions, which we naturally had to answer, indiscretions of all kinds in the press and the legitimate pressure of innumerable petitioners.*[75]

Furthermore, in a masterpiece of understatement, he explained that '[t]he petitioners have shown particular concern about work start' and had requested to be kept informed about the Commission's decisions.

THE UK'S FORMAL RESPONSE

The UK was required to respond to the letter of formal notice by midnight on 17 December 1991 and reportedly did so at the eleventh hour,[76] maintaining its position and declining to suspend work on the projects in question. In fact, even during the response period, the Department of Transport had taken further significant steps to progress the Twyford Down project, including the award of the contract for advance works.[77]

In fact, very quickly after the controversy over the Commissioner's intervention broke out, I was given a pointer as to the way things would develop. I was told informally by a Commission official that such had been the reaction within the college of Commissioners to the UK's initial response to Mr di Meana's intervention that it would be politically impossible for Directorate General XI to take any steps to protect the site pending the outcome of its Article 169 procedure. The Commission could not be seen to interfere in the run up to the forthcoming UK General Election.[78] I was also told that Directorate General XI was concerned that at the forthcoming Maastricht Conference there might be moves to limit or take away the Community's competence over certain environmental matters or to reduce the powers of the Commission over them on grounds of subsidiarity. I did not know at the time whether or not this fear was justified, but the message was ominous enough. In fact it is interesting to note that the Maastricht Conference did indeed subject EC environmental legislation in certain fields to a national veto. Significantly enough, the areas affected included in particular *'measures concerning town and country planning...[and]...land use...'*[79]

A *FAIT ACCOMPLI*

From the complainants' point of view, the political climate got worse rather than better in the months after the UK responded to the formal letter. The rejection of the Maastricht Treaty by the people of Denmark in their referendum on 2 June 1992 produced a climate in which the Commission was bound to be at pains to avoid further friction with the UK Government, especially as it was to assume the Presidency of the EC Council on 1 July of that year (so that its support would be crucial if the Maastricht Treaty were to be saved). Furthermore, having rejected Mr di Meana's plea to suspend work on the highway projects, the Government was clearly determined to press speedily ahead with work on the Twyford Down site; on 23 January 1992 bulldozers commenced 'preliminary' work, removing trees and preparing to root up hedges.[80] In February 1992 the Department's contractors attempted to demolish two bridges on the site but were delayed by protesters.[81] Such indeed was the opposition from protesters that a Department of Transport spokesman was reported on 3 March 1992 as saying that the Department would take *'whatever action is necessary'* to ensure that construction began on time, including the seeking of a High Court injunction. On 16 March 1992, bulldozers began to tear down trees and strip the turf off the River Itchen Water Meadow SSSI.[82]

Thus, long before the Commission had come to a view on the UK's response to the formal letter, the Twyford Down site had been irreparably damaged. This despite the fact that in January 1992 Mr di Meana had publicly said that he rejected the UK Government's restatement of its position on the pipe-line point and thought it likely that the cases would fall to be resolved by the Court of Justice.[83] In the event, by mid-March 1992, all that he could do was to describe himself as *'extremely disappointed'* at the UK's behaviour and to comment, rather forlornly, that legal proceedings *'certainly cannot be ruled out'*.[84]

A NEW COMMISSIONER

On 29 June 1992 it was reported that Mr di Meana had resigned.[85] He was replaced by Mr Karel Van Miert who took over as acting Environment Commissioner. Thus the Commission's stance on the enforcement procedures against the UK, the most controversial of which (including Twyford Down) concerned major highway projects, would thereafter be determined by the erstwhile Transport Commissioner; a fact which, whether intentionally or not, conveyed an ominous message to the complainants.

On 31 July 1992,[86] no less than seven months after the UK had responded to the formal letter, the Commission finally came to a decision, which it announced by means of a press release[87] ('the Press Release'). This stated that, on a proposal from Mr Van Miert, the Commission had decided to terminate its procedures relating to the M3 motorway and four of the other projects that had been the subject of the letter of formal notice. It had decided to send Reasoned Opinions (the next step in the enforcement procedure) in respect of two remaining projects and in connection with the 'pipe-line point' generally.

In light of the earlier history of the case, the justification given by the Commission for terminating the Twyford Down procedure was extraordinary. The Press Release did not claim that, having examined the UK's response, the Commission had concluded that there had in fact been no breach of the Directive. On the contrary it stated that

> [b]ecause the United Kingdom failed to comply with the proce-
> dures laid down for implementation of [the] Directive in the case
> of [the] five specific projects, the Commission [had] initiated pro-
> ceedings against it on 17 October 1991.

So far as the Twyford Down Project was concerned, Mr Van Miert had now proposed termination of the enforcement proce-dure because

> the British Government was able to demonstrate that it had
> sought guarantees **equivalent** to those given by the impact
> assessment provided for in the Directive. (emphasis mine)

Thus the Commission, while maintaining its view that the law had not been observed, nonetheless decided to terminate its procedures because it now believed that the UK had 'sought' 'guarantees' which, although unspecified, were thought by the Commission to be in some way 'equivalent' to those required by the Directive.

More specifically, the Press Release indicated that the Twyford Down enforcement procedure had been commenced because

> it appeared that no non-technical summary in accordance with
> the Directive...had been provided...

but that the case had now been closed because

> *the documentation provided in the UK's response to the Letter of*
> *Formal Notice included **an equivalent** to the non-technical sum-*
> *mary, acceptable on the facts of this case, which had not previ-*
> *ously been submitted to the Commission.* (emphasis mine)

This explanation is far from convincing. Are we really to believe that, despite the extensive discussions which took place between the Commission and the UK authorities in the seven months before despatch of the letter of formal notice, a document *'equivalent'* to the key non-technical summary had simply been overlooked by the Departments concerned? That would imply a staggering degree of ineptitude on the part of the UK authorities. The Commission's statement was implausible in other respects. First, the Press Release failed to identify the new document. Secondly, it made clear that the new document was not actually a non-technical summary but merely 'an equivalent', but it failed to explain in what respects it differed from the summary required by the Directive. Did it differ as to content, and if so how? Or did it differ as to the extent to which it was made available to the public concerned by the development? Why was this document *'acceptable on the facts of this case'*? What were the relevant facts and how did they serve to justify acceptance of the *'equivalent'* document in place of the summary required by the Directive?

The Commission did not even bother to explain these important points. It could get away with such a cursory approach because of the opaque nature of the enforcement process itself. Although a Member State is entitled to know the allegations made against it by complainants and by the Commission, complainants are not themselves entitled to know what evidence the Member State puts before the Commission, still less to comment upon or to rebut it. Thus, if the Commission wishes to terminate a procedure commenced in response to a complaint it can blandly assert that on the basis of the (unspecified) 'evidence', it is satisfied that no infraction of Community law has occurred. Neither the complainant nor the Court of Justice can go behind such an assertion. Such was the case with Twyford Down. Since there was no possibility of judicial review of the Commission's decision, the complainants could not challenge it or complain about the inadequacies of the reasons given.

Since the position could not be clarified by legal action the suspicion remains that the Commission's decision was not in fact the result of the discovery of a new document but was the result of a change of policy. If there was such a change of policy the question would then arise as to the motivation behind it and, specifically, as to whether it was prompted by the political pressure exerted by the UK Government. If that were indeed the case, it would raise serious constitutional questions about whether the Commission had observed its duty of independence under Article 157 of the Treaty of Rome and had properly carried out its duty under Article 155 of that Treaty *'to ensure that the provisions of this Treaty and the measures taken...pursuant thereto are applied'*.

In fact, the Commission has, in response to questions in the European Parliament and in correspondence with the Twyford Down Association, provided some further explanation of its position. Such explanation has, however, been incomplete and inconsistent with the version of events given in the Press Release. Important questions remain unanswered.

1.   **If there had been no change of policy by the Commission, why was it now prepared to accept 'equivalent' guarantees to those sought by the Directive when it had not earlier been prepared to do so?**

The UK Government had argued from the outset that even if there had been, strictly speaking, no non-technical summary, the planning procedures in respect of Twyford Down took full account of the environmental impact of the project and gave equivalent protection. Indeed, the Secretaries of States' decision letter of 20 February 1990 expressly made this assertion and contended that the Secretaries of State were satisfied that information which would now be included in an 'Environmental Statement' had *'been made available during the consultation and inquiry stages'*.[88] Had the Commission been prepared to accept such an 'equivalent protection' argument, it could have done so from the outset. Instead, it had insisted in its formal letter upon the necessity of a non-technical summary. Clearly, however, by the time the Commission came to dispose of the case things had changed.

2.   **Why did the Commission later change its story?**

The Press Release made it clear that the critical new document was not itself a 'non-technical summary' but was in some way 'equivalent' and offered 'equivalent' 'guarantees'. As we shall see, when it later elaborated upon its position the Commission changed its tune. It stated not that the new document was 'equivalent' to a non-technical summary, but that it actually constituted such a summary. It gave no explanation of this revisionism. This hardly adds to the credibility of its position. A witness who changes a fundamental part of his testimony cannot expect to be believed. Indeed, if the version of events stated in the Press Release were true, the subsequent interpretation simply could not be correct. If the subsequent interpretation were correct, the Press Release could not have been right. Such fundamental inconsistency casts doubt on the credibility of the Commission's story as a whole.

3.   Why did the Commission's further explanation not address the fundamental issue?

The Commission ultimately stated, in response to correspondence from the Twyford Down Association and to questions raised in the European Parliament, that the critical new document was a Statement of Reasons produced by the Departments of Transport and the Environment in May 1985. The first and most striking thing about that document is its limited circulation, which is made clear by the very first paragraph of its Preamble, which states that

> **This statement is that required to be served**, *in accordance with Rule 5 of the Highways (Inquiries Procedure) Rules 1976,* **on each statutory objector** *(as defined in the Rules) not less than 28 days before the date of the Public Inquiries. Part 7 of this statement lists documents which the Department may refer to or put in evidence at the Inquiries, together with addresses where these documents may be inspected.*[89] (emphasis mine)

Thus it is clear (and must have been clear to the Commission throughout) that the Statement of Reasons was not intended to be made available to the public in general but only to the very limited number of those who were statutory objectors. How could such a document properly be regarded as constituting, or even being 'equivalent' to, the non-technical summary required by Article 5.2? That would seem to fly in the face of the Directive itself, which requires that Member States must ensure that the information required from the developer (including the non-technical summary) is *'made available to the public'* and that *'the public concerned is given an opportunity to express an opinion before the project is initiated'*.[90] If the purpose of making available the developer's information, and in particular the non-technical summary, is to alert the public concerned to the environmental implications of the project and so allow it to make representations on an informed basis, it seems perverse to suppose that a document made available to a small number of people who were statutory objectors could possibly fulfil that role. Nonetheless, such a proposition is implicit in the Commission's decision. How can a document having such a limited circulation possibly constitute a non-technical summary or serve the purpose of such a summary? That is the key issue to which the Commission's explanations give rise, and yet it is a point which the Commission, even when questioned in the European Parliament, has repeatedly failed to address.

In fact the Commission's first opportunity to clarify its position came in correspondence with Mr David Croker of the Twyford Down Association. Writing to Mr Croker, Dr Ludwig Kramer (Head of Legal Matters and Application of Community Law in Directorate General XI of the Commission) explained that

> It is not the Commission's normal practice to give detailed reasons for the decisions it takes in the context of proceedings under Article 169 of the Treaty, as content of correspondence with the Member States in [such] proceedings is...confidential between the Commission and the Member States.

Nonetheless Dr Kramer was prepared to set out briefly the view taken by the Commission on the specific points raised in the complaint. In several respects his interpretation of the Directive did not differ fundamentally from that originally advanced by the Association itself. But his ultimate conclusion that there had been no infringement of the Directive depended in each particular upon a mere assertion that the Commission was so satisfied on the basis of the 'evidence' put before it, evidence which was unspecified and which (as we have seen) the Association would not have the opportunity to test, challenge or rebut.

Dr Kramer said that the Commission continued to agree with the Association's contention on the 'pipe-line point', namely that the Directive did indeed apply to relevant projects for which development consent is given after 3 July 1988, regardless of whether or not the application for consent was first made before that date. He then referred to the Association's argument that the information required from the developer should be provided in a comprehensive and self-contained form (whether in a single document or a series of documents) and should be provided at an early stage in the development consent procedure. He stated that

> With regard to the form of the information supplied, Article 5.1...requires a Member State to ensure that information is supplied in 'an appropriate form'. With regard to the content of the information supplied, the minimum information to be supplied is set out in Article 5.2. *If the information supplied in a particular case were in a clearly inappropriate form,* or if it failed to contain the data required by Article 5.2 then there would be a breach of the Directive. The information before the Commission did not suggest that there was such a breach in this case. (emphasis mine)

It is worth noting at this point that, although Dr Kramer acknowledged that the Directive required Member States to ensure that the information required of the developer is provided in 'appropriate form', he did accept this did not confer an absolute discretion on the Member States. If the information were supplied in a *'clearly inappropriate form'* there would indeed be a breach of the Directive. That of course begs the question as to what would indeed be regarded by the Commission as appropriate or inappropriate. All that we know is that on the basis of the (again unspecified) information before the Commission it had concluded that there had been no breach in the present case.

In response to the contention that the information required from the developer must be provided at an early stage in the consent process, Dr Kramer stated that

> [w]ith regard to the time at which the information must be supplied, the Directive requires in Article 2 that the assessment must be carried out before development consent is granted. Articles 6 and 8 require that the information be supplied in time for there to be public consultation, and for the results of the consultation to be taken into account in the development consent procedure.

Once more, however, he was unforthcoming as to the factual basis upon which the Commission had applied these principles to the case in question. Once more, a bland assertion that

> *[t]he evidence before the Commission did not suggest that these*
> *requirements of the Directive had been breached in this case.*

It came as no surprise, of course, that the Commission did not
support the complainants' points as to the form in which, and
the time at which, the information required from the developer
should have been provided. After all, the letter of formal notice
had not pursued those points but had been based exclusively
upon the allegation that no non-technical summary had been
provided as required by Article 5.2.

Dr Kramer's letter concluded by addressing the question of
the non-technical summary. He wrote that

> *[y]ou allege. . .that the developer failed to supply a non-technical*
> *summary. The Commission decided that the Statement of*
> *Reasons furnished by the Departments of Transport and the*
> *Environment met the requirement for a non-technical summary*
> *in Article 5.2 of the Directive.*

Thus Dr Kramer's explanation boils down to a mere assertion
that the Commission had decided that the Statement of
Reasons '*met the requirements of a non-technical summary*' (not as
originally claimed that it was only 'equivalent' to such a summary) without offering any explanation as to why it was so
regarded. No explanation was given as to how it was thought
to meet the requirements of Article 5.2 either as to its content
or, *critically*, as to the extent to which it had been made available to the public.

Mr Van Miert himself had the opportunity to offer such an
explanation when he later responded to a question[91] in the
European Parliament. The questioner wanted to know, among
other things:

> *What new documents were supplied by the British authorities in*
> *response to the formal notice from the Commission?*

> *To what extent did the new documents not correspond to the doc-*
> *umentation required pursuant to Article 5 of the Directive, and*
> *in accordance with what criteria and on what grounds were these*
> *documents deemed equivalent?*

Mr Van Miert's answer confirmed that the new document, on
the basis of which the Commission had terminated its procedure,

was indeed the Statement of Reasons. Although he did refer in cursory manner to the content of the Statement, his response[92] (like Dr Kramer's earlier letter) completely failed to deal with the limited extent of its circulation to the public.[93] Furthermore, like Dr Kramer before him, Mr Van Miert also departed from the Commission's original claim that the new document was merely 'equivalent' to the required non-technical summary. He now claimed that the Statement of Reasons actually constituted such a summary.

4. How could the Commission's acceptance of the Statement of Reasons be consistent with its earlier approach?

Since the Commission has not seen fit to explain the point, one can only speculate as to why it may have thought (depending upon which explanation is to be believed) that the Statement of Reasons was capable of being 'equivalent to' or of actually constituting the necessary non-technical summary. It may have based its view on Article 6.3 of the Directive which provides that

> [t]he detailed arrangements for such information and consultation shall be determined by the member States, which may, in particular, depending on the particular characteristics of the projects or sites concerned;
>
> – **determine the public concerned,**
> – specify the places where the information can be consulted, **specify the way in which the public may be informed,** for example by bill-posting within a certain radius, publication in local newspapers, organisation of exhibitions with plans, drawings, tables, graphs, models,
> – **determine the manner in which the public is to be consulted,** for example, by written submissions, by public enquiry,
> – fix appropriate time limits for the various stages of the procedure in order to ensure that a decision is taken within a reasonable period. (emphasis mine)

Thus the Commission may have felt that, since it was up to the Member State to define the '*public concerned*', it was quite proper for the UK to publish the required information only to statutory objectors and not to make it easily accessible to the wider public in the locality of Twyford Down. For the Commission to adopt such an interpretation would, however, be both alarming and inconsistent. It would be alarming because it would amount to an acceptance that the Member States have an absolute and unfettered discretion to determine the 'public concerned', however narrow and unreasonable such a determination might be. It would potentially allow Member States to undermine the whole purpose of the information and consultation provisions of the Directive.

It would also be inconsistent with the Commission's previous position and with its general attitude to discretions conferred by the Directive upon Member States. In its letter of formal notice the Commission had, after all, rejected the idea that the Second Inspector's Report could be a non-technical summary *expressly* because it had been provided as advice to the Secretary of State and not in order to alert the public in simple and straightforward language to the environmental impact of the project, *and because*

> *although it had been made available to those who had attended the Second Inquiry,* **it had not been made more generally available to the public concerned by the project.** (emphasis mine)

If the circulation of the Second Inspector's Report was too narrow to allow it to serve as the non-technical summary, the same was true of the Statement of Reasons. This crucial point, which the Commission has not seen fit to address in its explanations to the European Parliament, clearly demonstrates that its claim not to have changed its policy between issuing the letter of formal notice and later terminating its procedure simply could not be correct. The Commission had at the very least changed its position on the critical issue as to the extent to which such a summary must be made available to the public. Furthermore, since the limited circulation of the Statement of Reasons must have been known to the Commission throughout, the question must be asked as to why it has not thought fit specifically to justify its position on the point. Was this because it simply overlooked the requirement that a non-technical summary must be made available to the public concerned? Or was it because it preferred not to address an issue which most clearly undermines its claim that its decision was based upon the finding of a new document rather than upon a change of policy?

Furthermore, the Commission's apparent but unacknowledged acceptance that Member States have an entirely free hand in defining the 'public concerned' to whom the summary must be made available seems inconsistent with the attitude which it took in the case of the East London River Crossing (the only one of the highway cases in which the Commission did not terminate its procedure). That project differed from the M3 development in one important respect. The M3 project was of a type ('construction of motorways or express ways') listed in Annex I to the Directive. It was therefore subject to mandatory assessment. The East London River Crossing development did not involve construction of a motorway or express way. It was not therefore an Annex I project but was instead of a type listed in Annex II ('construction of roads'[94]). Such projects are only subject to assessment, according to Article 4.2

> *where Member States consider that their characteristics so require*

and

> *[t]o this end Member States may inter alia specify certain types of projects as being subject to an assessment or may establish the criteria and/or thresholds necessary to determine which of the projects of the classes listed in Annex II are to be subject to an assessment...*

Despite the fact that the UK had regarded Article 4.2 as conferring upon Member States an absolute discretion to determine which cases should or should not be subject to assessment, the Commission insisted that the Member States did not have an absolute discretion but were duty bound to determine whether Annex II cases were objectively likely to have significant environmental effects and, if so, that they were then obliged to subject them to assessment. Thus the apparently 'open' nature of the wording of Article 4.2 did not prevent the Commission from insisting upon an assessment where the Member State's determination was thought to be objectively inconsistent with the purpose of the Directive. The same could be said of any determination made by the UK Government under Article 6.3 that the 'public concerned' by the Twyford Down development consisted only of the statutory objectors rather than the general public in the area of the site.

In other words, if the Commission was intent upon ensuring that the Member States exercise their discretion under Article 4.2 in a way which would achieve the purpose of the Directive, why should it now be prepared to accept that statutory objectors to the M3 project could properly be regarded as the 'public concerned', a determination which could have no objective justification and which would be almost calculated to undermine the effectiveness of the information and consultation aspects of the Directive?

5. How could the form and content of the Statement be regarded as conforming to the objectives of the Directive?

If the Statement of Reasons appears to be a rather spurious non-technical summary in point of its circulation, the same can be said of its form and content. In order to comply with the Directive it should have amounted to a 'non-technical summary' of the following information:

- *a description of the project comprising information on the site, design and size of the project,*
- *a description of the measures envisaged in order to avoid, reduce and, if possible, remedy significant adverse effects,*
- *the data required to identify and assess the main effects which the project is likely to have on the environment...'*

It is true that among the information contained in the Statement of Reasons was information which might be categorized as falling within these provisions. The site, design and size of the project were indeed described in words and by reference to Deposit Documents. Data was indeed included which could help identify and assess the project's main environmental effects. But was the description adequate? Or should it have been regarded, in the words of Dr Kramer's letter, as being in a 'clearly inappropriate' form? It is striking, for example, that although the case in large part concerned the impact of the proposed motorway upon the landscape no map indicating the line of the road was included in the Statement itself. Nor did it contain any plan or illustration showing the elevation of the road nor the scale or impact of the Cutting to be made through Twyford Down. Surely a non-technical summary in such a case should include at least these elements.

Difficulties also arise with the Statement of Reasons as much from the extraneous information which it did contain as from the material which it omitted. It was a 64-page document and much of the information it contained related to matters other than those required to be summarized by the Directive. In other words, the prescribed information, so far as it was summarized by the Statement of Reasons, was buried among other information, which could only serve to detract from the accessibility of the prescribed information.

To these points could be added doubts as to whether a 64-page document containing the material comprised in the Statement of Reasons could properly be said to be a 'summary', still less a 'non-technical summary' of the prescribed information. These considerations prompted a further question in the European Parliament asking

> *Can a 63-page* [sic] *Statement of Reasons for a road Scheme be an equivalent to the non-technical summary required under the environmental impact directive?*[95]

The question was answered on behalf of the Commission by Commissioner Paleokrassas (who succeeded Mr Van Miert as Environment Commissioner). His response was that

> *Article 5.2 of [the Directive] does not require the non-technical summary to be a document on its own. It may be integrated into another document.*

He continued that a Statement of Reasons may meet the requirements for a non-technical summary if it meets three conditions, namely, if

- *it provides all the information set down as required by the Directive,*
- *it is made available to the public in a way to be determined by the Member State and the public is given an opportunity to express an opinion on its contents,*
- *it is taken into consideration by the competent authorities before development consent is given to the project.*

Although all concerned, including the Commissioner, must have known that the question was a reference to Twyford Down, the fact that the question did not specifically refer to the case meant that he was not required to explain why and on the basis of what evidence the Commission believed these criteria to be satisfied in that case. Nor did he (any more than Dr Kramer or Mr Van Miert before him) think fit to explain further how the Statement of Reasons could, in point of its limited circulation, possibly qualify as having been *'made available to the public'*. On the other hand, his reference to the need for the summary to be made available *'in a way determined by the Member State'* does seem to imply that the Commission was now prepared to accept that Member States have an absolute discretion as to how they disseminate the prescribed information to the public concerned.

6.   **If there was no change of policy, how can the Commission's decision be reconciled with earlier statements by Mr di Meana made before he left office?**

We have seen that in January 1992 Mr Di Meana, when still Environment Commissioner, had said (having received the UK's response to the letter of formal notice on 17 December 1992) that he rejected the UK Government's restatement of its position on the pipe-line point and that he thought it likely that the cases would have to be resolved by the Court of Justice. By mid-March 1992, he said that he was *'extremely disappointed'* by HM Government's behaviour in respect of Twyford Down and that legal proceedings *'certainly [could] not be ruled out'*. These were hardly the words of a Commissioner who was expecting the enforcement procedure to be terminated. It is of course possible that at the time he was speaking, nearly three months after receiving the UK's response to the formal letter, the Commission had not yet discovered the Statement of Reasons or appreciated its purported significance. On the other hand, the suspicion has been voiced in the European Parliament that the Commission's decision was really the product of a political deal and marked a change of approach from that adopted by Mr di Meana. A change of approach which, if it occurred at all, coincided with the change of Commissioner.

Mrs Aglietta, for example, posed the following question in the Parliament:[96]

In light of the Commission's decision to take no further action in the proceedings instituted against the UK for 5 cases of infringement of [the Directive]...and of the utterances, made by the British Prime Minister, John Major, at the time when the pro-

ceedings were first instituted, can the Commission comment on the supposition – expressed not least in the British press in the days following the decision – that it came to a political under-standing with the British authorities to block the infringement proceedings, thereby overstepping its specific powers?

Other questions have suggested that the Commission's decision to terminate its procedures in the discontinued cases marked a new trend whereby the environment would be allowed to suffer because of disagreement between the Member States and the Commission over the extent of subsidiarity[97] (the respective spheres of competence of the Community and the Member States) and that it amounted to a new interpretation of the Directive departing from that previously adopted by Mr di Meana.[98] Questioners also asked, more directly, why the Commission had terminated its procedures and how it pro-posed to keep Parliament properly informed in such cases.[99] Mr Paleokrassas, who answered these questions on behalf of the Commission,[100]

strongly reject[ed] the suggestion of the Honourable Members that the decisions were taken as a result of any political agree-ment.

He claimed that

In each case proceedings were closed because the Commission decided that no breach of Community law had occurred.

But so far as Twyford Down was concerned he added nothing to the answer already given by Mr Van Miert, an answer which, as we have seen, did not address the central question of the lim-ited circulation of the Statement of Reasons.

CONCLUSIONS

After the Commission terminated its Twyford Down procedure, work on the site continued apace. The motorway link will be completed and drivers will be able to speed through the cutting which now deeply scars the Down and so hasten their journeys between Winchester and Southampton. So far as the environ-ment is concerned the damage is done. But the campaign to save Twyford Down, which in large part focused upon the

European complaint, has deeply affected public consciousness. It has been one of the factors which has brought about widespread opposition to the Government's road building plans. At sites as geographically and socially diverse as Hackney,[101] Salisbury Hill[102] and Newbury,[103] the byword of those opposing major highway developments is that the site which they seek to protect should not become 'another Twyford Down'.

Twyford Down is also a case-study in the application of Community environmental law which lays bare the many faults in the system. It shows the inadequacy of proceedings in the national courts as a means of enforcing Community rules protecting the non-owned environment. Furthermore, nothing could more clearly demonstrate the weakness of the Community system than the UK Government's flagrant determination to press ahead with works on the Down after the Commission had initiated its enforcement procedure (by issuing the letter of formal notice) and in the face of Mr di Meana's personal plea that work should be suspended. This, coupled with the Commission's inability at the critical time to expedite its procedures or to take measures to protect the site pending their outcome, calls into question the very idea of the effective application of Community environmental law.

Furthermore, Twyford Down shows the urgent need to reform the workings of the enforcement procedure; to introduce greater transparency and to make the Commission properly accountable for the enforcement decisions it takes. The fact that the Commission could terminate its procedure without being obliged first to allow the complainants to know what new 'evidence' was being relied upon and to comment upon that evidence and without being obliged to give full reasons to the complainants is bad enough. Especially since the Commission itself emphasizes the importance of citizens' complaints in the enforcement of Community law (especially environmental law).[104] If it is bad that the Commission need not give full explanations to complainants it is even worse that they should have no recourse to judicial review. Worse still, however, is the fact that the Commission was able to act as it did without being forced to give a *complete* account to the European Parliament. Despite the many questions raised in the Parliament, neither Mr Van Miert nor Mr Paleokrassas actually explained the key issue in the Twyford Down case. Indeed, the Commission's approach to the Parliament in respect of Twyford Down and the other British cases is amply demonstrated by a further fact. The Directive itself[105] required the Commission to report to the Parliament and Council on its application and effectiveness within five years of its being notified to the Member States. In the European Parliament's debate on Environmental Impact Assessment of 25 October 1991[106] (which was mainly preoccupied with the British cases, including Twyford Down) Members of the European Parliament called for the Commission to expedite its Report. Notwithstanding all that, the Report was not in fact made until nearly three years later.[107] Despite the crisis which the British cases (especially Twyford Down) had caused in relations with the UK, despite the importance of the issues of interpretation and implementation involved, despite the obvious need for the Commission to give an account of its handling of the cases, they are not even mentioned in the Report. Perhaps Twyford Down and the other cases are problems which the Commission would prefer to forget.

The lack of effective accountability to the European Parliament is all the more objectionable because it appears that national Parliaments are no more entitled to know what passes between the Commission and national Governments in enforcement cases than are complainants or members of the public generally.[108] The convention that enforcement procedures are matters only between the Commission and Member States, and that what passes between them is confidential, may be very convenient for the Ministers, Commissioners and officials involved, but in the real world it reflects no credit upon the Community at all and, as with Twyford Down, risks bringing the whole system into disrepute.

POSTSCRIPT

So far as the pipe-line point itself is concerned, the Commission's Press Release promised that a Reasoned Opinion (the next step in the enforcement procedure) would be issued. Such proceedings will give the Commission the opportunity to vindicate its position on the point of law *in the abstract*. If it succeeds it will obtain a ruling that, by exempting pipe-line cases from the Directive, the UK has failed to honour its obligations under Community law. By then, however, many of the pipeline

projects will, like Twyford Down, be completed or near completion. Even if the Commission succeeds, therefore, its victory will
be largely meaningless. It will be able to say that it has insisted
upon the proper transposition of the Directive. But it will only
have done so in an abstract or hypothetical sense, and not as
regards the many real projects which were 'in the pipe-line'
when the Directive should have been transposed and which
will impact upon the real environment. The Commission did
indicate that it would issue a Reasoned Opinion in respect of
one of the road cases covered by its letter of formal notice,
namely the East London River Crossing. That project was in fact
cancelled by the Department of Transport on 7 July 1992, thus
relieving the Commission of the need to proceed further.[109]

NOTES: CHAPTER 13

[1] *Official Journal of the European Communities*, OJ 1985, L175/40.
[2] Articles 100 and 235 of the Treaty of Rome.
[3] The Directive, art 12.
[4] *'Development consent'* is defined as meaning *'the decision of the
competent authority or authorities which entitles the developer to proceed with the project'*; ibid. art 1(2). The *'competent authority or
authorities'* is that or those which the Member States designate as
responsible for performing the duties arising from the Directive;
ibid. art 1(3).
[5] It is interesting to note that the complainants alleged that for
the purposes of the Directive consent was given for the project
on 16 March 1990, when the definitive schemes and orders
authorizing the development were made. The Commission's letter, however, suggests that consent was granted on 20 February
1990, but neither the letter nor subsequent press releases explain
that choice of date. 20 February 1990 was, however, the date
upon which the Department of Transport wrote to those who
had attended the second Public Inquiry, notifying them that the
Secretaries of State had decided to make the definitive schemes
and orders. If the Commission did indeed regard that letter as
amounting to the grant of consent in this case, it would involve
an interesting interpretation of art 12 of the Directive, which
defines *'consent'* as meaning *'the decision of the competent authority
or authorities **which entitles the developer to proceed with the project'*** (emphasis mine). Notwithstanding the letter of 20 February

1990, the Secretary of State for Transport in his capacity as '*developer*' was not entitled to proceed until (as 'competent authority') he and the Secretary of State for the Environment had actually made the definitive schemes and orders. It is submitted that the word 'decision' in art 12 refers to the legal act authorizing a project and not merely to a decision that such an act will in time be made. Of course, however, even taking 20 February 1990 as the consent date, consent was given many months after the Directive's transposition deadline.

⁶ Art 3 of the Directive.

⁷ Ibid, art 2.2

⁸ Ibid, arts 3, 4.1 & 4.2.

⁹ The '*developer*' is '*the applicant for authorisation for a private project or the public authority which initiates a project*'; ibid, art 1.2.

¹⁰ Annex III lists the following information:

  1. Description of the project, including in particular:

    – a description of the physical characteristics of the whole project and the land use requirements during the construction and operational phases,

    – a description of the main characteristics of the production processes, for instance, nature and quantity of the materials used,

    – an estimate, by type and quantity, of expected residues and emissions (water, air and soil pollution, noise, vibration, light, heat, radiation, etc.) resulting from the operation of the proposed project.

  2. Where appropriate, an outline of the main alternatives studied by the developer and an indication of the main reasons for his choice, taking into account the environmental effects.

  3. A description of the aspects of the environment likely to be significantly affected by the proposed project, including, in particular, population, fauna, flora, soil, water, air, climatic factors, material assets, including the architectural and archaeological heritage, landscape and the inter-relation between the above factors.

  4. A description of the likely significant effects of the proposed project on the environment resulting from:

    – the existence of the project,

    – the use of natural resources,

    – the emission of pollutants, the creation of nuisances and the elimination of waste; and the description by the developer of the

forecasting measures used to assess the effects on the environment.

5. A description of the measures envisaged to prevent, reduce and where possible offset any significant adverse effects on the environment.

6. A non-technical summary of the information provided under the above headings.

7. An indication of any difficulties (technical deficiencies or lack of know-how) encountered by the developer in compiling the required information.

[11] Ibid, art 5.1.

[12] Ibid, art 5.2.

[13] Ibid, art 6.1.

[14] Ibid, art 6.1.

[15] Ibid, art 6.1.

[16] Ibid, art 7.

[17] Ibid.

[18] Ibid, art 8.

[19] Art 9, after all, makes it the competent authority's responsibility to publicize and in some circumstances to give reasons for the decision ultimately taken.

[20] Ibid.

[21] Ibid.

[22] Ibid.

[23] On the grounds that, because of the alleged infringement of the Directive either the scheme was *'not within the powers of the Act'* or *'there had been a failure to comply with a requirement of the Act'*; Paragraph 3 of Schedule 2 to the Highways Act 1980.

[24] In a judgment reported in [1992] 1 CMLR 276.

[25] Ibid, paras [30] to [53].This aspect of the judgment is discussed further below.

[26] Ibid, para [44].

[27] Ibid, para [45].

[28] Ibid, para [46].

[29] Ibid, para [40].

[30] Ibid, emphasis mine.

[31] [1982] 1 CMLR 499.

[32] Ibid, para [48]. In His Lordship's view the *'same considerations'* served to distinguish Case 152/84 *Marshall v Southampton and SW Hampshire Area Health Authority*, supra, which concerned a

directive on the equal treatment of men and women and the provision relied upon dealt with retirement on the ground of age; and Case 80/87 *Dik v College Van Burgemeester en Wethouders Arnhem and Winterswijk*, [1989] 2 CMLR 963, which concerned equal treatment in the field of social security.

[33] And in the other cases cited at note 32, supra.

[34] The restrictive nature of this power of derogation is further emphasized by the Directive's thirteenth recital, which itself states that

> *it may be appropriate in **exceptional cases** to exempt a specific project from the assessment procedures laid down by the Directive, **subject to appropriate information being supplied to the Commission**.* (emphasis mine)

[35] The Commission is then required to forward such documents to the other Member States and to report annually to the European Council on the application of art 2.3.

[36] In Case C-396/92 *Bund Naturschutz in Bayern eV and Others* v *Freistaat Bayern and Others, Proceedings of the Court of Justice No 23–94, 9 August 1994, pp. 8, 9*, it was later held by the European Court of Justice that the Directive '*must be interpreted as not permitting a Member State which has transposed the directive into national law after 3 July 1988, the deadline for transposition, to waive, by a transitional provision, for projects in respect of which the consent procedure was already initiated before the entry into force of the national law transposing the directive, but after 3 July 1988, the obligations concerning the environmental impact assessment required by the directive.*' That decision does not, however, directly deal with those cases which entered the planning pipe-line before 3 July 1988 but which were granted development consent after that date.

[37] [1992] 1 CMLR 276, paras [54] to [68]. In His Lordship's view this requirement was implicit in the judgments of the European Court of Justice in Case 8/81 *Becker* v *Finanzamt Munster-Innenstadt* and in Case 152/84 *Marshall* v *Southampton and SW Hampshire Area Health Authority*, both supra. Whether these judgments in fact justify such a conclusion is an interesting question but one which is outside the scope of the present work. His Lordship did not elaborate upon what he meant by the

need for the applicants to have '*suffered*' other than by referring to the need for an applicant to have '*suffered in some way from the failure to accord him his rights*'; ibid, para [60].

[38] Ibid, paras [69] to [78]. This point is discussed further below.

[39] Ibid, paras[69] to [78].

[40] Ibid, paras [79] to [87].

[41] Discussed below.

[42] Kramer 'Focus on European Environmental Law' p. 209.

[43] This might particularly have been the case if the House were to regard the question as to the applicants' standing to sue as being entirely a matter of English rather than European law; and if it were then to uphold Mr Justice McCullough on the point. The House might then have dismissed the appeal purely on that ground without giving the European Court the opportunity to consider the European legal issues involved, including the question of the impact of Community law principles on English rules as to standing.

[44] Although a directive is not to be interpreted in light of the national measures which transpose it, it is nonetheless interesting to note that sub-section 105A of the Highways Act, 1980 itself adopted the position that (in cases not excluded by reason of sub-section 105A (7)) the information required from the developer is relevant at the outset of the consent procedure and must be provided by the Secretary of State for Transport (as developer) in a single comprehensive document. This follows from sub-section 105 A (2) which provides that where the Secretary of State determines that a project 'should be subject to assessment in accordance with the Directive '*...he shall publish not later than the date of publication of details of the project an environmental statement, that is, statement containing...*' [the information required by art 5 of the Directive].

[45] As required by art 6.2.

[46] Published in the *Official Journal of the European Communities*, OJ 1991, S131/27.

[47] In practice, once a contract was awarded, it would be more difficult for the Commission to prevent work on the site, since the disruption of private contractual rights which that would involve would weigh against suspension.

[48] In light of the dialogue which had by this stage taken place between the Commission and the Government this assertion seems, to say the least, rather odd.

[49] Although not expressed, it is clearly implicit in this statement that the Department of Transport had no reason, other than the fact that the Commission had invited comments, to believe that the Commission would pursue the matter further. Once more this is difficult to reconcile with the account of events given by Mr di Meana. Apart from anything else, Mr di Meana has stated that Mr Rifkind himself sent him an *aide-mémoire* at the end of July, which was followed by *'other exchanges of information and meetings as well as a long, direct telephone conversation'* between the two (Debates of the European Parliament No 3-410 p. 226 first column). On that basis the Department of Transport must by then have known that the Commission was taking the pipe-line point and the road cases to which it was relevant, including Twyford Down, seriously.

[50] Note 49, supra.

[51] This statement again seems rather odd since, according to Mr di Meana, there had been *'...a meeting at a high level between the two administrations'* at the beginning of September 1991 at which di Meana had himself participated (Debates of the European Parliament No 3-410 p. 226 first column). If Mr di Meana's account is accurate one would have to be very 'economical with the truth' to assert without qualification that there had been *'no communication from the Commission'*.

[52] For a report of this work see, for example, 'Rescue Diggers Salvage Landscape Endangered by M3 Extension' *The Daily Telegraph*, 9 September 1991.

[53] Given under section 11(1) of the Compulsory Purchase Act 1965.

[54] EC Press Release IP/91/928 of 17 October 1991; the projects referred to are the seven projects subject to the formal letter.

[55] Which took place in December 1991.

[56] Mr Rifkind himself was reported as having described the intervention as *'foolishness'* at which he was *'rather irritated'*. Sir David Howell MP (Conservative Chairman of the Commons Foreign Affairs Select Committee) suggested that the Commission's powers needed to be restricted. Noted 'Eurosceptics' were more robust in their criticism. Lord Tebbitt, former Cabinet Minister and Chairman of the Conservative Party, was reported as having described di Meana as a *'cardboard Commissioner'* and as saying both that the affair had *'an element of farce about it'* and that it

was a *'terrible warning'* as to the scope of Commission power. Sir Teddy Taylor MP said that the intervention showed that the Commission had gone *'power mad'*; See 'Tory Anger At EC Order To Halt Building Schemes' – *The Daily Telegraph*; 'EC Environmental Directive on Seven Projects Raises New Summit Obstacle' – *The Guardian*; 'EC Intervention Over Channel Tunnel Rail Link May Damage Political Agreement' – *The Guardian*; 'Tories Try to Avoid Damage Over EC' – *The Times* (all of 19 October 1991).

[57] 'Environment Row Threatens EC Treaty, Says Prime Minister' – *The Independent*; 'Prime Minister Attacks EC Freeze on M-Way Works' – *The Guardian*; 'British Prime Minister Protests At Environment Commissioner's Demands On Transport Projects' – *The Times*; 'British Prime Minister Protests At EC Meddling In Internal Plans' – *The Daily Telegraph*; 'British Prime Minister Protests At Environment Commissioner's Demands In Transport Projects – *The Times* (all of 22 October 1991). For a less polite criticism reportedly made to the press by an unnamed UK official see 'Environment Commissioner Blind to Mess In His Own Backyard' – *The Sunday Times* of 20 October 1991.

[58] A UK Minister, Lord Brabazon of Tara, stated on 11 November 1991 that *'[f]ollowing receipt of the Article 169 letter, My Right Honourable friend the Prime Minister wrote to M Delors about the way the Commission handled the matter and received a satisfactory reply'*; House of Lords Official Report, Vol. 198, Cols. 160–162. See also Mr Baldry (as Under Secretary of State for the Environment) *'I am glad to say that the Government have received a satisfactory reply from Mr Delors'*; House of Commons Official Report 8 November 1991 Col. 751.

[59] See, for example, 'Major Hits At Brussels Handling of Environment Affair' – *The Financial Times* and 'British Prime Minister Protests At EC Meddling In Internal Plans' – *The Daily Telegraph* (both of 22 October 1991).

[60] For this criticism see, in particular, 'More "Nooks and Crannies" Meddling On Way – EC Intervention' – *The Times*, 8 November 1991; *'It was his personal request to stop work until the dispute had been settled, which he had no authority to make at this stage, that infuriated the Government'*.

[61] A criticism made by Mr Hurd on television and reported inter alia, in the article cited at note 60, supra.

[62] See Mr di Meana, Debates of the European Parliament No 3–410/225.

[63] *'while Vice President Marin and President Jacques Delors were engaged in the EFTA debate in the plenary [session of the Parliament], the Commission expressed its complete solidarity with me, led by my colleagues Sir Leon Brittan and Bruce Milan'* (the British Commissioners); ibid.

[64] Debates of the European Parliament, No 3-410/214.

[65] According to the letter of formal notice, the ELRC complaint was lodged with the Commission on 24 June 1989, the Commission wrote to the UK authorities on 24 October 1989 seeking their response to the complaint, and the UK Government responded by letter of 22 December 1989. The M11 complaint was lodged on 12 February 1990; the Commission wrote to the UK Government about it on 21 June 1990 and received a reply dated 14 August 1990. The Twyford Down complaint was lodged on 19 November 1990, the Commission wrote to the UK Government about it on 26 March 1991 and the Government responded by letter dated 21 May 1991. The Government later confirmed this initial correspondence although the dates which it gave for its replies to the Commission differ by a few days from those stated above: See Mr Chope, House of Commons Official Report Vol. 199, Col. 12.

[66] The press coverage included the following articles: 'EC to Prosecute Britain Over M3 Road Plans for Twyford Down' – *The Observer*, 19 May 1991; 'Commissioners Press for Studies On Impact of New Motorway on British Environment' – *The Independent*, 1 June 1991; 'EC Supports Protest Over Government Plan to Extend M3' – *The Daily Telegraph*, 30 August 1991; 'Campaign to Save Twyford Down Wins Backing From EC Over Road Schemes' – *The Times*, 30 August 1991; 'Challenge to British Law on Planning' – *The Daily Telegraph*, 28 September 1991; 'Commission Poised to Act on East London River Crossing' – *The Independent*, 28 September 1991; 'Environmentalists' Campaign Against The East London River Crossing Goes To EC' – *The Daily Telegraph*, 28 September 1991.

[67] Since the Department of Transport replied to both of these letters, it could not claim that they had not been received. Indeed Lord Brabazon of Tara confirmed, on 11 November 1991, that *'a private individual in the United Kingdom sent the Department a letter he had received from a Commission official saying that action was in prospect'*; House of Lords Official Report Vol. 198, Cols. 160–161.

[68] Indeed, the Government subsequently admitted that the personal telephone conversation between Mr Rifkind and Mr di Meana, and the meeting on 16 October did in fact take place; Lord Brabazon of Tara has stated that on these occasions '[d]iscussions covered the legal interpretation of Directive 85/337 and the method of environmental assessment of road schemes in this country'; Written Answer dated 11 November 1991, House of Lords Official Report Vol. 198, Cols. 160–161.

[69] Debates of the European Parliament No 3-410 at p. 225, second column.

[70] Ibid. He recalled in particular 'recent cases in Portugal and Spain' and specifically referred to the case of the Italian Expo 2000 in Venice and the construction of a dyke which would have destroyed a birds' habitat in Germany.

[71] As the other points of grievance originally stated by Mr Major were shown to be groundless, the UK Government came increasingly to focus its dissatisfaction with Mr di Meana on the point that he had publicized his personal letter to Mr Rifkind; Mr Baldry (as Parliamentary Under-Secretary of State for the Environment) stated that 'Our dispute is simply a straightforward matter of good manners. Having sent what was purportedly a personal letter to the Secretary of State for Transport, the Commissioner then leaked it to the press and to various environmental groups before the Secretary of State knew it was coming'; House of Commons Official Report, 8 November 1991 Col. 751; On another occasion, Mr Simon Hughes MP asked whether, in light of the contacts between the Government and Commission, Mr Major's statement in Harare (that the Government had no prior knowledge that the Commission was going to intervene and that the Commission had not discussed the relevant facts with the Government beforehand) was not 'simply untrue'. The Government's response was merely to assert that 'no notice was given by the Commissioner of his strenuous efforts to obtain extensive publicity of his letter...No warning was given at all'; Mr Yeo (as Parliamentary Under-Secretary of State for the Environment) House of Commons Official Report Vol. 198, Cols. 432–433.

[72] The quoted text seems rather odd inasmuch as it appears to suggest that the personal letter to Mr Rifkind was sent to the UK Permanent Representative seven minutes before being sent to Mr Rifkind himself. In fact, the report of this part of the speech may be inaccurate, because at least one MEP present (Mrs Daly) understood Mr di Meana to mean that letters had been sent at 'three minutes past five and ten past five'.

[73] House of Commons Official Report Vol. 202, Col. 302, where Sir George Young (as Minister for Housing and Planning) accepted a questioner's proposition that *'by agreeing the directive the Government are not saying that the European Environment Commissioner can dictate planning decisions but formalising best planning practice...'*

[74] Debates of the European Parliament No 3-410, page 226, first column.

[75] Ibid. The Commissioner identified the following as being included among the petitioners: Lord Clinton Davies (former Environment Commissioner) and MEPs such as Peter Price (MEP for London South East, and who supported the ELRC complaint), Anthony Simpson, Alex Falconer, Richard Balfe, Stan Newens and Ken Collins (Chairman of the European Parliament's Committee on Environment and Consumer Affairs) and others; and *'important non-governmental organisations like the World-wide Fund for Nature'.*

[76] According to Mr Heseltine (then Secretary of State for the Environment) *'the UK responded to the Article 169 letter on 17 December within the two months requested by the Commission';* House of Commons Official Report Vol. 201, Col. 172. The two month deadline expired at midnight on the 17th. See also 'Environment Wrangle Over Transport Schemes May Go To European Court' – *The Guardian;* 'EC Objections Will Not Halt Road Schemes' – *The Daily Telegraph;* 'EC Defied Over Road Building Projects' – *The Independent;* 'Brussels Fails to Halt Road Schemes' – *The Times* (all of 18 December 1991).

[77] The contract was awarded 'on Friday' see 'Rifkind Defies Europe Over Twyford Down' – *The Observer,* 22 December 1991.

[78] Ultimately called for 9 April 1992.

[79] Art 130s of the Treaty of Rome as amended by the Treaty on European Union.

[80] 'Twyford Down Work Begins Despite Protest From EC and Environmentalists' – *The Daily Telegraph;* 'Bulldozers Move in On Twyford Down in Defiance Of EC Environment Commissioner' – *The Independent* (both of 24 January 1992).

[81] 'M3 Motorway Protesters Refuse to Budge' – *The Times,* 15 February 1992; 'Six Arrested At M3 Protest' – *The Financial Times,* 17 February 1992.

[82] 'British Government Defies EC Over Beauty Spot' – Reuters, 16 March 1992; 'Bulldozers Strip Off Twyford Meadow' – *The Daily Telegraph,* 17 March 1992; 'Bulldozers Hit Twyford Down To Begin Work on M3 Extension' – *The Independent,* 17 March 1992; 'Unlikely Allies Confront Bulldozers As Motorway Crosses

Water Meadow' – *The Independent*, 18 March 1992; 'Last Ditch Stand On Cobbett's Patch – Bulldozers Move in On Twyford Down' – *The Guardian*, 20 March 1992.

[83] 'EC Chief Rejects Reply By Britain On Construction Projects' – *The Daily Telegraph*, 10 January 1992; 'Environment Commissioner Says European Court Could Stop British Motorway Extensions' – *The Guardian*, 10 January 1992; 'EC Renews Warning on Land Development' – *The Independent*, 10 January 1992.

[84] 'Start of Twyford Work Dismays EC Environment Commissioner' – *The Guardian*, 19 March 1992.

[85] Agence Europe No 5761 (n.s.), 29 June 1992.

[86] The last day before the Commission took its August vacation.

[87] European Commission Press Release IP/92/669, dated 31 July 1992.

[88] This passage of the decision letter was expressly drawn to the Commission's attention in the Twyford Down complaint itself.

[89] The Statement of Reasons, May 1985, paragraph 1.1.1.

[90] Ibid, art 6.1.

[91] Written Question 2415/92 (Amendola), 6 October 1992, (93/C 86/37), OJ C86, 26.3.93 p. 22.

[92] 22 December 1992, OJ C86, 26.3.93 p. 22.

[93] His answer was framed as follows:

1. *The Commission alleged in the Letter of Formal Notice notified to the UK that the Secretary of State for Transport, as developer, had failed to supply a non-technical summary of environmental information as required by Article 5.2 of the Directive. It was not alleged, nor do the documents supplied to the Commission suggest, that there was otherwise a failure to meet the requirements of Article 5.*

2. *The UK enclosed with its reply to the Letter of Formal Notice a substantial number of documents. Of these the Statement of Reasons dated May 1985 and produced by the Departments of Transport and the Environment constituted a non-technical summary as required by Article 5.2.*

The document was not entitled 'non-technical summary'. However, it contained, in non-technical language, a summary description of the project and of the measures envisaged in order to reduce and remedy significant adverse effects, and a summary of the data required to identify and assess the main effects which the project was likely to have on the environment. It therefore fulfilled in this case the requirements for a non-technical summary.

[94] Section 10(d) of Annex II to the Directive.

[95] Written Question 255/93 (Pollack), 23 February 1993, (93/C 258/92), OJ C258, 22.9.93 p.50.

[96] Written Question 45/93, 8 February 1993, (93/C 202/06), OJ C202, 26.7.93 p.3.

[97] Written Question 44/93 (Aglietta and Colajanni), 8 February 1993, (93/C 202/65), OJ C202, 26.7.93 p.3, which asked:

In view of the debate over the Community's power and responsibilities with respect to the environment and especially in light of the new definition of subsidiarity set out in the Maastricht Treaty...and the divergent interpretations to which it has given rise – can the Commission say whether the decision to take no further action in the infringement proceedings instituted in 5 cases against the UK by a former Member of the Commission, Mr Ripa di Meana, heralded a new trend whereby the environment is to suffer consequences of the Council and Commission's failure to reach agreement?

[98] Written Question 46/93 (Aglietta and Colajanni), 8 February 1993, (93/C 202/07), OJ C202, 26.7.93 p.3, which asked:

In light of the Commission's decision to take no further action in the proceedings instituted against the UK for 5 cases of infringement of [the Directive] on environmental impact assessment and bearing in mind the interpretation which the former Member of the Commission, Mr Ripa di Meana, gave when the infringement proceedings were debated [See Debates in the European Parliament No 3-410/214, 25.10.91.]*, in which he pointed among other things to the importance of consulting the public with regard to implementation of the Directive and of the procedure for putting back its date of entry into force, as well as in connection with projects falling due for consideration during the time between the date of adoption of the Directive and the date of its entry into force in the different Member States, can the Commissioner say whether the above interpretation is to be considered incorrect? If so, why and what is meant to be the new interpretation?*

[99] Written Question 418/93 (Angletta, Colajanni and Roth-Behrendt), 8 March 1993, (93/C 202/08) which asked: *Following the decision of the Commission to terminate 5 infringement procedures regarding the implementation of [the Directive] against the British Government and having regard to the need to keep the European Parliament informed of the progress of Article 169 procedures as well as to take account of the high level of press and public interest in these matters, will the Commission now report to the European Parliament 1. on why it has terminated those procedures and*

2. on its intention so far as reporting to the European Parliament on Article 169 procedures and on the general progress of that Directive.

[100] 30 April 1993, OJ C202, 26. 7. 93 p.4.

[101] The site for construction of the M11 Link road.

[102] The site for construction of the Bath bypass.

[103] The proposed Newbury bypass.

[104] The lack of transparency of the system contrasts sharply with the philosophy of the Community's own Directive 90/313, O.J. 1990 L158/56, which requires Member States to ensure public access to environmental information held by national authorities.

[105] Art 11.

[106] Debates of the European Parliament No 3-410/214 of 25.10.91.

[107] The report should have been made by 3 July 1990, but was in fact made only on 2 April 1993; COM(93) 28 final, 2 April 1993.

[108] When requested by an MP to lodge a copy of the Letter of Formal Notice in the House of Commons library Mr Major declined on the grounds that '[c]orrespondence between the Commission and Member States about alleged infraction of European law is generally conducted in confidence' House of Commons Official Report Vol. 199, Col. 521 w.

[109] Bull EC 4-1993 point 2.2.2. A Reasoned Opinion was issued in respect of the Directive in 1993 under the title 'Failure properly to apply Directives in practice'.

Part Four

The Environmentalist's Conclusions

14

Twyford Down: the aftermath

From August 1992 onwards I tried to avoid going back to Twyford Down. Or ever having to drive on the M3. This was a conscious choice. I might very well have chosen to get involved in the continuing efforts of the Dongas and other direct action campaigners, or to remain semi-actively involved in the Twyford Down Association. But I didn't.

I felt comprehensively defeated, angry with myself that I hadn't done more, devastated by the devastation of Barbara Bryant, Merrick Denton-Thompson, David Croker and all those who had been at it for ten years or more. I couldn't summon up any enthusiasm whatsoever for the idea of perpetuating the protest through non-violent direct action, which seemed to me at the time almost self-indulgently futile. My campaigning zeal was exhausted; I wanted to move on, find new energy somewhere else, and put Twyford Down behind me.

Exactly two years later I was on my way to a conference in Southampton for which I'd had to hire a car. Nothing had prepared me for the visual shock of what had been done in the interim to Twyford Down – not even the Department of Transport's most grotesque photomontage of the desecration it was planning to carry out. All the anger, all the pain, all the sheer disbelief at such wanton vandalism came roaring back – and I had a hard time making an even half-way coherent speech when I eventually arrived at the conference.

This book has been written with the most admirable restraint. I got to know Barbara pretty well over the few years I was involved in the campaign, and came to admire her impassioned moderation and never-say-die dedication more than I can express. (Indeed, I wouldn't be writing this now if it weren't for her skills of persuasion!)

Though she has allowed the reader the occasional glimpse into the emotional maelstrom that such a campaign involves, she has characteristically understated the degree to which almost unbelievable levels of self-sacrifice are required of all those involved. In a national debate which is quite properly driven by reasoned debate, state-of-the-art science, cost-benefit analysis and so on, the media often find it difficult to capture the mood, the gut feelings that drive people beyond both reason and endurance to pit their puny personal strength against a system that could have been purpose-built to destroy such individuals.

We rightly admire the astonishing commitment of those who put their bodies where their beliefs are, in a succession of high-profile anti-road campaigns, but tend in the process to overlook the equally astonishing commitment of those who find it more fitting to do their bit in the backroom, in the Public Inquiry or even along the corridors of power.

Part of that commitment is to work out every single seam of opposition until it is irrevocably exhausted or blocked off. Hence the overwhelming importance of the European dimension in the latter stages of the Twyford Down campaign.

Perhaps we were naïve to pin such faith in the bureaucratic battalions in Brussels, but they seemed to offer by far the best chance we had at that time. Perhaps we should have foreseen that the more explicitly interventionist Carlo Ripa di Meana (the Environment Commissioner) became, the more firmly Twyford Down's fate was sealed. It wasn't just a question of the usual loss of face involved in a Government having to change its mind, but of national pride. Better by far to assert our inalienable sovereignty by destroying one of the most important conservation and archaeological sites in the country than to be forced to recant by a bunch of meddling Euro-Federalists.

But we were naïve. We didn't foresee how hard the subsidiarity card would be played, or how easy it would be for a newly-elected Conservative Government to stitch up a deal with Jacques Delors in the run up to Maastricht. 'EC retreat brings end to Twyford Down battle' proclaimed *The Daily Telegraph* of 1 August 1992. So it did, for all the rearguard heroics of the Dongas.

There were galling stories circulating at that time of celebratory parties within the Department of Transport itself. I find it hard to believe now, but there were plenty of insiders (civil servants, politicians and road lobby evangelists) who saw Twyford Down as the *final* battle in the war to rout the antis. It was going to be plain sailing from then on in terms of expanding and accelerating the roads programme. We may have been naïve; they were both arrogant and stupid. Far from being the final battle, Twyford Down was but the first, and without being too vainglorious about it ourselves, many campaigners now believe we are well on the way to winning the war.

The trauma of Twyford Down galvanized thousands of people into a host of actions that might otherwise never have taken place. It was just so horrific, so visible, so palpable. Even now, there is no amount of cosmetic landscaping and tree planting that can conceal the sheer scale of the wound inflicted on the countryside. It screams out at you, and will go on screaming out to all with ears to hear and eyes to see.

Ruling politicians and their self-serving advisers consistently underestimate the power of symbolism in politics. Long after the Twyford Down campaign was lost, and the Dongas had been brutally routed, Twyford Down continues to work its magic as a symbol of opposition to undemocratic, ecologically wanton road-building, wherever it is taking place.

What's more, it has reinforced all the anger and incredulity many people have felt but suppressed for years; it has legitimized a far more explicit avowal of passionate feelings for the British countryside in all its glory and vulnerability. Nothing has ever been the same since then.

The first clear signal of this came with the Government's U-turn on the East London River Crossing and the salvation of Oxleas Wood – the last surviving remnant of ancient woodland in London, and a much loved, much used community woodland. After years of tedious rhetoric about the 'inestimable strategic significance' of this particular road, it was deeply galling for the Department of Transport to be forced to acknowledge that it wasn't actually needed after all in the light of the Government's 'new priorities'.

Just as no one proposal for a new road is like another, so no protest campaign is quite like another either. But the Oxleas Wood campaigners learned a great deal from the Twyford Down campaigners, both directly and indirectly, and by the time the Government announced its volte-face on 7 July 1993, their armoury was as well provisioned as it is possible to imagine. For all its national prominence, Oxleas had remained predominantly a local campaign, guided, inspired and administered by local people. But it was backed (both financially and logistically) by most of the big national environmental organizations, with solid support from the local council and MPs, and the threat of EU intervention never far from the frame.

On top of all that, literally hundreds of people had specifically signed a direct action pledge to chain themselves to certain trees in the event of the bulldozers moving in. And the Department of Transport was kept very well informed of precisely how many had signed the pledge.

It was an unbeatable combination, a rare but enormously powerful example of *force majeure*, even though the odds never looked that good right up until the last moment. Other victories followed including the decision to 'tunnel' the A3 at the Devil's Punchbowl and the withdrawal of one of the biggest motorway proposals in the entire road programme, the M1/M62 link in Yorkshire. The rationale for such withdrawals has always been as opaque and secretive as the initial proposals. One can't help but speculate, therefore, about how Department of Transport/Highways Agency officials might weigh up the different factors associated in coming to such a decision: what value might they attach to the unbending opposition of at least eight Conservative MPs in electorally vulnerable seats – as was the case with the recently withdrawn proposals to widen the M25. Or to the prospect of another ferocious direct action campaign – as with the highly controversial Newbury bypass, which was put on hold by the Transport Secretary, Brian Mawhinney and then given the go-ahead as his last act before the cabinet reshuffle.

The simple point is that no major road scheme has been stopped once the first sod has been turned by the contractors. The threat of large-scale civil disobedience may therefore be much more effective in practice than the actual direct action campaigns themselves, which invariably come too late in the day to make any difference to the completion of that particular scheme. Where they do make a difference is to the prospects for future schemes elsewhere in the country.

As far as the Twyford Down campaign itself is concerned, the transition from conventional campaigning tactics (consciousness-raising, legal representation at Public Inquiries, political lobbying, high-profile events) to non-violent direct action was not an easy one. The rationale behind such a transition was overwhelmingly clear: in February 1992, TDA activists and Friends of the Earth (who had been working closely together for more than a year) argued that the Government was itself breaking the law in proceeding with preliminary works *before* the EC had ruled on the complaint before it concerning breaches of the Environmental Impact Assessment Directive. This unlawful behaviour entirely justified the use of responsible, non-violent direct action to slow down or even prevent that work continuing. A railway bridge due for demolition was therefore occupied on 14 February by Friends of the Earth.

At the same time, members of the organization called Earth First! felt this was not upfront enough, and six of them were subsequently arrested in mid-February after occupying one of the cranes involved in the works. Relationships between Earth First!, Friends of the Earth and the Twyford Down Association were strained, with accusations flying around of 'anarchists parachuting into the campaign' with no local knowledge and no local feeling. Many members of the TDA were nervous about *any* direct action; as this book has consistently made clear, Winchester is a very conservative area, and some forms of protest come more naturally to local people than others.

In the end, however, it was clearly the right way for things to develop. In mid-March, Friends of the Earth had injunctions served against most of its objectors, who had managed to hold off contractors for five days. At that point, FoE felt duty bound to abide by those injunctions, and the 'constitutional focus' shifted to the organization of a tactical voting campaign in the approaching General Election. Friends of the Earth said later that it had come to regret that decision, but personally I still think it was the right one.

Earth First! members decided to stick it out (as one of them said at the time, 'Voting doesn't get you anywhere. Direct action is the only way forward'), evolving over the next few months into the Dongas Tribe who took up permanent residence on the Down.

The rest, as they say, is history. That's where the new-style, anti-roads protest was born, and for those of us who looked on from afar, it's impossible not to feel the deepest admiration for that kind of courage and commitment. The experience gained there has fed through to one campaign after another, particularly the protests over the M11 link road in East London, at Solsbury Hill outside Bath, the M77 at Pollok in Glasgow, and most recently over the M65 extension near Blackburn.

Not everyone approves of this campaigning style. There are some who argue that it erodes the credibility of the whole environment movement, tarring everyone with the brush of subversive, illegal confrontationalism. There seems to be little evidence for that in fact. Just as many members of the Twyford Down Association came to respect and even quietly support the efforts of the Dongas, so respectable England seems to have acknowledged the validity and integrity of what today's direct action campaigners are trying to achieve.

A Gallup Poll at the beginning of June 1995 reveals that 68 per cent of people in this country would be prepared to entertain the idea of civil disobedience in defence of the cause they believed in – 14 per cent up on a similar poll in 1984. Of Tory voters 52 per cent agreed with the proposition that there are times 'when people may be justified in disobeying laws to protest against things they find very unjust or wrong.'

This caused *The Daily Telegraph* to take the majority of its own readers furiously to task, likening them to the Gadarene swine bent on hurling themselves into an abyss: 'This is the road to chaos and barbarism. Virtually every necessity or convenience of life is capable of being objected to by somebody with an axe to grind. But how much civilisation is left once people decide to disobey any law they disagree with, and reserve the right to prevent others going about their lawful affairs because they have taken exception to them?'

The Spectator tried a similar tack: 'We live in an age of emotional incontinence, in which it is assumed that no emotion (such as anger) should remain without its behavioural expression. In other words, anger in itself justifies all.'

Those who choose to disregard the power of emotion (and, indeed, its relative honesty in an age of double-talk and chronic political sleaze) have only themselves to blame when they fail to foresee the inevitable. People who've followed the rational route to protesting against roads are just worn out and worn down by the inherent inequities of the system.

For someone who has spent years battling away with the Department of Transport, in countless meetings and Public Inquiries, buried under piles of weighty, worthy reports and correspondence, it can come as a blessed relief to hear someone cutting straight through all those rationalizations simply by declaring: 'This land is sacred, it *matters* to local people and to us. Future generations have the right for it to matter to them too. So take your bulldozers and your chainsaws, your cost-benefit analyses and impact assessments, and sod off!'

But it's in the nature of that style of protest that it should remain flexible, light on its feet, non-hierarchical, spontaneous – everything, in short, that the large environmental organizations in the UK aren't! Those same organizations can help by providing money, information networks, political support and so on. But essentially they have other tasks to carry out, earlier in the piece, trying to change policy and prevent road proposals from getting to the point where the only recourse for concerned citizens is direct action.

This is very much the conclusion of an important conference held in Oxford in December 1994, bringing together the direct action groups with the established environmental organizations. A considerable measure of reconciliation was achieved at the conference, but no one should ever pretend that so diverse a range of tactics and organizations can hold together without a certain amount of internecine strife.

In the meantime, anti-road campaigners have become far better organized and far more supportive of each other. ALARM UK, the national alliance against new road building, has somewhere between 250 and 300 groups as members, kept in touch through an excellent newsletter and a suprisingly impressive electronic information service. The Camcorder Action Network has more than 100 trained activists on its books ready to film protests at a moment's notice, and videos of direct action campaigns are widely circulated, helping to improve training sessions and increase the sophistication of the tactics to be used. The best known of these is *Undercurrents* ('showing the news that isn't on the news'), distributed by Small World, one of a new generation of organizations taking advantage of the potential of new information and communication technology.

This can only become more important as the state system becomes more oppressive. The Criminal Justice Act is already having a highly damaging effect on the legitimate activities of anti-roads groups, with new public order and trespass offences in force since July 1994. Anyone found guilty of the criminal offence of aggravated trespass is liable to a fine of up to £500 and as much as three months' imprisonment. Whitehall sources have made it clear that they have every intention of these laws being used to deter all anti-roads organizations – though it has to be said that it seems to be having exactly the opposite effect at the moment.

What's more, surveillance operations are now standard on any major road scheme, and civil liberties are being infringed on an absolutely regular basis. If you think it's improbable that someone like Barbara Bryant should have her telephone tapped at the height of the campaign, think again. It is, I'm afraid, all too common.

With all this ferment of anti-roads activity going on, one might almost imagine that little had changed on the policy front since Twyford Down. Nothing could be further from the truth. Government Ministers have in fact experienced as much of a conversion on the Motorway to Damascus as they're ever likely to get.

Back in 1992, the road lobby was still in full cry. By their account, more cars and more lorries (based on a predicted increase in traffic of between 83 per cent and 142 per cent by the year 2025) quite simply required more roads, and that should be the sole goal of a sound transport policy. In just three years, that prevailing orthodoxy had been systematically shredded, first at the hands of the 1994 Roads Review and then with the publication of two highly damning reports at the end of the year.

The Review of the 1989 Roads Programme (announced with a great fanfare back in 1989, consisting then of 330 trunk road and motorway schemes costing up to £2 billion a year) provided the clearest indication yet of the kind of pressure that the Department of Transport had been coming under. Pressure from the Treasury (ever more keen to wield the axe to help balance the budget); from the Department of the Environment (increasingly concerned that its strategy for sustainable development and the various pledges made at the Earth Summit in Rio de Janeiro in 1992 could not be delivered unless the Department of Transport drew in its bulldozing horns); and from local authorities (many of whom wanted to spend their money on other transport options instead of just roads, roads and more roads).

More than 50 schemes were dropped under the Review, and many more put on the back burner. Together with the transfer of responsibilities for all new roads to the ill-starred Highways Agency, the impact of this has been dramatic. In the coming financial year (1995/96) only 19 new roads are to be started – the lowest figure for many years – of which a mere six are completely new schemes. Far from reducing the levels of protest around the country (which must have been one of the Department of Transport's intentions in selling the Review as a 'green package'!), it's actually intensified the determination of many local groups to stop the road building juggernaut in its tracks.

These developments were powerfully reinforced by the publication of the Royal Commission on Environmental Pollution's report on Transport and the Environment in October 1994. The Report called for a halving of the roads programme and a doubling in the real price of petrol over the next ten years. It also set out a series of targets including: reducing the proportion of urban journeys undertaken by car by 15 per cent by the year 2020; quadrupling cycle use to 10 per cent of urban trips by the year 2002; increasing the proportion of passenger kilometres carried by public transport from 12 per cent in 1993 to 30 per cent by 2020; and increasing rail's share of tonne-kilometres from 6.5 per cent to 20 per cent over the next 15 years.

As Sir John Houghton, chairman of the RCEP, commented in launching the report: 'We hope the overall vision we have presented will generate the impetus and commitment required to realise the benefits of a new transport strategy. The prize is a transport system which will be much less damaging to health and the environment, and at the same time more efficient in providing the access that people want for work and for leisure.'

As yet, the Government has failed to produce any comprehensive response to the RCEP's report, but this is the one body that it will find difficult to dismiss in the way it might once have been inclined to do. There is a clear need for a wider transport debate and a more balanced transport strategy, recognizing that the era of 'this great car economy of ours' is dead and buried.

This has been reinforced in these revolutionary thoughts by the report on traffic generation from the Standing Advisory Committee on Trunk Road Assessment. This may sound like a rather boring issue being considered by a rather boring backroom committee, but its report goes to the very heart of the current debate about meeting the demand from motorists for new roads. For years, the Department of Transport categorically denied the rather obvious suggestion that new roads might themselves generate (or induce) new traffic. But that's exactly what SACTRA has now told them: 'induced traffic can occur, probably quite extensively, though its size and significance is likely to vary widely in different circumstances.'

The reason this little statement is so important is that it dramatically affects the whole cost-benefit analysis process that plays so large a part in the promotion of every new road scheme. Many new roads are justified in financial terms on the grounds that they will relieve traffic congestion elsewhere on the road network. But if those new roads induce new traffic themselves, then that 'congestion relief' is significantly reduced and may even be cancelled out. Which raises a huge question mark over the so-called benefits of *any* new road.

The Government has accepted SACTRA's main conclusion that new roads induce new traffic. They have issued new guidance to the road planners to take account of SACTRA's findings, and ordered an extra assessment of 270 schemes, two-thirds of the existing roads programme.'

ALARM UK succintly summarized the overall significance of the SACTRA report: 'What this means for the roads programme is not yet clear. It should spell the end for urban road building (urban schemes will now be almost impossible to justify in traffic terms) [and] the motorway widening programme and [cause] a serious re-think on the many corridor upgrades in the roads programme.'

Two months later (in April 1995) those words proved very prescient when the Government announced it was dropping plans to widen parts of the M25 to 14 lanes.

The M25 was only completed in 1986; local people had been promised that it would spell the end of their own particular congestion problems throughout that area. But within just a few years, they found themselves threatened all over again with a massive (and equally disruptive) widening scheme, with exactly the same carrot on offer: only this kind of widening would help relieve their congestion problems!

It was just one con-trick too far. The particular stretch of the M25 to be widened fell slap-bang in Tory heartland, filled to bursting point with what's come to be known as 'the inhabitants of Middle England', only too ready to give a Conservative Government a good kicking in the marginals for so insensitively misconstruing their real interests, and so directly threatening their quality of life. A scheme that made no sense in traffic management terms was doomed from the word go by its political naïvety.

Many predict that this is just the start of the rising-up of Middle England, particularly around a series of piecemeal schemes all along the South Coast, which would amount in effect to a 230 mile superhighway, from Folkestone in Kent to Honiton in Devon, driven through some of Britain's most outstanding countryside. In the old days, each scheme would have been opposed by a separate group fighting its separate campaign to protect its particular backyard. Now, 40 local action groups have already joined forces to form SCAR – South Coast Against Roads.

It's a very different world today in which to be opposing a new road scheme from that in which the Twyford Down Association set out to persuade the Department of Transport to invest in a tunnel under the Down rather than a cutting through it. There must be a lot of 'if onlys' in the minds of those who lost out at Twyford Down: 'if only we could have delayed things for another couple of years'; 'if only Middle England had found its voice a little earlier'; 'if only we'd had a Government with even a semblance of foresight and decency'.

For Twyford's scarred warriors, it's all much too late. But it is all the more despairing for people involved in *current* actions, with their local environment still getting it in the neck even *after* the big picture seems to have changed so dramatically.

The 'Pollok Free State' protesters in Glasgow look on in disbelief as their own local authority (Labour-controlled Strathclyde) drive through the hugely destructive four and a half mile M77 extension, which will bring an estimated daily flow of 53 000 vehicles by the year 2007 right into their backyard.

And even as this book goes to press, protesters seeking to block the path of the M65 extension in Lancashire were being evicted by 300 police and security men (none too gently either) from the treehouses they'd set up in the spectacularly beautiful Stanworth Woods near Blackburn. As one protester put it: 'All this desecration, even now, just to allow a few stressed-out businessmen to get from A to B five minutes faster than they're able to now. They'd be so much better off spending that five minutes walking through the very woods that are now being destroyed on their behalf.'

Exactly. Road building has always been about trading-off costs against benefits: increased speed, mobility, efficiency versus impaired quality of life, community, ecological value, and so on. Until now, the deck has been stacked in favour of the benefits, with the costs either under-valued or not valued at all. That has now changed irreversibly.

But so too has Twyford Down. And for many of those caught up in the final battles between 1992 and 1994, they still have the Department of Transport on their backs. Officials have estimated that the protests of the Dongas added an extra £3 million to the £26 million cost of the M3 extension. Initially, they sought to retrieve £1.9 million of that by bringing civil claims against 67 protesters ('We are merely protecting the interests of the taxpayer against the unlawful protest action taken by so many'), but had to drop that claim in the face of outright ridicule.

They are now seeking to 'settle the whole thing once and for all' by billing the 67 protesters for £1000 each, which is clearly more about face-saving than due legal process. Elsewhere in the courts, claims brought by 40 protesters for wrongful arrest are still being pursued, and in January this year the first ten protesters won £50 000 in compensation from Hampshire Police.

It's all so transparently vindictive. By contrast, in May this year, those same officials must have been fuming when one of the world's most prestigious environmental prizes (the Goldman Prize, worth around £47 000) was awarded to Emma Must. Emma is a former children's librarian from Winchester who played on the Down as a child. She became one of the central figures in the protests against the road when she was gaoled in 1993 for one month for defying injunctions to stay away from Twyford Down. Since then, she has inspired and encouraged hundreds of other people to take up non-violent cudgels against many different road schemes, as a co-founder of Road Alert and an indefatigable campaigner. As she says: 'this award is recognition of the whole spectrum of protest, from people with beads in their hair, to middle aged ladies with pleated skirts.' That's exactly the surprising but powerful combination which first started coming together, at first with a lot of uncertainty and apprehension, at Twyford Down.

For more than ten years Twyford Down has been the local prism through which the national transport debate has been refracted. During that time, what was once a small group of dedicated opponents of the Government's road building plans has grown into a huge army of dissenters drawn from every walk of life. That dissent is both rational *and* emotional: whichever way you look at it, the price we are being asked to pay for a futile and self-defeating policy objective (to get rid of traffic congestion by building more roads) has been judged too high.

The loss of Twyford Down is of course part of that price. For those who gave ten years of their life to trying to avoid its loss, there is at least some compensation in seeing what has happened since 1992, and knowing the impact that their campaign has had on transport policy in general.

But the pain is still there. One can't help but be moved by Barbara Bryant's account of the valedictory meetings of the Twyford Down Association. Even as defeat stared its members in the face, a proposal was made to convert the Association into a permanent Trust with one principal objective: to remain the keeper of local knowledge, love and expertise about Twyford Down as it was before its destruction, and to raise funds to ensure that this knowledge can be turned to good effect whenever the decision is made to restore the Down to its former glory.

In a way that nobody ever wanted, the destruction of Twyford Down has become a symbol of everything that is senseless and sacrilegious about this country's obsession with road building. As we move into rather saner times, albeit hesitantly and inconsistently, with a rather more rational transport policy at least under serious discussion, the kind of commitment shown by the Twyford Down Association to repairing the damage we have caused offers a powerfully countervailing symbol – a symbol of everything that is wise and compassionate in our emerging desire to act as true and trusted stewards of the gift of life and the beauty of the Earth.

Glossary

AREA OF OUTSTANDING NATURAL BEAUTY (AONB)
Areas designated under the National Parks and Access to the
Countryside Act 1949 as being areas which are not in National
Parks but are of such outstanding natural beauty that they
should be designated as AONBs. The purpose of designation is
to identify, conserve and enhance the beauty of landscapes so
designated. Designation is by the Countryside Commission (see
below) but thereafter their role is advisory rather than executive.
PPG7 (January 1992) encourages the formation of advisory committees of local authorities and local interests, but actual powers
to protect AONBs remain extremely limited.

COBA (Cost-Benefit Analysis) Department of Transport's computer programme designed to produce economic evaluations of
its proposed road schemes.

COUNCIL ON TRIBUNALS Independent advisory body set
up following the Franks Committee on Administrative Tribunals
and Inquiries (Cmnd 218, HMSO 1957). It has supervision over
the constitution and working of tribunals/inquiries set out in the
Tribunals and Inquiries Act 1992. Responsible to the Lord
Chancellor's office.

COUNTRYSIDE COMMISSION Originally the National Parks
Commission. Its powers were increased and title changed to
Countryside Commission following the Countryside Act 1968
and it is now responsible to the Secretary of State for the
Environment. It designates National Parks and Areas of
Outstanding Natural Beauty, may grant aid proposals for recre-
ation or access to the countryside and for action to conserve the
countryside and is responsible for keeping under review all
matters relating to the general well-being of the countryside and
for advising ministers and public bodies on such matters.

COUNCIL FOR THE PROTECTION OF RURAL ENGLAND (CPRE) An independent conservation organization established in 1926 to protect the countryside. Monitors Government and its agencies and encourages national policies to protect and enhance the countryside. Submits representations on local matters at local level.

DEPARTMENT OF THE ENVIRONMENT(DoE) Government department with wide powers over planning and land use, development and construction, countryside matters, conservation areas, environmental protection and the general administration of local government.

DEPARTMENT OF TRANSPORT (DoT) Overall responsibility for land, sea and air transport. More particularly is responsible for construction and maintenance of motorways and trunk roads and transport planning of local authorities including central government grant-aid.

ENGLISH NATURE Replaced the former Nature Conservancy Council following the Environmental Protection Act 1990. Advises Government on nature conservation, promotes the conservation of wildlife, designates National (as opposed to local) Nature Reserves and more particularly identifies and notifies Sites of Special Scientific Interest (SSSIs) for their biological or geological interest under the Wildlife and Countryside Act 1981.

EUROPEAN COMMISSIONER A Commissioner nominated by a European State to the European Commission. He may be invited to accept a portfolio to manage a relevant function relating to EC responsibilities, e.g. Environment Commissioner.

FRANKS COMMITTEE See Council on Tribunals above.

GUIDANCE NOTES FOR INSPECTORS Notes produced administratively by the Planning Inspectorate of the DoE for the guidance of Inspectors holding Highway Inquiries.

LANDSCAPE ADVISORY COMMITTEE (LAC) Group of members with expertise in a wide range of relevant skills, appointed by the Secretary of State for Transport to advise on the general acceptability of proposals for new or modified trunk roads or motorways, with particular reference to their overall environmental impact whether in town or countryside.

NATURE CONSERVANCY COUNCIL (NCC) See English Nature above.

PARLIAMENTARY PRIVATE SECRETARIES (PPS) Back-bench Members of Parliament chosen by individual ministers to assist them in their parliamentary duties.

PREFERRED ROUTE (PR) The route selected by the Department of Transport from a group of possible options following the technical appraisal report and public consultation.

PUBLIC INQUIRIES INTO TRUNK ROAD AND MOTOR-WAY PROPOSALS Statutory proceedings for objectors to put their case to an independent Inspector. Such Inquiries may consider the draft Statutory Orders (including Compulsory Purchase Orders) for the line of the proposed route (PR) and/or for the relevant Side Road Orders. They are conducted in front of a single Inspector recommended by the Lord Chancellor's Office and nominated by the Planning Inspectorate. The appointed Inspector may, at his own discretion, be assisted in complex cases by a technical assessor. The Inspector will have available substantial written information resulting from the Deposit Documents submitted by the DoT as part of the justification for the route, together with Proofs of Evidence from the Promoter as well as from objectors. Additional papers may be called for during the Inquiry and the DoT may be called upon to undertake additional appraisals of counter-proposals submitted by objectors.

RECOMMENDATION Inspector's recommendations following a Public Inquiry.

SCHEDULED ANCIENT MONUMENT A Schedule of Ancient Monuments is prepared, maintained and monitored by English Heritage under the Ancient Monuments and Archaeological Areas Act 1979 as amended by the National Heritage Act 1983. The official Schedule contains more than 20 000 entries. A monument is defined as comprising any building, structure or work, whether above or below ground level, or any cave or excavation, or their site, or the remains of any movable structure. Once a site or structure has been scheduled certain works set out in the Act may not be undertaken without official consent.

SCHEME A proposal for a new road or an improvement to an existing road.

SITES OF SPECIAL SCIENTIFIC INTEREST (SSSIs) Sites identified by English Nature as of special interest by virtue of their flora and fauna or geological or physiographical interest. Once identified, English Nature has a duty to notify all owners and occupiers of the land, the local planning authority and the Secretary of State under S.28 of the Wildlife and Countryside Act 1981. This Act was amended by the Wildlife and Countryside (Amendment) Act 1985, which for the first time provided some element of protection to SSSIs and which takes effect immediately upon notification.

TRUNK ROAD A major all-purpose road for which the Secretary of State for Transport is responsible.

Appendix

List of Secretaries of State for Transport and Ministers for Roads since 1980

PARLIAMENTARY UNDER SECRETARIES

Kenneth Clarke	7 May 1979 – 5 March 1982
Richard Eyre	5 March 1982 – 13 June 1983
Lynda Chalker	5 March 1982 – October 1983
David Mitchell	13 June 1983 – 23 January 1986
Michael Spicer	10 September 1984 – June 1987
Earl of Caithness	2 September 1985 – September 1986
Lord Brabazon of Tara	10 September 1986 – July 1989
Peter Bottomley	23 January 1986 – July 1989
Robert Atkins	25 July 1989 – 23 July 1990
Patrick McLoughlin	25 July 1989 – 14 April 1992
Christopher Chope	23 July 1990 – 14 April 1992
Kenneth Carlisle	14 April 1992 – 28 May 1993
Steven Norris	14 April 1992 –
Robert Key	28 May 1993 – 20 July 1994
Lord Mackay of Ardbrecknish	11 January 1994 – 20 July 1994
Viscount Goschen**	20 July 1994 –

** Minister of Aviation and Shipping

Reproduced faithfully from parliamentary records

Correct as of August 1995

Index

Page numbers appearing in *italic* refer to figures and tables.
An N following a page number refers to Notes.

OTHER TITLES AVAILABLE FROM E & FN SPON

The Channel Tunnel Story
G. Anderson and B. Roskow

Urban Transport Policy Today
B. Simpson

The Idea of Building
S. Groák

Passenger Transport after 2000 AD
Edited by G. Fielden, A. Wickens and I. Yates

Project Management Demystified
G. Reiss

The Ecology of Urban Habitats
O. Gilbert

Countryside Conservation: second edition
B. Green

Transport, the Environment and Sustainable Development
edited by D. Banister and D. Button

Transport and Urban Development
D. Banister

Guidelines for Landscape and Visual Impact Assessment
Institute of Environmental Assessment